VAGUENESS IN LAW

Vagueness in Law

TIMOTHY A. O. ENDICOTT

OXFORD
UNIVERSITY PRESS

Great Clarendon Street, Oxford OX2 6DP

Oxford University Press is a department of the University of Oxford.
It furthers the University's objective of excellence in research, scholarship,
and education by publishing worldwide in

Oxford New York

Auckland Bangkok Buenos Aires Cape Town Chennai
Dar es Salaam Delhi Hong Kong Istanbul Karachi Kolkata
Kuala Lumpur Madrid Melbourne Mexico City Mumbai Nairobi
São Paulo Shanghai Taipei Tokyo Toronto

Oxford is a registered trade mark of Oxford University Press
in the UK and in certain other countries

Published in the United States
by Oxford University Press Inc., New York

© Timothy A. O. Endicott 2000

ISBN 0-19- 826840-8

Cover illustration: © Joseph Raz

for Jane

Acknowledgements

In this book I offer some arguments developed during doctoral research at Oxford. If they sometimes sound peremptory, I hope that it is because I have tried to state them as clearly as I could, and not because I have disregarded the thoughtful criticisms of many students and teachers.

Joseph Raz supervised my work. I could not have started it without his guidance, or finished it without his criticism and his encouragement. Gordon Baker, Mark Sainsbury, Timothy Williamson, and Dorothy Edgington each supervised my research for one term, and I am grateful to each of them for their generous help (and in particular to Professors Sainsbury, Williamson, and Edgington for showing me unpublished work).

I am grateful to José Juan Moreso, Pablo Navarro, Cristina Redondo, and Steve Smith for extensive discussions and encouragement, and for advice and criticism from Roger Crisp, Ronald Dworkin, John Finnis, John Foster, John Gardner, Hanjo Glock, David Lametti, Gideon Makin, Graeme McLean, and Sir Peter Strawson. I presented part of Chapter 8 to Professor Francisco Laporta's graduate seminar entitled 'El Imperio de la Ley' in Madrid, and I benefited from his comments and those of his colleagues. I am grateful for the help and support of Oxford University Press, and for the generous comments and criticisms of anonymous referees.

My research was supported by a doctoral fellowship from the Social Sciences and Humanities Research Council of Canada, and by an overseas research scholarship from the Committee of Vice-Chancellors and Chancellors.

The book includes revised versions of the following papers: 'Linguistic Indeterminacy' (1996) 16 *Oxford Journal of Legal Studies* 667 (Chapter 2), 'Vagueness and Legal Theory' (1997) 3 *Legal Theory* 37 (Chapter 4), 'Putting Interpretation in its Place' (1994) 13 *Law and Philosophy* 451 (Chapter 8.4–8.6), 'The Impossibility of the Rule of Law' (1999), 19 *Oxford Journal of Legal Studies* 1 (Chapter 9). I benefited from the comments of anonymous reviewers for the *Oxford Journal of Legal Studies* and *Legal Theory*.

My friend Michael Spence kept me going, and his support and advice made it possible for me to complete this project. I could not have done the work without the constant support of Julianne and Orville Endicott. George and Anne Wilson gave invaluable help. Naomi and Peter Endicott were a constant encouragement and put things in proportion, more or less.

As for Jane Endicott, words fail me.

Contents

Abbreviations

1

Introduction

LAW is very commonly vague, so that the requirements of the law in particular cases are frequently indeterminate. I will call that familiar though controversial claim the 'indeterminacy claim'. My purpose is to explain it, to defend it, and to test its implications for an understanding of law and of adjudication. While the book addresses the vagueness of language, I should emphasize that it is not merely a book about legal language. I argue that vagueness, and resultant indeterminacies, are essential features of law. Although not all laws are vague, legal systems necessarily include vague laws. When the law is vague, the result is that people's legal rights and duties and powers are indeterminate in some (*not* in all) cases.

The indeterminacy claim seems to make the ideal of the rule of law unattainable: to the extent that legal rights and duties are indeterminate, we cannot be ruled by law. The indeterminacy claim is a threat to what I will call the 'standard view of adjudication': the view that the judge's task is just to give effect to the legal rights and duties of the parties. These drastic consequences have made the indeterminacy claim into an important focus of controversy in legal theory in this century. Legal theorists who take the standard view of adjudication have rejected the indeterminacy claim. The controversies have addressed one of the two characteristic marks of vagueness: the fact that doubt and disagreement arise over the application of vague expressions in some cases ('borderline cases').[1]

Here I seek to put those controversies in a new light, by addressing the second characteristic mark of vagueness—the 'tolerance principle'. Vague words appear to tolerate insignificant differences: it seems that any heap of sand will still be a heap if you remove one grain of sand (and no one goes bald by losing one hair, and no sea becomes an ocean when one drop of rain falls, and so on). The 'sorites paradox', or the paradox of the heap, is an argument that applies an apparently sound principle of this form repeatedly, until it arrives at the false conclusion that, for example, there is still a heap when all the grains of sand have been removed. I argue that an understanding of the tolerance principle, and of the sorites reasoning that it generates, raises an objection to some popular theories of law and of adjudication, and poses challenges that any theory of law or of adjudication must face.

That objection and those challenges are serious, if indeterminacy is a

---

[1] In the Index I mark in italics the places where I explain my use of such more or less technical terms.

significant feature of law. It would be senseless to try to quantify the indeterminacies that arise from vagueness in any legal system. But I argue that we should accept the general claim that they are significant (see Chapters 3.12, 5.4, 5.5, and 7.3).

In trying to defend various controversial views in the theory of law, I have found it necessary to make and defend some controversial claims in the philosophy of language and philosophical logic. I have avoided technicalities, but I have not omitted any that seemed necessary to the argument. Some readers may prefer to overlook some technical passages (e.g. Chapters 4.3, 5.2, 5.3, 7.1, and 7.2) and to read instead the introductions and conclusions in those chapters, and in this chapter.

1. What is in the Book

Chapter 2 clears the ground by rejecting the incoherent notion that the application of language is radically indeterminate. I hope that Chapter 2 will make it clear that the indeterminacy claim that I defend and discuss is not a *sceptical* claim: unlike radical indeterminacy claims, it casts no doubt on the sense of the practice of law, or on the meaningfulness of statements of law. Chapter 2 highlights the point that the application of vague language is indeterminate in *some* cases but *not in all* cases. The rest of the book aims to explain the implications of that fact.

The notion of 'indeterminacy' is introduced in Chapter 2: the law is indeterminate when there is no single right answer to a question of law, or to a question of the application of the law to the facts of a case.[2] The foundations for the rest of the book are laid in Chapter 3, which introduces the notions of borderline cases and tolerance, and tries to clarify the relation between the two notions. Links are drawn between tolerance and various forms of doubt and disagreement about the application of words, in order to justify the book's focus on vagueness. The reason for that focus is that vagueness is a paradigmatic source of indeterminacy in law, and a very important source. Along with express grants of discretion and conventions giving judges power to develop the law, it is one of the most important sources of judicial discretion. And unlike other sources of indeterminacy such as ambiguity, it is a necessary feature of law.

Chapter 4 addresses the implications of vagueness for understanding the nature of law, and the nature of adjudication, through an argument that 'higher-order' vagueness (the vagueness of phrases like 'clear case' and 'borderline case') poses an overwhelming objection to various popular accounts

---

[2] I address the problem of the extent to which questions of the application of law are questions of law in 'Questions of Law' (1998) 114 *Law Quarterly Review* 292.

of adjudication that take the standard view of adjudication (notably Ronald Dworkin's account). Those theories apply to law a version of the 'principle of bivalence' (the principle that every meaningful assertion is either true or false). Dworkin and Hans Kelsen claim that it is either true or false of every judicial decision to say that it was made according to law. Like others — notably H. L. A. Hart and Joseph Raz — I reject that application of bivalence. But Raz and others have supported the indeterminacy claim by arguing that propositions of law are 'neither true nor false' in borderline cases; I argue that this traditional formulation should be rejected: it is a misleading way to put the indeterminacy claim (Chapter 4.3).

Chapter 4 also discusses a characteristic feature of legal practice which I label 'juridical bivalence' — the practice of treating people as if the application of the law to their situations were bivalent. John Finnis has pointed out the importance of this feature of legal practice, and has called it a 'technical device'. I argue that his characterization of juridical bivalence is supported by an understanding of vagueness in law.

Chapter 5 examines higher-order vagueness more closely, by pointing out problems that it poses for philosophers of logic who seek to solve the sorites paradox. I suggest that an understanding of higher-order vagueness gives reason to think that no theory should seek a solution: the reasons are the appeal of the notion that there are no sharp boundaries to the application of vague words, and the fact that a theory that solves the paradox needs to postulate sharp boundaries.

Chapter 6 addresses aspects of one theory of vagueness in detail, for a particular purpose. The epistemic theory of vagueness claims that there are sharp, unknowable boundaries to the application of vague expressions. I address some features of Timothy Williamson's elaboration of the epistemic theory, and propose reasons not to take the epistemic view. There are two reasons for that extended discussion. The first is that the epistemic theory confronts and rejects the claim that there are indeterminacies in the application of vague language. If it succeeds, the indeterminacy claim is false. If it fails, its failure may help us to understand the indeterminacy claim.

The second reason for examining the epistemic theory is Williamson's account of the relation between meaning and use. He allows that use determines meaning, but argues that that only means that the correct application of words depends on the dispositions of speakers. That view of meaning and use supports what I will call the 'boundary model'. The boundary model is a theory of meaning: it explains the application of vague words as determined by a social choice function (from dispositions of speakers to correct and incorrect applications of words). I sketch a contrasting account of the relation between meaning and use, which supports what I will call the 'similarity model' of vagueness. The similarity model claims that there is no more satisfactory way of picturing the application of vague expressions than to say that they apply to objects that are sufficiently similar to paradigms. The similarity model is barely a model, and is *not* a theory: it gives no general explanatory account of the application of vague expressions. In Chapter 6 I link the similarity model with two very general, controversial claims. First, the meaning of a word can be seen either as a rule for its use, or as sharing fundamental normative characteristics with rules. Secondly, general evaluative and normative expressions are necessarily vague.

Chapter 7 further compares the similarity model with the boundary model. I argue that no social choice can determine sharp boundaries, but also that we should not say that the location of boundaries is indeterminate. We should say that the notion of a location of boundaries is misleading. If we think of the correct application of words as determined by a social choice of boundaries to their application, we can use Kenneth Arrow's 'impossibility theorem' to show that, under certain attractive assumptions, such boundaries *cannot* have a precise location. The social choice argument might be modified to claim that the location of boundaries is *roughly determined* by social choice; the possibility is examined and rejected through a critique of James Griffin's views on the rough equality in value of incommensurable options (Chapter 7.3). That argument uses the work of Joseph Raz and John Finnis on incommensurability, and adds a claim that incommensurabilities in the application of vague language show that the indeterminacies that arise from vagueness are significant.

The indeterminacy claim faces a potential objection from Dworkin's interpretivist theory of law. The interpretivist objection to the indeterminacy claim is that the law has resources that eliminate indeterminacies in the application of the words with which legal standards are formulated. I defend the indeterminacy claim first by addressing Dworkin's views about the interpretive resources of the law (Chapter 8.1–8.3), and then by presenting a 'simple account' of the nature of interpretation that is opposed to Andrei Marmor's theory of the role of interpretation in law (Chapter 8.4–8.7). Whether interpretive considerations are part of the law or not, there is no reason to think that they tend to eliminate indeterminacy. The appeal of the notion that interpretation is a way of reducing or eliminating indeterminacies can be explained as a facet of the general legal technique of juridical bivalence: that notion is attractive in the same way that the standard view of adjudication is attractive.

By upsetting the standard view of adjudication, the book reaches conclusions that some people find horrible: when the law is vague, judicial decision-making will in some cases be unconstrained by the law. It is impossible in principle for judges always to treat like cases alike. Predictability in the law is to some extent unattainable. Moreover, I argue in Chapter 9.2 that vagueness cannot be eliminated from law. These conclusions might seem to imply that the rule of law is, at least to some extent, conceptually *impossible*.

Avoiding that conclusion requires a revised account of the ideal of the rule of law, which asks, 'What counts as a *deficit* in the rule of law?' That question has been little discussed in the long history of debates over the rule of law. Yet we need to be able to answer it in order to understand the ideal. Answering it raises some new puzzles about the nature of arbitrary government. Chapter 9 addresses those puzzles, in support of a claim that vagueness (and judicial decision-making that is not guided by law) is not necessarily a deficit in the rule of law. That conclusion requires us to account for the resolution of unresolved disputes as an important and independent duty of judges—a duty that is itself an essential component of the ideal of the rule of law.

We cannot say in general that even a *very* vague legal rule represents a deficit in the rule of law. But vagueness *is* a deficit when it enables authorities to exempt their actions from the reason of the law, or when it makes it impossible to conceive of the law as having any reason distinguishable from the will of the officials.

2. What is not in the Book

Those are, in outline, all the substantial claims that the book makes. It is important to see what the book does not claim. First, the indeterminacy claim that I defend is not the notion that there is no right answer to a controversial question. That incoherent idea has been effectively criticized by Ronald Dworkin, among others. The indeterminacy claim that I defend receives no support from the mere fact that people disagree: it is consistent with the view that there are right answers to some questions (including questions of the application of vague expressions in borderline cases) on which reasonable people disagree. Of course, reasonable people disagree over cases in which someone might reasonably be in doubt. Such cases are 'borderline cases' (see Chapter 3.1). But the book does not claim that there is no right answer to any question of the application of a vague expression in a borderline case; it argues that some such questions have no right answer.

Secondly, I do not claim that vagueness is a purely linguistic feature of law. And the book relies on no claim about the relation between law and language. These points must be stressed, because vagueness is commonly thought of as a linguistic phenomenon. And, indeed, most of the discussion in the book concerns the vagueness of linguistic expressions. But the indeterminacy claim *is not just a claim about language* (so I argue in Chapter 3.12). So, for example, the claim in Chapter 6 that general evaluative and normative expressions are necessarily vague is not just a claim about the word 'good' and the word 'right'; it is a claim about any linguistic expression in which we could conceivably express general evaluative and normative judgments. It therefore includes a claim about what is good and what is right.

Because of the discussion of linguistic expressions, it might seem that the argument of the book rests on a naive view that there is indeterminacy in the law just when there is indeterminacy in the application of expressions in which a purported authority has purported to formulate a law. I make no such claim. I do not think that there can be a theoretical (i.e. a general, explanatory) account of the relation between the application of a lawmaker's words and the content of the law. This point is addressed in Chapter 8, but the argument of the book does not rely on it. The book *does* rely on the claim, which may be surprising, that we have grounds for saying that the linguistic *and* non-linguistic resources of the law are typically vague (see Chapters 3.10, 3.12, 8.1, and 8.2).

The third point that I wish to emphasize is related. The book offers arguments for rejecting certain positivist and certain anti-positivist theories of law. But I think that the claims of the book are consistent with some positivist *and* some anti-positivist theories. I do not argue in favour of any general position on the old, convoluted disputes among legal positivism, natural law theory, and other anti-positivist theories (or among forms of legal positivism).

At least since the rise of legal philosophy in the United States, disputes between positivists and anti-positivists have often proceeded by asking what considerations judges act on or ought to act on, and then formulating a view as to which of those considerations are legal considerations. The question concerns the limits of the law. It may seem that I am supporting a positivistic theory about the limits of law, relying on some form of 'sources thesis' which views indeterminacy in the language used by lawmakers as entailing indeterminacy in legal rights and duties. But that is no part of the argument, just as it is no part of the argument to express a general view about the relation between language and law. I express no view as to the limits of the law. For the purposes that I have outlined in this chapter, that is unnecessary because of the argument of chapter 8.1 and 8.2.

Disputes between legal positivists and natural law theorists have concerned not only the relation between law and adjudication, but also the relation between law and morality. Here I take no general position on the intrinsic moral value of law. I *do* rely on the claims that law can be valuable to a community, and that justice and the rule of law are two ideals which a community can intelligibly pursue as political virtues. Even those claims are controversial (Kelsen and some of the theorists discussed in Chapter 2 have controverted them). But I do not defend them here.

This work aims to show that the indeterminacy claim does nothing to threaten the pursuit of justice and the rule of law. Those ideals cannot be well understood if we try to make them depend on determinacy in the requirements of the law.

2

Linguistic Indeterminacy

No person shall take or possess, in the County of Lanark or the Regional
Municipality of Ottawa-Carleton, any bullfrog unless the tibia thereof is
five centimetres or more in length.

(Regulation under the Ontario Game and Fish Act, O. Reg. 694/81)

W E can think of cases in which liability for catching bullfrogs in Ottawa is
indeterminate — that is, cases in which the law does not determine whether
an offence has been committed. What if a bullfrog has one tibia longer than
5 cm and one shorter? What if the length of a tibia is pushed over 5 cm by a
rare growth? What of a bullfrog with a curved tibia that is 4 cm long when laid
beside a ruler, but measures 6 cm with a tape?

Countless indeterminacies appear in linguistic formulations of legal rules:
lexical ambiguities (does 'person' include a company?), syntactical ambiguities (does the person have to be in Ottawa? does the bullfrog?), uncertainty
as to whether 'take' adds anything to 'possess', and so on.

Bullfrog hunters and their lawyers might face further legal indeterminacies that do not arise from the language of the regulation: if there is an unresolved conflict between the bullfrog regulation and another rule, or if the
power to make the regulation or the procedures by which it was promulgated
or enforced are suspect, or if it is unclear whether proof of some mental state
is required for conviction, or whether principals are liable when agents take
bullfrogs. And the lawyers and the bullfrog hunters may face further uncertainties that are neither linguistic nor legal, such as whether the authorities
will exercise their discretion to prosecute, whether a particular witness will
make it to court, and so on.

Those non-linguistic indeterminacies arise because life and legal systems
are complicated. But people can choose their words, and it would be reassur-
ing to think that linguistic indeterminacy, at least, could be eradicated by
careful use of language. Perhaps the drafters of the bullfrog regulation set out
to do this by avoiding imprecise terms like 'adult bullfrog' or 'large bullfrog'.
What does their failure to eliminate linguistic indeterminacy show about law
and language? Indeterminacy seems pervasive and obdurate.

This chapter addresses the claim that language (and therefore law) is
radically indeterminate: that no question of the application of a linguistic
expression has a single right answer. I conclude not only that the claim is
wrong, but that, in spite of appearances, no one actually makes it. Those
two conclusions raise the more important question of what to make of the

allegations that legal sceptics of various types do make about linguistic indeterminacy. To get to that question, we need to start by identifying what legal theorists are talking about when they talk about indeterminacy.

1. The Twilight Zone

A metaphor popular in twentieth-century legal theory pictures linguistic indeterminacy as a penumbra, a shadowy purlieu between the clear applicability of an expression and its clear inapplicability. The metaphor is traditionally credited to H. L. A. Hart.[1] But Benjamin Cardozo had written in 1921 of 'the borderland, the penumbra, where controversy begins',[2] and Glanville Williams used the metaphor in a review of legal problems about the meaning of words, written in 1945: 'Since the law has to be expressed in words, and words have a penumbra of uncertainty, marginal cases are bound to occur.'[3] Cardozo implicitly and Williams expressly presaged Hart's claim that the judge has a law-making role in penumbral cases.[4]

Since Hart popularized the metaphor of core and penumbra,[5] many legal theorists have insisted that the notion falsely attributes to words some kind of certainty, or absoluteness, or independence of context, or immunity to change, and that indeterminacy is more than a fringe or margin. They have questioned not the notion of a penumbra, but the notion of a core.

Is meaning like a partial eclipse of the sun—all penumbra? What can be made of claims that the meaning or application of words is entirely indeterminate? One response would be to reject those claims as obviously wrong: everyone knows that there are cases in which words apply without any doubt or disagreement, just as there are situations in which it is unclear whether

---

[1] e.g. by Ken Kress, 'Legal Indeterminacy' (1989) 77 *California Law Review* 283, 287; Margaret Jane Radin, 'Reconsidering the Rule of Law' (1989) 69 *Boston University Law Review* 781 793–4 (*LL* 285–6); David Lyons, 'Constitutional Interpretation and Original Meaning' (1986) 4 *Social Philosophy and Policy* 75, 83 (*LL* 221); Frederick Schauer, 'Formalism' (1988) 97 *Yale Law Journal* 509, 514 (*LL* 434).

[2] Benjamin N. Cardozo, *The Nature of the Judicial Process* (New Haven: Yale University Press, 1921), 130.

[3] 'Law and Language—III' (1945) 61 *Law Quarterly Review* 293, 302 (*LL* 139). Hart acknowledged Williams's use of the notion: *CL* 278. The penumbra metaphor is at least as old as Bertrand Russell's description of vagueness: 'All words are attributable without doubt over a certain area, but become questionable within a penumbra, outside which they are again certainly not attributable' ('Vagueness' (1923) 1 *Australasian Journal of Psychology and Philosophy* 84, 87). Willard Quine also used the penumbra metaphor in *Word and Object* (Cambridge, Mass.: MIT Press, 1960), 128.

[4] Williams, 'Law and Language—III' 303 (*LL* 140).

[5] 'We may call the problems which arise outside the hard core of standard instances or settled meaning "problems of the penumbra" . . .', 'Positivism and the Separation of Law and Morals' (1958) 71 *Harvard Law Review* 593, 607. Cf. the discussion in *The Concept of Law* of 'a core of certainty and a penumbra of doubt' in the application of the general terms used in formulating legal rules (*CL* 123).

they apply. Another response would be to reject such claims as nonsensical — they declare themselves to be not exactly altogether true.

But the first lesson of jurisprudence is not to dismiss obviously wrong or nonsensical claims (e.g. 'what the officials do *is* the law' said by a legal realist, or 'an unjust law is not a law' said by a natural law theorist). Instead, it is worth asking what new emphasis or neglected insight a theorist is embellishing with absurdity. Nonsense in legal theory deserves lenience, just as someone deserves lenience if we ask whether it's raining and they say, 'yes and no'.

Lenience recommends interpreting radical indeterminacy claims as hyperbolic objections to immodest claims (or to inarticulate assumptions) of determinacy. And, indeed, intriguing and crazy claims of indeterminacy tend to crumble into sensible and less intriguing positions. In fact, the sensible positions typically accompany the crazy claims, as express concessions. I will argue that, when the concessions to determinacy are accounted for, every claim about indeterminacy that we will see is consistent with what Hart said about language: 'There will indeed be plain cases . . . to which general expressions are clearly applicable . . . but there will also be cases where it is not clear whether they apply or not.'[6] Then the debate is over whether determinacy is vast and typical (as Hart occasionally suggested[7]), or scarce, and likely to delude unimaginative theorists.

What is Indeterminacy?

Legal theorists say that the law is indeterminate when a question of law, or of how the law applies to facts, has no single right answer.[8] I will call such indeterminacy 'legal indeterminacy', and I will use 'linguistic indeterminacy' to refer to unclarity in the application of linguistic expressions that could lead to legal indeterminacy. I will generally treat 'indeterminacy' as a feature of the application of the law, or of an expression, to a particular case (or cases), and 'vagueness' as a feature of the law and of expressions. So, for example, the law on bullfrog hunting is vague if the boundaries of the area affected by the bullfrog regulation are unclear; but there is no indeterminacy when a bullfrog is taken in the centre of that area. There is indeterminacy (if any) only in borderline cases.

---

[6] *CL* 126. In *The Concept of Law* Hart was concerned to oppose the 'rule scepticism' of American legal realists; Brian Leiter has pointed out that in general their indeterminacy claims were not linguistic in form, but relied on the diversity of legal principles available for judges' use in any case ('Legal Realism', in Dennis Patterson (ed.), *Blackwell's Companion to Philosophy of Law and Legal Theory* (Oxford: Blackwell, 1996), 261). But those indeterminacy claims are also consistent with Hart's view: in Leiter's terms the legal realists thought that 'the law is rationally indeterminate locally not globally' (265).

[7] *CL* 124, 134, 154.

[8] See e.g. Kress, 'Legal Indeterminacy', n. 1 above, 283; Brian Bix, *Law, Language and Legal Determinacy* (Oxford: Clarendon Press, 1993), 1.

Concerning the application of the language in which laws are formulated, legal theorists make claims of *practical* indeterminacy and claims of *theoretical* indeterminacy. Practical indeterminacy arises in language when competence in the language is not enough to know whether an expression applies to known facts, and in law when legal competence is not enough to know the legal consequences of a known situation. A *radical* claim of practical indeterminacy would allege that competent speakers of a language can never know whether an expression applies, and that competent lawyers can never know what the law requires and permits. Theoretical indeterminacy claims do not outrage naive notions in that way. They allege that the meaning or correct application of words is determined not in the way that people might have thought, but in some manner so different that it is misleading even to call them determinate. Some theorists argue that the current debate about indeterminacy is entirely about what I call theoretical indeterminacy.[9] Such theorists will not necessarily find any more practical indeterminacy in a legal system than, for example, Hart did; this sort of theoretical indeterminacy thesis represents not a claim about the extent of legal uncertainty, but the working out of a philosophical agenda.[10] I do not mean to assess theoretical indeterminacy claims. That job would require a fully fledged theory of meaning, and no one has ever found enough feathers to fledge a theory of meaning.

The purpose of this survey is not to analyse the theories of language that back the indeterminacy claims that will be encountered. And no attempt will be made to refute a radical indeterminacy claim—it would refute itself, since it would amount to saying, 'No statement means anything, including this one'. My purpose is to point out some features which support the interesting conclusion that, in spite of appearances, no one actually sustains a radical indeterminacy claim. The fact that such a claim would refute itself does not in itself explain this fact, as the legal deconstructionist David Gray Carlson has shown: 'That deconstruction is self-refuting—a fact it fully grasps, emphasizes, and even exploits—by no means proves that deconstruction is wrong about meaning.'[11] Carlson is right that self-refutation does not show that deconstruction is wrong about meaning; instead, it shows that deconstruction *says nothing* about meaning, so that it calls for the lenience I suggested above.

I will start by discussing a current consensus on the nature of interpretation (Section 2) and deconstruction (Section 3). Radical indeterminacy claims that issue from those theoretical perspectives tend to degenerate into

---

[9] See e.g. Robert Justin Lipkin, 'Indeterminacy, Justification and Truth in Constitutional Theory' (1992) 60 *Fordham Law Review* 595, 611.

[10] In Lipkin's case, to 'rid ourselves of the notion of truth'. Ibid. 609 n. 56.

[11] David Gray Carlson, 'Liberal Philosophy's Troubled Relation to the Rule of Law' (1993) 43 *University of Toronto Law Journal* 257, 278.

concessions of determinacy. What is left after radical indeterminacy claims are discounted by the concessions? Often, a claim that meaning depends on *context*. So Section 4 will discuss the relation between context and indeterminacy. Section 5 will review the extraordinary indeterminacy claims that have emerged from the furore over Wittgenstein's remarks on following rules.

2. Interpretive Orthodoxy and the Critical Predicament

A consensus has emerged about interpretation and, specifically, about its role in law: that understanding *is* interpretation and, specifically, that every application of the law requires an interpretation of the law. This notion, which Dennis Patterson has called 'the current interpretive orthodoxy',[12] is particularly associated with Stanley Fish. He thinks that *everything* that people do with other people's utterances is interpretation:

in my argument, interpretation *is* conventional understanding.[13]

. . . communications of every kind are characterized by exactly the same conditions — the necessity of interpretive work, the unavoidability of perspective, and the construction by acts of interpretation of that which supposedly grounds interpretation, intentions, characteristics and pieces of the world.[14]

Some people disagree with Fish about most of the latter claim, but agree on 'the necessity of interpretive work' in understanding and applying linguistic expressions and the law. The striking range of theorists who hold similar views establishes a wide interpretivist consensus:

Owen Fiss: Adjudication is interpretation: Adjudication is the process by which a judge comes to understand and express the meaning of an authoritative legal text and the values embodied in that text.[15]

Frederick Schauer: ordinary talk appears to reserve the word 'interpretation' for those cases in which there seems to be a problem. In this respect, common linguistic usage is potentially misleading, for *every* application of a rule is also an interpretation.[16]

Margaret Jane Radin: every application of them [rules] is a reinterpretation.[17]

Ronald Dworkin: So I am drawn to the interpretive answer to the question: what makes a proposition of law true? Even in easy cases, that is, even when it goes

---

[12] 'The Poverty of Interpretive Universalism: Towards the Reconstruction of Legal Theory' (1993) 72 *Texas Law Review* 1.

[13] 'How Come you Do me Like you Do? A Reply to Dennis Patterson' (1993) 72 *Texas Law Review* 57, 62.

[14] *Doing What Comes Naturally* (Durham: Duke University Press, 1989), 43–4.

[15] Owen Fiss, 'Objectivity and Interpretation' (1982) 34 *Stanford Law Review* 739, 739.

[16] *Playing by the Rules* (Oxford: Clarendon Press, 1991), 207.

[17] Radin, 'Reconsidering the Rule of Law', n. 1 above, 819 (*LL* 311).

without saying what the law is . . . we do better to explain that phenomenon by speaking of a convergence on a single interpretation.[18]

Michael Moore: I do not intend by the word ['interpretation'] to distinguish between finding the meaning of a law, and applying that law to the facts of some case. . . . Whatever I must do to connect the law to the facts in the manner earlier sketched is what I mean by 'interpretation'.[19]

Jacques Derrida: Each case . . . requires an absolutely unique interpretation.[20]

This is a bizarre consensus among people who agree on nothing else. It survives their different views on how to interpret, on whether an interpretation can intelligibly be called right or wrong, on the nature of truth and meaning, and so on. They all think that no legal question can be answered except by an interpretation.

The consensus itself shows that fascination with interpretation does not compel any particular view on indeterminacy. Ronald Dworkin, for instance, seems to view law as more determinate than anyone else does.[21] And we should even hesitate to attribute any sort of indeterminacy claim to Stanley Fish. In a reply to Patterson called 'How Come you Do me Like you Do?' he seems hurt by the imputation.

In the world I describe, readers are situated (not by choice, but by histories that have befallen them) in communities whose traditions are constraints in the strongest way . . . they structure the individual consciousness, providing it with a limited set of meanings and routes of interpretive action. . . . This is about as far as one could get (short of an out-and-out determinism) from a condition in which 'everything is permitted' . . .[22]

The interpretive consensus does not entail any indeterminacy claim; it holds that interpretation is needed when the application of language seems quite determinate—in situations where, if we are interpreting, there is only one correct interpretation. It claims that when you drive up to a stop sign, you cannot respond to the sign without interpreting.

The consensus seems to stretch the notion of interpretation over instances of understanding that are not interpretive at all. In Chapter 8 I offer an account of interpretation that supports this view of the consensus. But I have

---

[18] 'On Gaps in the Law', in Neil MacCormick and Paul Amselek (eds.), *Controversies about Law's Ontology* (Edinburgh: Edinburgh University Press, 1991), 84, 88. And cf. the claim in *Law's Empire* that 'Law is an interpretive concept . . .' (*LE* 87). Dworkin argues that a judge must use the same interpretive method to decide *any* case (*LE* 265–6, 353–4). John Finnis has argued cogently against Dworkin's interpretive universalism in 'On Reason and Authority in *Law's Empire*' (1987) 6 *Law and Philosophy* 357, 358–63.

[19] 'A Natural Law Theory of Interpretation' (1985) 58 *Southern California Law Review* 277, 284–5.

[20] 'Force of Law: The "Mystical Foundation of Authority"', in Michel Rosenfeld and D. G. Carlson (eds.), *Deconstruction and the Possibility of Justice* (London: Routledge, 1992), 3, 23.

[21] See Ch. 4.3 below.   [22] (1993) 72 *Texas Law Review* 57, 61–2.

no quarrel with the use of the word 'interpretation': we could say that there is only one admissible interpretation in some cases, and that determinacy is the inadmissibility of all other interpretations. Or we could say that in such cases no interpretation is needed—that an understanding of the law and the facts leaves no room for interpretation. 'Interpretation' seems useful (and is often used) as a term for making choices as to the meaning of an expression or a text. And while there are choices to be made when driving up to a stop sign (e.g. whether to stop), there are none to make about its meaning. On this use of the term 'interpretation', we interpret when we can reformulate a rule in a way that clarifies its meaning. But we do not interpret stop signs.[23]

People are free to use 'interpretation' as a synonym for 'understanding', or for a creative process of making choices. But interesting things happen when they use it for both at once. It is precisely because the use of the word 'interpretation' to describe a creative process is common and attractive that the interpretive consensus lends itself to indeterminacy claims. If you think that every application of the law is an interpretation, and if you can simultaneously hold in your head the idea that interpretation is a matter of making choices among open alternatives, the result is indeterminacy. Thus, Sanford Levinson constructs an indeterminacy claim by invoking Richard Rorty's pragmatism. Rorty thinks that an interpreter 'simply beats the text into a shape which will serve his own purpose', and he insists that there is no distinction between that activity and understanding a text.[24]

Levinson joins a band of critical theorists who 'reject the very search for finality of interpretation',[25] and concludes that one can never say that a constitutional case 'was "wrongly" decided, for that use of language presupposes belief in the knowability of constitutional essence'.[26] And although he would like to criticize some of John Marshall's work as dishonest, he considers such criticisms 'irrelevant', because they assume 'the existence of a privileged discourse that allows me to dismiss Marshall as "untruthful" rather than merely different'.[27] Levinson stops short of asking what privileged discourse enables him to say that Marshall is 'different', or to say anything at all.

To be unable to say that a case was wrongly decided (or, of course, rightly) is an appalling predicament for a lawyer to land in, and Levinson occasionally voices despair about it.[28] Ironically, the predicament besets some theories

---

[23] These claims are discussed further in Ch. 8.

[24] Levinson, 'Law as Literature' (1982) 60 *Texas Law Review* 343, 385 (*LL* 355), quoting Richard Rorty, *Consequences of Pragmatism* (Brighton: Harvester, 1982), 139. Cf. Rorty, 'The Pragmatist's Progress', in Umberto Eco, *Interpretation and Overinterpretation*, ed. Stefan Collini (Cambridge: Cambridge University Press, 1992), 89, 93: 'On our view, all anybody ever does with anything is use it. Interpreting something, knowing it, penetrating to its essence, and so on are all just various ways of describing some process of putting it to work.'

[25] Levinson, 'Law as Literature' 384 (*LL* 354).   [26] Ibid. 386 (*LL* 356).

[27] Ibid. 389 (*LL* 359).   [28] Ibid. 401–3 (*LL* 371–3).

that set out to be critical. By touting indeterminacy, legal theorists squander the possibility of criticizing anything.

There are various techniques for coping with this critical predicament, besides Levinson's despair. A standard response is to cleave to the belief that challenging the status quo is good in itself, even if the form of the challenge makes it absurd to propose a change to the status quo.[29] This approach relies on the rhetorical potential of nonsense.

Pragmatists like Richard Rorty make a more subtle response: they try to distinguish 'between knowing what you want to get out of a person or thing or text in advance and hoping that the person or thing or text will help you want something different—that he or she or it will help you to change your purposes, and thus to change your life'.[30] But a stop sign, for example, cannot help you to change your purposes, if all you ever do with a stop sign is to beat it into shape *for* your purpose.[31] The resolution of this tension in Rorty's work has to be some sort of interplay between text and purpose, which is only possible if some texts resist being beaten into some shapes. That resolution would be a concession of determinacy.

The critical predicament is more agonizing in legal theory than in literary theory, because the urge to say that an interpretation of a constitution is right or wrong is generally more pressing than the urge to say that an interpretation of a poem is right or wrong. And in spite of Levinson's intermittent despair, he takes to the most common recourse of legal indeterminacy theorists: concessions of determinacy: 'To be sure, none of the radical critics defend the position that any interpretation is just as good as any other.'[32] The concession contradicts Levinson's denial that he can criticize John Marshall: to do so he would only have to give reasons why Marshall's interpretations are not as good as the alternatives. Levinson's indeterminacy claim turns out not to be as radical as it seems.

We can say the same of interpretivist indeterminacy theorists generally. A *radical* interpretivist indeterminacy claim would have to say that all applications of linguistic expressions are interpretations, and that no interpretation is ever better or worse than any other interpretation. No doubt it would be possible to make both claims, but it is hard to find anyone who does. If examples are to be found at all, we might seek them at the apogee of interpretivism: deconstruction.

[29] For an argument against such a tactical use of indeterminacy arguments, see Kress, 'Legal Indeterminacy', n. 1 above, 336.

[30] 'The Pragmatist's Progress', n. 24 above, 106.

[31] Stefan Collini points out this 'tantalizing' aspect of Rorty's philosophy: 'Introduction', in Eco, *Interpretation and Overinterpretation*, n. 24 above, 1, 12.

[32] Levinson, 'Law as Literature', n. 24 above, 384 (*LL* 354).

3. Deconstruction

Deconstruction inverts whatever anything seems to mean, by reversing the 'privileging' of one interpretation over another. That is the technique of the guru, Jacques Derrida; 'deconstruction' is also occasionally used in a wider sense as more or less equivalent to what is sometimes called 'post-structuralism', or 'critical theory', or even just 'theory'. Perhaps deconstruction is a sophisticated intellectual apparatus for disclosing ironies that pervade thought and language and experience. Perhaps it is bravura. Deconstructionists themselves do not differentiate: 'No conception of deconstruction can be advanced with confidence, as every such conception is subject to further deconstruction' (Michel Rosenfeld).[33] 'All sentences of the type "deconstruction is X" or "deconstruction is not X", *a priori*, miss the point, which is to say that they are at least false' (Jacques Derrida).[34] Derrida's own reflections on justice allege radical indeterminacy—at least in the application of the word 'just'. The result is newspeak: 'one cannot ... say "this is just" and even less "I am just", without immediately betraying justice'.[35] He concludes that 'Deconstruction is justice'.[36]

Derrida's insistence on the impossibility of calling anything 'just' arises from a paradox he creates: to be just, a decision must be responsible, and also free. So it must 'be both regulated and without regulation: it must conserve the law and also destroy it or suspend it . . . .'.[37] The attractive way to take Derrida's paradox is as a recommendation of modesty in making claims of justice, and as a warning against hypocrisy and moral blindness. But the same deconstructionist principle that applies to 'just' also applies to 'unjust', either (i) by parity of deconstruction, or (ii) in virtue of the fact that if *no* decision can be just, no decision can be distinguished as unjust. 'Unjust' becomes either applicable to no decision, or meaninglessly applicable to every decision (it could not be used, for example, to distinguish the conviction of a prisoner who has been framed from the acquittal of a prisoner who has been framed). There is no attractive way to take the proposition that no one can ever say 'this is unjust' without betraying justice.

Warnings against moral blindness should not be taken lightly. In some cases no just decision may be possible: suppose that an accused is manifestly guilty on admissible evidence of serious criminal charges properly brought, and suppose that the penal system is abusive. It might be unjust to acquit, and

---

[33] Michel Rosenfeld, 'Deconstruction and Legal Interpretation: Conflict, Indeterminacy and the Temptations of the New Legal Formalism', in Rosenfeld and Carlson (eds.), *Deconstruction and the Possibility of Justice*, n. 20 above, 152, 199 n. 22.

[34] Jacques Derrida, commenting on how the word 'deconstruction' might be translated into Japanese, in 'Letter to a Japanese Friend', in David Wood and Robert Bernasconi (eds.), *Derrida and Différance* (Coventry: Parousia Press, 1985), 7.

[35] Derrida, 'Force of Law', n. 20 above, 10.   [36] Ibid. 15.   [37] Ibid. 23.

unjust to convict, and a juror cannot make things better by assuming that the less bad option (if there is one) is just. But Derrida's paradox claims to prove more than that there may be no just decision on offer: it claims to prove that it is a betrayal of justice to say that any decision is just.

Curiously, Derrida's argument coincides with a concession of determinacy in *law*: 'every time that we placidly apply a good rule to a particular case, to a correctly subsumed example, according to a determinant judgment, we can be sure that law (*droit*) may find itself accounted for, but certainly not justice'.[38] If examples can be subsumed correctly, if rules can be applied to particular cases, linguistic determinacy is conceded. If law finds itself accounted for as a result, legal determinacy is conceded. If legal determinacy is conceded, it is more straightforward to say that justice lies in rightly deciding whether to apply the law than to say that justice must both conserve the law and destroy the law. It is more straightforward, and it accounts for the sound, non-deconstructible burden of Derrida's argument, which is that it is not necessarily just to follow a rule — that 'Law (*droit*) is not justice.'[39]

But perhaps the concessions of determinacy are, in deconstructionist argot, erasable. Perhaps Derrida was only saying that his claim about justice would hold *even if* any legal judgment *were* certain. If talk of subsumption and correctness is erasable, we should be able to find concession-free assertions of indeterminacy in deconstruction if anywhere. And deconstructionists do make very gratifying claims of radical indeterminacy: 'the meaning of a text could possibly be anything except that which it presently appears to be' (Michel Rosenfeld).[40] 'If I may write under erasure, the so-called radical indeterminacy thesis is clearly correct' (David Gray Carlson).[41] Yet even deconstructionists flinch:

Deconstruction is not licentiousness or promiscuity at all . . . Nor does deconstruction deny the phenomenon of successful communication. Without question, every day provides examples of spoken sentences understood by listeners in the way the speaker would have them understood. But there is no guaranty of the successful arrival of the message, because language has a life in context that is beyond the control of the speaker. (David Gray Carlson)[42]

It seems that nobody will say that anything goes. Deconstructionists take pains to escape the critical predicament: along with the concessions of determinacy, they rely on the value of an open mind. 'Deconstruction is not a denial of the legitimacy of rules and principles; it is an affirmation of human possibilities that have been overlooked or forgotten in the privileging of

---

[38] Derrida, 'Force of Law', n. 20 above, 16.   [39] Ibid. 16.
[40] 'Deconstruction and Legal Interpretation', n. 33 above, 157–8.
[41] 'Liberal Philosophy's Troubled Relation to the Rule of Law', n. 11 above, 282. But note that Carlson seems to use 'radical indeterminacy thesis' as I use 'theoretical indeterminacy thesis'. Ibid. 278 n. 51.   [42] Ibid. 282–3.

particular legal ideas' (J. M. Balkin).[43] '. . . inversions of hierarchical opposions expose to debate the institutional arrangements that rely on the hierarchies and thus open possibilities of change' (Jonathan Culler).[44] Deconstruction exposes law to debate, but not to argument. It suggests new possibilities of change, but allows no claim that the reasons in favour of a change are better than the reasons against it. It points out the privileging of ideas, but it cannot say what ideas *should be* privileged. In favour of this approach, it can be said that it gives underprivileged ideas (and therefore, presumably, the people whose ideas they are) a kind of equality with the privileged. But the way in which it makes ideas equal is indiscriminate: its inversions lead only to further inversions.

Derrida shows a concern for the critical predicament, and takes a sophisticated version of the open-mind response. He insists that deconstruction is not 'a quasi-nihilistic abdication before the ethico-politico-juridical question of justice and before the opposition between just and unjust',[45] and claims that 'constantly to maintain an interrogation of the origin, grounds and limits of our conceptual, theoretical or normative apparatus surrounding justice is on deconstruction's part anything but a neutralization of interest in justice, an insensitivity towards injustice'.[46] But how does deconstruction's interest in justice and sensitivity towards injustice express itself? In the denial that any decision is just. Here Derrida sees a solution to the critical predicament that is more positive than mere concessions of determinacy: he thinks that there is 'nothing more just than what I today call deconstruction'.[47] His claim seems to be that deconstruction has such paradoxically high standards that it rates nothing as just. But if deconstruction cannot say that any decision is *unjust*, it also has paradoxically low standards. As a technique for deciding what to do, it would be like a mad Robin Hood who gives the booty to the poor, and returns in the night to steal it back.

4. Context

When indeterminacy theorists make concessions to determinacy, they often retreat to assertions that the indeterminacy claim was actually a reminder of the context dependence of meaning:

There are still rules. But there are no rules that can be understood apart from the context . . . (Margaret Jane Radin)[48]

---

[43] J. M. Balkin, 'Deconstructive Practice and Legal Theory' (1987) 96 *Yale Law Journal* 743, 763 (*LL* 405).

[44] *On Deconstruction* (London: Routledge & Kegan Paul, 1982), 179, quoted by Balkin, 'Deconstructive Practice and Legal Theory' 776 (*LL* 418).

[45] Derrida, 'Force of Law', n. 20 above, 19.   [46] Ibid. 20.

[47] Ibid. 21.   [48] 'Reconsidering the Rule of Law', n. 1 above, 817 (*LL* 309).

... if the meaning of a signifier is context bound, context is boundless—that is, there are always new contexts that will serve to increase the different meanings of a signifier. (J. M. Balkin)[49]

Deconstruction ... stresses that meaning is context bound—a function of relations within or between texts—but that context itself is boundless: there will always be new contextual possibilities that can be adduced, so that the one thing we *cannot* do is to set limits. (Jonathan Culler)[50]

A general response to claims that the meaning of language is indeterminate because it depends on context would need to show (1) that meaning is not radically dependent on context, or (2) that context dependence does not typically lead to indeterminacy.

Is Meaning Acontextual?

Frederick Schauer has developed this response to indeterminacy claims. Schauer writes that 'ruleness' (a rule's capacity to demand different behaviour from the behaviour required by the rule's justification[51]) requires 'the possibility that a form of decision-making could conceivably be guided by the meaning of the formulated generalization rather than by the optimal particularized application of the justification behind that formulation'.[52] He argues that this possibility depends on 'semantic autonomy', which is the possession of 'acontextual' meaning. So Schauer's account of rules includes a claim that they can be applied without knowledge of context.

It is obvious that the meaning of an utterance is not merely a particularity of the single event in which it occurs. Yet the ways in which Schauer elaborates on the idea seem to run into trouble.

The main trouble is that no one can use the symbols of a language independently of particular goals and occasions. But Schauer says that the waves of the ocean could do so:

Suppose I go to the ocean and while there notice a group of shells washed up on the beach in a pattern that looks something like C-A-T. I will think then of small furry house pets and not of zeppelins or zebras, despite the fact that in this case there is no user of language whatsoever. My ability to think cat when I see 'C-A-T', and the fact that all speakers of English would have a rather closely grouped array of reactions to that same shell pattern, demonstrates the phenomenon I call semantic autonomy, the way in which language carries something by itself, independent of those who use it on particular occasions.[53]

---

[49] 'Deconstructive Practice and Legal Theory', n. 43 above, 781 (*LL* 423).

[50] Jonathan Culler, 'In Defence of Overinterpretation', in Eco, *Interpretation and Overinterpretation*, n. 24 above, 109, 121. See also the quotation from David Gray Carlson in the text at n. 42 above.

[51] *Playing by the Rules*, n. 16 above, 102.   [52] Ibid. 61–2.   [53] Ibid. 56.

In fact there *is* a user of language on the beach. Schauer has not demonstrated that the meaning of language is autonomous, because he is one of 'those who use it on particular occasions'.

The truth in Schauer's discussion of cats is that the word 'cat' does refer *to cats*, and no one can understand the word without knowing that it does. To understand the word 'cat', you *do* need to be able to do various things such as distinguishing a cat from a dog, explaining the word's meaning by pointing to a cat or by describing a cat, and so on. But for meaning to be autonomous from context, it would have to be possible to grasp the meaning of a word without any grasp of the facts that make up contexts. It would have to be possible to know the meaning of the word 'cat' without knowing anything about cats. Thus, in another formulation of the idea of semantic autonomy, Schauer says that 'there is at least something, call it what you will, shared by all speakers of a language that enables one speaker of that language to be understood by another speaker of that language even in circumstances in which the speaker and understander share nothing in common but their mutual language'.[54] In fact, there is no such something, because there are no such circumstances. The circumstances Schauer pictures are contradictory: a speaker and an 'understander' cannot share a language, and share nothing else—just as no one can know the English language, and know nothing else. The people Schauer imagines would not share *any* knowledge about cats, or about rain, or sleep, or food, and yet they would know the meaning of the words 'cat', 'rain', 'sleep', 'food'. In fact, people who share a knowledge of the meaning of those words also share a lot of knowledge about cats, rain, sleep, and food.

But Schauer concedes that people who share a language must share 'numerous contextual understandings',[55] and that 'contextual factors are presupposed in attributing even the barest amount of meaning to an utterance'.[56] That concession puts the idea of semantic autonomy in a new light: meaning is not a mere transitory feature of a particular situation. Yet the meaning of an expression is not independent from the context in which it is used.[57]

Is Context Dependence Indeterminacy?

We have to try to reconcile the good sense of Schauer's reminder that the meaning of a word on an occasion of its use is not merely particular to that occasion with the problems that arise in attempts to articulate the notions of

---

[54] Ibid. 55–6.   [55] Ibid. 57.   [56] Ibid. 56.

[57] I discuss the importance to legal theory of the context dependence of meaning in 'Law and Language', in Jules L. Coleman and Scott Shapiro (eds.), *Handbook of Jurisprudence and Legal Philosophy* (Oxford: Oxford University Press, 2001).

semantic autonomy and acontextual meaning. It is worth remembering that children learn the meaning of a word from its use in particular situations, and learn to use it in similar situations. Then the meaning of a word may be thought of as its usefulness in particular situations. That usefulness could be called contextual (because words can only be used *in a context*), or acontextual (because they can be used in *various* contexts that are different as well as similar); but it can be misleading to call it either. Children often use words in surprising contexts that they see as similar enough to justify using the word. They cannot use any word in any context without making judgments of the aptness of such similarities. Yet this radical context dependence cannot be a form of radical indeterminacy: children are not only *very frequently right* that a new situation is sufficiently similar in relevant respects for the word to be used; they are also capable of *understanding* the point of using a word.

Such reflections on the nature of meaning may seem unsatisfying in a discussion of context. It seems paradoxical to talk in general terms about 'context', which is only whatever characterizes a particular situation. The fact that there is a word 'context' for all that should not mislead us into thinking that we can generalize in a helpful way about it. Nevertheless, there *is* a general response to claims that context dependence means indeterminacy: the context can and characteristically does answer questions of (i.e. determine) the application of words. The word 'large' is radically context-dependent: if we are given the dimensions of an object, we are in no position to say whether 'large' applies to the object unless we know what sort of object it is. And we cannot say whether, for example, a house of a particular size is large unless we know a lot of facts about, for example, its location, the way of life of people in its community, the houses it might be compared with, and so on.[58] But radical context dependence does not make the meaning of 'large' radically indeterminate. In context, we can say whether a particular house is large or not, except in borderline cases that fit Hart's claims. The word 'tomorrow' is radically context-dependent: it has a different reference every day! But its meaning is not radically indeterminate.[59]

This is an argument that the resort to context is a retreat from radical indeterminacy, and it needs to be weighed against the insistence of indeterminacy theorists that, if meaning varies with context, it cannot be trusted: 'Because "meaning is context-bound, but context is boundless", natural law's facticity is invaded by subjective interpretation, and liberalism loses its status as a philosophy.'[60] Context dependence does not necessarily lead to 'subjective

---

[58] The implications of this point are discussed in Chs. 3.10 and 6.5 below.

[59] And this is not to make any radical *determinacy* claim about the meaning of 'tomorrow'— an indeterminacy could arise in a particular use. If you tell me, 'she said she would do it tomorrow', it may not be clear whether 'tomorrow' means the day after she spoke, or the day after today.

[60] Carlson, 'Liberal Philosophy's Troubled Relation to the Rule of Law', n. 11 above, 282.

interpretation', because context may give objective reasons for applying or not applying an expression to something. Suppose that a boat owner asks you to recommend 'a good painter'.[61] On the one hand, just knowing the meaning of 'good' and 'painter' will not allow you to help them. On the other hand, the context will typically determine whether they need an artist, or a decorator, or a rope for a boat. It may be perfectly clear that the boat does not need painting, that it does need a rope, and that the owner hates art. Then there are objective reasons for taking the boat owner to be asking about a rope.

Far from amounting to a source of indeterminacy, it can be tempting to think that the context determines whether anything is 'a good painter', since it can determine both (i) what sort of painter is in question, and (ii) what is needed, in the case in question, from that sort of painter (i.e. what is a 'good' painter). In fact, context may not be as determinative as that. It may make various incommensurable standards relevant (a rope's strength and its weight...). Indeed, the context may not even make it clear whether someone wants a decorator or a rope. Then you are faced with a genuine uncertainty arising from linguistic indeterminacy. But context dependence would make the application of linguistic expressions radically indeterminate only (1) if people were typically ignorant of the relevant and important features of the context in which an expression was used, or (2) if those features typically left facts such as whether someone needs an artist, a decorator, or a rope unclear. Since neither (1) nor (2) is the case, indeterminacy claims that merely point out the context dependence of meaning are not radical. It does not matter if an indefinite range of different contexts could be imagined for a particular use of a word, as long as there are reasons for deciding what contextual factors are relevant to applying the expression.

So, even though it is risky to generalize about contexts, we should not underrate the extent to which they make meaning clear—just think how, if someone asks the meaning of an odd word, we instinctively ask for the sentence in which it was used. A context can even determine when somebody means something other than what they said. Here is an example, ironically, from the papers of C. S. Peirce, one of the founders of the philosophy of indeterminacy:

no sign can be absolutely and completely indeterminate . . .*

* Though the writing is unmistakable this should be 'determinate'. (Editors' note)[62]

Peirce's editors were *right*: the context in which the sentence appears makes it *determinate* that he meant that no sign can be 'determinate'.

---

[61] An example of ambiguity discussed by Mark Sainsbury in *Logical Forms* (Oxford: Blackwell, 1991), 35.
[62] *Collected Papers of Charles S. Peirce*, ed. Charles Hartshorne and Paul Weiss (Cambridge, Mass.: Harvard University Press, 1934), sect. 5.506.

5. Wittgenstein

Some proponents of legal indeterminacy have followed Saul Kripke in interpreting Wittgenstein's remarks on following rules as posing a sceptical paradox;[63] their opponents argue that they have been confused by a misleading
philosophical question, and that Wittgenstein, far from answering that question sceptically, wanted to dissolve confusions that underlie the question.[64]
Frederick Schauer, meanwhile, has argued that Wittgenstein's remarks show
that formulated rules are not radically indeterminate, but unformulated
rules are.[65]

The scenario that leads to all this perplexity is simple: suppose that you are
teaching a pupil who has learned to count, and is now learning to recite the
even numbers. Everything goes smoothly as far as 1000, after which the pupil
says '1004, 1008, 1012'. You find yourself at a loss, because all the examples
of adding 2 which you had given (and which the pupil had mastered) seem
unable by themselves to determine that 1002 comes after 1000. You meant
them to be examples of 'add 2', but they could just as well have been examples of, for instance, 'add 2 as far as 1000, and then add 4'. It seems that
something extra is needed to connect a rule like 'add 2' with instances of its
application. What can that something extra be?

This philosophical question ('What connects a rule with its applications?')
has consequences for the indeterminacy debate. On the sceptical interpretation, Wittgenstein is pointing out that, because there is no extra something,
there is an unbridgeable gap between a rule and its applications. That is to say
that there is no such thing as rules: 'There can be no such thing as meaning
anything by any word. Each new application we make is a leap in the dark;
any present intention could be interpreted so as to accord with anything we
may choose to do.'[66] The sceptics deal with this paradoxical situation by saying that the consensus of a community licenses us to talk as if a rule existed:

---

[63] See Charles M. Yablon, 'Law and Metaphysics' (1987) 96 *Yale Law Journal* 613; Sanford
Levinson, 'What do Lawyers Know (And What do they Do with their Knowledge)? Comments
on Schauer and Moore' (1985) 58 *Southern California Law Review* 441, 447–8; Radin, 'Reconsidering the Rule of Law', n. 1 above; Christopher L. Kutz, 'Just Disagreement: Indeterminacy
and Rationality in the Rule of Law' (1994) 103 *Yale Law Journal* 997.

[64] See Brian Langille, 'Revolution without Foundation: The Grammar of Scepticism and
Law' (1988) 33 *McGill Law Journal* 451; Scott Landers, 'Wittgenstein, Realism and CLS:
Undermining Rule Scepticism' (1990) 9 *Law and Philosophy* 177; Brian Bix, *Law, Language
and Legal Determinacy* (Oxford: Clarendon Press, 1993); 38–41; Andrei Marmor, *Interpretation
and Legal Theory* (Oxford: Clarendon Press, 1992), 146–54. These legal theorists draw on the
non-sceptical response to Kripke developed by G. P. Baker and P. M. S. Hacker in *Scepticism,
Rules and Language* (Oxford: Blackwell, 1984) and *Wittgenstein: Rules, Grammar and Necessity*
(Oxford: Blackwell, 1985).

[65] *Playing by the Rules*, n. 16 above, 64–8.

[66] Saul Kripke, *Wittgenstein on Rules and Private Language: An Elementary Exposition*
(Oxford: Blackwell, 1982), 55.

'following a rule' is another way of saying 'doing what members of the community say is following a rule'.

The non-sceptical interpretation claims that Wittgenstein was trying to dissolve a philosophical muddle rather than to generate one. The remarks on following rules are an articulation of the relation between meaning and use that Wittgenstein pointed out. On this view, he was not arguing that nothing bridges a gap between rule and application; he was arguing that understanding the rule 'add 2' is knowing how to use the examples that the teacher gave.[67] You could understand 'add 2' and yet not be able to count to 1000, or know that '1000, 1002' is an application of the rule (because the teacher has told you so) without understanding the rule. But understanding the rule and knowing its applications need nothing to connect them: you cannot know how to count to 1002, and understand the rule 'add 2', without knowing that '1000, 1002' is a correct application of the rule. So learning a rule is neither finding something to bridge the gap, nor merely happening to do the same thing as other people, but grasping a way of using the examples that the teacher gives.

Understanding this debate is basic to understanding the problems of law and language, because the philosophical question about what connects a rule with its applications amounts to the question of what connects a word with its applications (as both Kripke and the non-sceptical Wittgensteinians recognize). We have a *rule* of calling baby dogs 'puppies'. It is not just a habit—we tell children that that is the right thing to call them. If a child calls a kitten a 'puppy', it is not just unusual, it is wrong. The debate over Wittgenstein's remarks on rules is a debate about what makes it wrong to call a kitten a 'puppy', just as it is a debate about what makes '1000, 1004' wrong when you are counting by twos.

If the non-sceptical view is correct, Wittgenstein cleared away the misconception that something other than the rule determines what counts as an application, but he did not suppose that if nothing other than the rule determines its applications, its applications are indeterminate. He cleared away the misconception that philosophers have the job of finding the something, if there is anything, that mediates between the word 'puppy' and baby dogs. This has consequences for some of the views that we have surveyed:

1. The interpretive orthodoxy, for all the consensus, is mistaken: as Wittgenstein put it, 'there is a way of grasping a rule which is *not* an *interpretation*'.[68]

---

[67] Cf. Baker and Hacker: 'we *define* the series "+2", for example, in terms of the sequence "... 998, 1000, 1002, 1004". The rule and its application are internally related, for we define the concept "following this rule" by reference to *this* result.' *Wittgenstein: Rules, Grammar and Necessity*, n. 64 above, 148.

[68] *PI* 201. John McDowell has made a persuasive argument against Kripke's views that focuses on this point. See, 'Wittgenstein on Following a Rule' (1984) 58 *Synthese* 325.

That remark is an obstacle, which no one has cleared away, to the use of Wittgenstein's remarks to support scepticism about rules.

2. Sceptical claims that nothing *guarantees* that a decision has followed a rule are put to rest.[69] They are claims that there is no bridge, where in fact there is no gap.

3. The critical predicament evaporates. In some circumstances, particular actions can and should be criticized for failing to follow a rule (if the rule ought to have been followed)—or, equally, for following a rule (if the rule ought not to have been followed).

It seems that the non-sceptical view, if it is right, defeats not just radical practical indeterminacy claims, but all theoretical indeterminacy claims. But if the sceptical view is right, Wittgenstein's argument *is* a theoretical indeterminacy thesis: he has shown that there could only be rules if there were some unimagined connection. There is none, but we are licensed to talk *as if* there were rules when there is something *like* a connection—the consensus of a community. Rule-following is essentially social.

It is easy to see the attraction of the social view for people interested in law and language. Languages are social practices, and law is a social practice, and so their rules must be social practices. A rule is not a legal rule if it has no role in the practices of a society. The only mistake is to jump from those propositions to a view about the connection between rule and application. That is, it is tempting to jump *from* questions such as whether there is a rule, what it is, who made it, who follows it, and so on (which are questions of social fact) *to* the question of what connects a rule with its applications (which is a philosophical question), and to conclude that the philosophical question is a question of social fact. Note that Wittgenstein's discussion is not about whether the rule that the pupil was supposed to apply was 'add 2', nor is it about whether 1002 comes after 1000 when that rule is applied. Wittgenstein's discussion takes it for granted that the answer to both those questions is 'yes'. The question is more basic: what *connects* '1000, 1002' with the rule 'add 2'? Wittgenstein's technique in such a situation was to resolve the confusion that leads a philosopher to ask the question.[70] The sceptical view supposes that the philosophical question should be changed into a question of social fact; the non-sceptical view is that the question is based on confusion.

Margaret Jane Radin makes the jump from the social nature of law and language to the social view of rule-following. She characterizes Wittgenstein as a rule-sceptic[71] who thought that rule-following is 'an essentially social phenomenon'.[72] She does not mean simply that social rules (such as the rules of law and of language) are social practices, but that there is no such thing as

---

[69] e.g. Carlson, in text above at n. 42.   [70] *PI* 47.

[71] 'Reconsidering the Rule of Law', n. 1 above, 798 (*LL* 290).

[72] Ibid. 799 (*LL* 291).

a rule unless people agree in following it: 'Rule-following can only be understood to occur where there is reiterated human action both in responding to directives and in observing others respond.'[73] This seems to say that no action can follow a rule unless there is a community that says that it does. That sceptical view of the social nature of rules cannot be right: if you live alone with a cat, and make it a rule to give her breakfast before you make yours, you are following a rule even if no one else ever finds out. There is no community consensus. Even if you and the cat form a community, you do not need her agreement to follow that rule. What if we say that you form a community of one, or that there is a hypothetical community of people like you who would counterfactually agree on what is an application of the rule? Then we dissolve the notion of a community, and admit that an action can follow a rule, or fail to do so, without any consensus.

In your practice of giving your cat breakfast first it is true that there are all sorts of manifestations of what you have learned from your community—the notion of duty, the notion of the interests of a cat, the notion of breakfast . . . We learn what rules are and how to follow them from being part of a real community; but that does not mean that following *a* rule is doing what the community says. Perhaps some who take the social view of rules simply mean to point out that we learn the *general* practice of following rules from a community—that we acquire the concept from a community. Or they might argue, more strongly, that that is the *only* way it is possible to learn how to follow rules. To reduce the social view to either claim would change it significantly from the sceptical Wittgensteinian view. If the social view of rules simply points out that you learned to follow rules from your community, or even if it argues that that is the *only* way to learn to follow rules, the social view would be watered down to something quite distinct from a view about what rules are. It would become consistent with the non-sceptical view that the question of what connects a rule with its applications is not unanswerable, but misconceived.

Radin herself, it seems, does not need to adopt the sceptical view on rules. Her position on Wittgenstein can be seen as much weaker than the sceptical view, because she only uses the discussion to refute 'traditional formalism'[74] about rules. The formalism that Radin opposes claims that rules can be applied by *deduction*, at least in core cases.[75] No one appears to hold that view, which would be absurd. If I ask you for an apple, and you choose an apple from the fruit bowl, you follow a rule.[76] But you need not make a deduction. Deductions need premisses, and here you only have an apple. 'This is an apple' could itself state a premiss in a deduction, but it is not a deduction. Could a traditional formalist say that it is necessarily the *conclusion* of a

---

[73] Ibid.   [74] Ibid. 792 (*LL* 284).   [75] Ibid. 793 (*LL* 285).
[76] For qualification of this claim, see Ch. 6.3.

deduction, in which the premises are propositions such as 'every object that has such and such characteristics is an apple', and 'this object has such and such characteristics'? No, because an absurd regress would result: the judgments that this is an object, and that it has any particular characteristic, would become conclusions of other deductions premised on the conclusions of other deductions . . . As Hart wrote, 'Logic is silent on how to classify particulars.'[77] If formalism is the view that classifying particulars is a process of deduction, Radin does not need rule scepticism to attack it.

It seems that the social view of rule-following is not a radical indeterminacy thesis, but a theoretical indeterminacy thesis.[78] In the social view a community could have a firm consensus. Like Stanley Fish, a sceptical interpreter of Wittgenstein could think that community consensus governs in a very strong sense what can be called 'following a rule'. The fact that the theoretically sceptical social view of rule-following can lead to just as much practical determinacy as the non-sceptical view becomes important in Frederick Schauer's approach to the debate. His conclusion is that something is needed to bridge the gap between rule and application, but since everyone agrees that there are actions in accord with a rule, that something *must* be there. And it does not matter what it is. This approach has a sensible ring: it relies on the difference between practical indeterminacy and theoretical indeterminacy, and postulates that the latter does not matter. But the approach runs into some bewildering problems.

Schauer emphasizes, and attributes to Wittgenstein, the claim that there is no unique correct answer to the question, 'What number comes next in the series 1000, 1002, 1004, 1006, ——?'[79] The answer could be 1008, or 1019, or anything. Schauer says that the point is that 'something other than the prior numbers in the series makes 1008 correct and 1019 incorrect',[80] and that the debate over rule-following is about what that 'something other' is. So, like the sceptics, he thinks that something *must* tie a rule to its applications, if there are to be rules.

But Schauer is not a sceptic. He says that if the series is accompanied by the 'verbally formulated instruction, "always add 2"', then '1008 becomes the right answer, and 1019 is simply wrong'.[81] He admits that this gambit seems to miss Wittgenstein's point, and that we might ask why 'always' could not mean

---

[77] *EJP* 67. In the same essay Hart wrote that in the penumbra of application of a legal rule, 'men cannot live by deduction alone' (64), seeming to suggest that men *can* 'live by deduction alone' in the core of application of a rule. That suggestion is simply misleading, as the rest of Hart's essay shows.

[78] Thus Radin says: 'Although the Wittgensteinian view thus certainly admits that there can be action determined by a rule, it is not the kind of determined-ness required by . . . the traditional formalist conception of the nature of rules.' 'Reconsidering the Rule of Law', n. 1 above, 292.

[79] *Playing by the Rules*, n. 16 above, 65.   [80] Ibid.   [81] Ibid. 66.

'but if $n > 1004$, add 13'. His response is that any reason will do: 'The reason it couldn't, of course, is again the topic of the debate about what it is that supplies the benchmark for following or breaking a rule *of language*, where the very characterization of that bedrock question makes it circular and question-begging to answer the question in terms of the existence of rules of language.'[82] This response is actually a cryptic tautology: the topic of a debate about X *is* X. So Schauer is only saying that *the reason why a particular application is in accord with a rule* is '*what it is that supplies the benchmark for following or breaking a rule*'. This is a significant tautology, because it is important to Schauer's approach that he does not need to specify a reason. The reason can be 'community practices or agreement, to refer (without endorsement) to just one possible answer'.[83] But there *must* be something that makes 'always' mean always, and once it has done so, rules of language can be the foundation for legal rules.

There are three interconnected difficulties with Schauer's argument:

1. 'Always add 2' is exactly as vulnerable to a sceptic as is 'give the next number in the series 0, 2, 4, 6, ..., 1000, 1002, 1004, 1006, ...'. The point of Wittgenstein's discussion is that we could not explain the meaning of 'always add 2' any better than by giving examples and saying 'and so on'. So 'always add 2' cannot 'entrench' the rule if 'give the next number in the series 0, 2, 4, 6, ..., 1000, 1002, 1004, 1006, ...' did not. This is the fact that Schauer was alluding to when he admitted that his argument seemed to miss Wittgenstein's point. His response is just to imply that it does not matter.

2. Schauer sees the 'verbally formulated instruction' (or 'linguistically formulated direction', or 'specific instruction in language'[84]) 'always add 2' as *entrenching* the rule that is expressed by 'something other than the prior numbers'. But 'give the next number in the series 0, 2, 4, 6, ..., 1000, 1002, 1004, 1006, ...' is verbally formulated, is linguistically formulated, is an instruction, is a direction, and is specific.

3. A contradiction emerges: 'there is no uniquely correct answer' to 'what comes next in the series 1000, 1002, 1004, 1006, ...?', so 'something other than the prior numbers in the series makes 1008 correct and 1019 incorrect'.[85] If something *makes* 1008 correct, it is not the case that there is no uniquely correct answer. Of course, the right choice is to say that 1008 *is* (uniquely) correct — and this seems to be the alternative Schauer would choose. In a footnote he says that in '1000, 1002, 1004, ——?' 'there *is* a rule — ... "add 2"', though the rule does not 'emerge uniquely from the series itself'.

Evidently, applications of a rule may be correct in the absence of an entrenching formulation. The very meaning of a formulation, we might say,

---

[82] *Playing by the Rules*, n. 16 above.   [83] Ibid.   [84] Ibid. 67.   [85] Ibid.

is such a rule.[86] Schauer says that 'The divergence between rule and justification, a divergence I take to be crucial to understanding the idea of a rule, is
possible only if formulated generalizations can have meanings differing from
the result that a direct application of the justification behind a rule would
generate on a particular occasion.'[87] That seems to be true—but it would be a
different matter to show that *only* a formulated rule can have a different
result from the direct application of its underlying justification. And Schauer
does not do so; by characterizing Wittgenstein's discussion as having to do
with formulations, he concludes that unformulated rules are left unex-
plained. In Schauer's view, the message of Wittgenstein's discussion is that
'The ability to explain the constraints *of an unformulated or unformulatable
rule* is a difficult task, and one quite different from the task of explaining the
potential constraint of a formulated rule.'[88] Schauer himself goes on to show
that there is nothing particularly difficult about explaining constraint by
unformulated rules.[89] He says, for example, that an unformulated customary
rule reflected in the normative practices of a community can exist 'in the
same way for that community as does a rule that actually has a canonical
inscription'.[90] And he develops a theory of precedent that demystifies the
constraint of unformulated rules.[91] After repeating the claim that Wittgenstein showed that constraint by non-formulated rules is mysterious,[92]
Schauer shows that, even if the generalizing characterizations (i.e. purported
rule formulations) of the precedent-setting court have no effect on the law,
precedents can constrain: some generalizations are 'more possible than
others'.[93] A precedent can be characterized as an instance of an indefinite
variety of different rules, but subsequent decision-makers may have compelling reasons for taking it to be an instance of one rule rather than another.
Schauer uses the example of *Donoghue* v. *Stevenson*,[94] which imposed liability on a manufacturer of contaminated ginger beer for harm to a consumer. It
would be wrong for a subsequent court to take that decision as an instance of
a rule that imposes liability only on manufacturers of ginger beer, and it
would be wrong to take it as an instance of a rule that imposes liability on
everyone who causes harm to another. Schauer concludes that 'nothing
about precedent-based constraint uniquely differentiates it from rule-based
constraint'.[95] This gives a quietus to the claim that the constraint of unformulated rules is difficult to explain and different from the constraint of formulated rules. In fact, it seems that there is no basis even for saying that common

---

[86] On whether the meaning of a word is a rule for its use, see Ch. 6.3.
[87] *Playing by the Rules*, n. 16 above, 61.   [88] Ibid. 67.   [89] Ibid. 68–71.
[90] Ibid. 71.   [91] Ibid. 181–7.
[92] '. . . the ability to identify the rule-based constraint in a series without a formulated generalization is deeply problematic.' Ibid. 185.
[93] Ibid. 186.
[94] [1932] A.C. 562.
[95] *Playing by the Rules*, n. 16 above, 187.

law rules are necessarily more indeterminate than rules with a canonical formulation: with all its indeterminacies, the rule that the defendant shall be liable when the facts are similar to those in *Donoghue* v. *Stevenson* is as determinate as many provisions in written constitutions, or even in statutes regulating contractual obligations.

6. Conclusion

There are no radical indeterminacy theses. Not only do radical indeterminacy claims implicitly contradict themselves; people who make them regularly contradict them explicitly, and turn them into theoretical indeterminacy claims. Theoretical indeterminacy claims are consistent with the sort of thoroughgoing practical determinacy that, for example, Stanley Fish asserts. And conversely, Hart's distinction between core and penumbra is consistent with widespread linguistic indeterminacy and legal indeterminacy.

Can we draw any general conclusions from a survey of indeterminacy claims? All we have established is that everyone more or less agrees, sometimes in spite of themselves, with Hart's platitude that there are clear cases and unclear cases of the application of linguistic expressions. The very great theoretical differences over the nature of clarity have not been resolved, and it is unclear how much is clear.

We can still learn some important lessons. First, judges and theorists should be modest in making claims of determinacy. Judges in particular should not take refuge in claims that the plain meaning of words compels a decision. But by the same token, if they do not want to do what, for example, a statute says to do, they should not take refuge in claims of indeterminacy, or claims that they are interpreting the words of the statute.

Theorists should accept that the application of linguistic expressions, in context, is sometimes determinate; this book supports the claim that the application of vague expressions is sometimes indeterminate — a claim that would make no sense if the meaning of language were radically indeterminate.

The survey of indeterminacy claims suggests a further point which can be made here, and which ought to be kept in mind in discussing vagueness in law. It is possible to know that the linguistic formulation of a legal rule applies to the facts of some cases, but that mundane knowledge does not tell a judge what to do. Knowing whether the case fits the formulation of a rule does not even tell the judge what the law requires: the judge also needs to know whether the law requires that the rule be applied. And knowing *that*, in turn, does not tell the judge whether the word 'just' applies to the result. Linguistic determinacy should not mislead judges into thinking that it will even be possible to make a just decision in every case. Though 'just' and 'unjust', too, have some clear cases.

3

Sources of Indeterminacy

IF the application of language is not generally indeterminate, what particular indeterminacies are there? Addressing that question offers opportunities to clarify some terms and to invent and discard others. Untangling the phenomena may also dispel the sense that it is unclear what vagueness and indeterminacy are, or that there may be more to them than we realize.

But the main purposes of this discussion are (i) to explain what is meant by 'vagueness' for the purposes of this book, (ii) to explain why I focus on imprecision, and (iii) to provide the groundwork for an argument that vagueness in the law leads to legal indeterminacy. An additional purpose is to introduce what I will call the 'similarity model', which claims that the most useful way to understand vague expressions is to think of them as applying to objects that resemble paradigms sufficiently in relevant respects. That approach yields a vague account of vague language. It does not deserve the label 'theory', because the notions of sufficiency and relevancy are open-ended. Those notions are crucial to an understanding of vague language, and they are both vague and, in a sense to be explained below, indefinite.

1. Vagueness: Introduction

An expression is vague if there are borderline cases for its application. Most of the job of an account of vagueness is to explain what borderline cases are. We can start to flesh out the notion by scrutinizing a vague definition of 'vague' offered by H. P. Grice: 'To say that an expression is vague (in a broad sense of vague) is presumably, roughly speaking, to say that there are cases (actual or possible) in which one just does not know whether to apply the expression or to withhold it, and one's not knowing is not due to ignorance of the facts.'[1] We can call the 'cases' Grice refers to 'borderline cases'. The definition needs two important qualifications, and a caveat.

The first qualification is that we ought to leave open the question of whether the uncertainty in borderline cases corresponds to indeterminacy in the

---

[1] *Studies in the Way of Words* (Cambridge, Mass.: Harvard University Press, 1989), 177. The definition is useful even though Grice was only trying to pin down a putative claim that ordinary language is unfit for conceptual analysis because it is vague. Cf. Mark Sainsbury: 'A vague word admits of borderline cases, cases in which we don't know whether to apply the word or not, even though we have all the kinds of information which we would normally regard as sufficient to settle the matter.' *Paradoxes*, 2nd edn. (Cambridge: Cambridge University Press, 1995), 24.

application of an expression, or is just ignorance of something that is determinate. To assume indeterminacy would beg the question against the 'epistemic' theory of vagueness (see Chapter 6). So we need to be clear about what it is that we do and do not know in a borderline case. If the vague word is 'tall', we should say that a borderline case is one in which, even if we do know *how tall someone is*, we do not know whether to say that they are tall or not tall.

The second qualification is that one's not knowing whether to apply the word must not be due to ignorance of the *meaning* of the expression: 'bald' is not vague just because someone learning English does not know whether to apply it to a man with no hair. This qualification has important consequences: if we think that it is possible to know the meaning of 'bald', and not to know whether it applies to some man, then we must distinguish between knowing the meaning of a word and knowing its correct application.[2] I will argue that nothing more precise can be said about the connection between meaning and correct application than that a vague word correctly applies to objects that are sufficiently similar in relevant respects to paradigms of its application; for this purpose, we can think of knowing the meaning of a vague word as knowing paradigms, and knowing how to use them.

The caveat about Grice's definition is that it is extremely broad: it applies to what we might call pragmatic vagueness as well as semantic vagueness. Not knowing 'whether to apply' an expression may mean (i) not knowing whether a statement applying it would be true, or (ii) not knowing whether it would be appropriate in the circumstances to make such a statement. If there is only a little coffee in the coffee pot and you ask me if it is empty, it would be clearly true, in a sense, to say, 'it's not empty', but it may be unclear whether it is appropriate (if there is only a drop of coffee, it will be clearly inappropriate). I will call problem (i) 'semantic vagueness', and problem (ii) 'pragmatic vagueness'. Vagueness in Grice's sense includes both; I will call it 'vagueness in the broad sense'.

Ordinarily, people use 'vague' to describe not expressions or concepts, but uses of language, such as promises, allegations, descriptions, threats, and insinuations. 'Vague' in this sense means something like uninformative or incomplete: wanting in useful details. Uses of language may be uninformative because they involve expressions that are vague in Grice's sense, but they need not. For example, we can make a vague allegation by suppressing the agent of an action with the passive voice ('money has been withdrawn from the pension fund') or a nominalization ('there has been a withdrawal from the pension fund'), or an indefinite subject ('someone has withdrawn

---

[2] Perhaps some philosophers might claim that to the extent that we do not know whether to apply the word 'tall' in known circumstances to a person whose height we know, we do not know the meaning of the word 'tall' (although epistemic theorists need not say that, and Timothy Williamson, whose epistemic theory is discussed in Ch. 6, does not say that). I do not propose to give the theory of meaning that would rebut such a claim.

money from the pension fund'). There are any number of ways of achieving this sort of vagueness: express vagueness ('roughly'), expression of doubt ('maybe'), exaggeration, understatement, self-contradiction, tautology, tone of voice, hesitation, concessions, parenthetical verbs ('I suppose', 'I guess'), indeterminacy of implicature (since every formulation of conversational maxims is vague), obscurity, irrelevance, confusion, terseness, wordiness, and any form of nonsense.

Perhaps the sense in which uninformative utterances are vague is the basic sense of 'vague', and expressions whose application is marked by borderline cases are called 'vague' because they lend themselves to use in, for example, guarded promises, non-committal descriptions, and innuendoes. To examine vagueness, then, would be to examine various sorts of language that are well adapted to such uses. In any case, the discussion will only indirectly address vagueness in the ordinary sense of uninformativeness.

I will start with imprecision, and then look at additional characteristics of expressions in virtue of which they might fit Grice's definition of vagueness. I will look at what various people have termed 'open texture', 'incompleteness', 'incommensurability' (and something I call 'immensurability'), 'contestability', and 'family resemblances', and ask how they differ from imprecision and, more importantly, how they are connected to imprecision. A brief look at 'dummy standards' will introduce a discussion of pragmatic vagueness. Ambiguity will be mentioned, because it might be viewed as a source of pragmatic vagueness; but I will try to distinguish it from vagueness.

2. Imprecision

The mark of vagueness is the apparent susceptibility of an expression to the 'tolerance principle'[3]—the principle that a tiny change in an object in a respect relevant to the application of the expression cannot make the difference between the expression's applying and not applying. I will call expressions to which the tolerance principle clearly does not apply 'precise'. I will call vagueness in the technical sense of apparent susceptibility to the tolerance principle 'imprecision', when it needs to be distinguished. But ordinarily I will just call it 'vagueness'. Imprecision is the typifying feature of words that are vague in the broad sense. Expressions displaying the semantic features that have interested philosophers of law (which they term 'open texture', 'family resemblances', 'contestability', etc.) are typically imprecise. It is possible to invent terms that display those features and are not imprecise;

---

[3] Wittgenstein spoke of a 'margin of tolerance' in his discussion of the 'Problem of the Heap' in *Philosophical Grammar* (Oxford: Blackwell, 1974), 236. Crispin Wright used the term 'tolerance' in 'Language-Mastery and the Sorites Paradox', in G. Evans and J. McDowell (eds.), *Truth and Meaning* (Oxford: Clarendon Press, 1976), 223, 229.

but imprecision is the common, characteristic feature of vague words in natural languages.

The tolerance principle generates a paradox, which we can illustrate using 'bald'. If the tolerance principle applies to 'bald', then any bald man will still be bald if he grows one hair. We can call the number of hairs on the man's head a 'dimension' for the application of 'bald', because a sufficient change on that dimension will affect the application of the word.[4] We can represent the tolerance principle as follows, where x_n is a man with n hairs on his head:

For any n, if x_n is bald, then x_{n+1} is bald.

Of course, x_0 is bald. So if the tolerance principle holds, we can substitute 0 for n and apply *modus ponens*, to yield the (true) conclusion that x_1 is bald:

x_0 is bald.

If x_0 is bald, then x_1 is bald.

x_1 is bald.

The tolerance principle applies in turn to x_1 (because *any* man who is bald will still be bald if he grows a hair), so x_2 is bald as well. In fact, the tolerance principle can be applied again and again, to generate the conclusion that a man with a full head of hair is bald:

(0) x_0 is bald.
(1) x_1 is bald.
(2) x_2 is bald.
...

(150,000) $x_{150,000}$ is bald.

The series from x_0 to $x_{150,000}$ is a 'sorites series'. I will use 'x' throughout the book for a case in a sorites series, with a subscript to indicate the number in the series.

The conclusion, (150,000), is paradoxical: it is false, yet we seem to have reached it by valid reasoning (repeat applications of *modus ponens*), from true premises (the 'categorical' premiss that x_0 is bald, and the 'conditional' premiss provided by the tolerance principle).

Legal theorists have been much concerned with borderline cases, but they have not dealt with the tolerance principle. If apparent susceptibility to the tolerance principle is the standard marker of vagueness, what is its relation with the notion of borderline cases (which I used to define 'vague')? This is

---

[4] I do not think that there is a determinate set of dimensions for the application of all vague words, or even that for any vague word F, there is necessarily a property G that has the denumerable character of a property like number of hairs, or height . . . I do not know of any such G for a word like 'pretty', although it is easy to formulate sorites paradoxes using such expressions; see Ch. 7.1.

puzzling, because the two notions seem logically inconsistent: it seems that, if the reasoning from (0) to (150,000) above were valid, it would not include any propositions that are any more doubtful than the proposition that a man with no hairs on his head is bald. And if we reflect that the tolerance principle seems as applicable to 'clearly bald' as to 'bald', then the tolerance principle seems to rule out borderline cases.[5]

The feature that connects the tolerance principle with borderline cases is a characteristic feature of vague expressions: that there seems to be no sharp boundary to their application. The tolerance principle is an assertion of the no-sharp-boundary claim; borderline cases are cases that are puzzling because we cannot identify a sharp boundary. We defined borderline cases in a way that takes no stand on whether the tolerance principle holds, but in such a way that it *appears* to hold. If we could identify a counter-example to the tolerance principle, of the form

x_i is bald, but x_{i+1} is not bald,

then there would be no cases (within the domain of this sorites series) in which we would not know what to say. For $n \le i$, we would know to say that x_n is bald, and for $n \ge i$ we would know to say that x_n is not bald.

Perhaps we can reconcile the notion of borderline cases with the tolerance principle if we can find a way of saying that (1) is true, that (150,000) is false, and that somewhere in between there are propositions which are neither true nor false, or not completely true and not completely false, or whose truth is indeterminate, or something similar.

The problems that the sorites paradox raises for an understanding of law and adjudication are identified in Chapter 4. The most important obstacle those accounts face is 'higher-order' vagueness. Whatever description philosophers of logic find for borderline cases, it seems that the tolerance principle will apply to that description as well. Losing or gaining a hair should not make the difference in the application of phrases such as 'borderline case for "bald"', or 'clearly bald', either. There are cases in which one would not know whether to apply those expressions—that is, there are second-order borderline cases. Philosophers use the phrase 'second-order vagueness' to describe the apparent absence of sharp boundaries between clear cases and borderline cases. They use 'higher-order vagueness' for the apparent absence of boundaries at the second order or higher. Chapter 5 will try to support the view that we should neither deny higher-order vagueness, nor assert a particular number of orders of vagueness, nor assert that a vague

[5] (1') x_1 is clearly bald.
   (2') x_2 is clearly bald.
   (3') x_3 is clearly bald.
   ...
   (150,000') $x_{150,000}$ is clearly bald.

word is vague at all orders. Chapters 5 and 6 will argue that a legal theory should not be based on an attempt to solve the paradox.

The Vagueness of Comparatives

Just as we may not know whether to call A 'bald', we may not know whether to call A 'balder than B'. The vagueness of comparative adjectives will play an important role in the argument (see in particular Chapter 7.3). If A is a borderline case for 'bald', it is unclear whether A is bald; if A is a borderline case for 'balder than B', it is unclear whether A is balder than B. If 'balder than' is vague, that means that there is no precise answer to a question of the form 'How bald is N?' We can make the reasonably safe assumption that if a comparative adjective is vague, then for any object A, there is some actual or possible object B such that we would not know whether to apply the comparative adjective to A as compared with B. Given this assumption, the vagueness of a comparative adjective entails the vagueness of the cognate positive adjective.[6] Common nouns like 'table' have contrived comparatives like 'better candidate for the application of "table"', or 'more clearly a table'; vagueness in those pseudo-comparatives entails that the noun is vague.

We can formulate sorites paradoxes for vague comparatives just as we can for vague positives. Imagine that A is hairless, and that B has a bit of hair, so that A is balder than B. The conditional premiss (i.e. the tolerance principle) in the comparative form of the paradox takes the form of the proposition that, after a trivial change, A will still be balder than B. Note that the premiss is false if the comparative is precise—if, for example, the only criterion of baldness is number of hairs, and everyone necessarily has a determinate number of hairs. But if 'balder' is vague, the conditional premiss seems attractive—it may not be the case that A becomes just as bald as B precisely when A acquires the same number of hairs. Imagine that A starts regaining his hair, and let n be the number of hairs. If the tolerance principle holds, it licenses deductions from each of the following premisses to the succeeding proposition in the series:

(0_c) A_0 is balder than B.
(1_c) A_1 is balder than B.
(2_c) A_2 is balder than B.
. . .

$(150,000_c)$ $A_{150,000}$ is balder than B.

This sorites reasoning with comparatives is paradoxical in the same way as

---

[6] We can demonstrate this point using 'bald': if 'bald' were not vague, we would be able to identify an actual or possible bald person, A, who is less bald than or just as bald as any other bald person, and balder than any non-bald person. But if 'balder' were vague, there would be some other actual or possible person, B, concerning whom we would not know whether A is balder than B.

sorites reasoning with positives: it leads to the false conclusion that A is still balder than B when A has much more hair than B.

Even if a comparative is vague, there are real or hypothetical domains within which there are no borderline cases for its application: 'red' is vague because it may be unclear whether a pinkish-red patch is redder than a purplish-red patch, but we can make a series of patches that change gradually from clearly pink to clearly red, in such a way that each successive patch is clearly redder. Within that domain there are no borderline cases for 'redder': every object is either clearly redder than or clearly not redder than every other object. But there are borderline cases for 'red'. The vagueness of comparatives is discussed in the section below on incommensurability (Section 5), and in Chapter 7.

3. Open Texture

As a term for the presence of a core of certainty and a penumbra of uncertainty in the application of general words, Hart introduced the term 'open texture' to jurisprudence.[7] It seems that Hart was searching for another metaphor that would support his notion of 'interstitial' law-making.[8] Perhaps the best interpretation of his use of the term is that he was looking for a term for vagueness in the broad sense. If that is what 'open texture' means, this book is about open texture.

Hart borrowed the term from Friedrich Waismann, who used it to describe a feature of the meaning of words like 'chair' that Wittgenstein had pointed out: that 'the application of a word is not everywhere bounded by rules'.[9] There is no answer to a question such as whether the word 'chair' applies to something that is like other chairs, except that it disappears and reappears now and then.[10]

Wittgenstein did not try to define vagueness, and he did not talk about open texture. Waismann wrote that open texture should be distinguished from vagueness, as 'something like *possibility of vagueness*'.[11] Legal philosophers following Hart have fastened on Waismann's distinction, and struggled to make something of it.[12] The distinction disappears by stipulation for the

---

[7] *CL* Ch. vii.1; *EJP* 274. [8] See *EJP* 'Introduction' 7. [9] *PI* 84. [10] *PI* 80.

[11] Waismann, 'Verifiability', in A. Flew (ed.), *Logic and Language*, 1st ser. (Oxford: Blackwell, 1952), 117, 120.

[12] e.g. Andrei Marmor, *Interpretation and Legal Theory* (Oxford: Clarendon Press, 1992), 132: 'vagueness should be distinguished from open texture. . . . Even terms which are not vague are potentially so . . .'. Michael Moore, 'The Semantics of Judging' (1981) 54 *Southern California Law Review* 151, 201: 'open texture is only the possibility of vagueness'. Frederick Schauer, *Playing by the Rules* (Oxford: Clarendon Press, 1991), 35: 'In contrast to currently identifiable vagueness, open texture is the possibility that even the least vague, the most precise, term will turn out to be vague . . .'.

purposes of this book: like Grice, I have defined 'vague' to apply to an expression if there are actual *or possible* borderline cases of its application. That stipulation seems to cost us nothing, because no one has ever shown that the distinction has any consequences at all for jurisprudence. And, in fact, open texture and vagueness cannot be distinguished *as properties of the meaning of expressions* by the contingency of whether there are actual borderline cases. Nothing about the meaning of 'bald' depends on whether borderline cases happen to exist. In any case, there is so much actual vagueness in law that possible vagueness does not need to concern us, and I will not use the term 'open texture'.

There is one respect in which Waismann's notion is useful, however. His concern was to show the essential incompleteness of empirical descriptions, to argue that verification of empirical propositions is impossible.[13] The notion of incompleteness is itself important for understanding vagueness — but it is important for understanding actual and not just possible vagueness.

4. Incompleteness

Suppose that a provision conferring criminal jurisdiction on a court empowers the court to try defendants on charges that they 'committed an offence in' the jurisdiction. And suppose that a defendant took part in an international telephone fraud that had some connections with the jurisdiction, so that it is unclear whether she 'committed an offence in' the jurisdiction. Even if the boundaries of the territory are perfectly precise, the phrase 'committed in . . .' seems to be vague. There is nothing obscure or nonsensical about the provision, and in most cases it will be perfectly clear whether an offence was committed in the jurisdiction. But there will be some cases in which, as Grice's definition of vagueness puts it, 'one just does not know whether to apply the expression ['committed in . . .'] or withhold it'.

We can call this form of vagueness 'incompleteness', because the provision purports to answer the question of which offenders are within the jurisdiction of the court, but that task seems unfinished. Compare the bullfrog regulation: it is not imprecise, yet in respect of a bullfrog with one tibia longer than 5 cm and one shorter, or a bullfrog whose tibia is pushed over 5 cm by a rare growth, it seems that the statutory formulation gives an incomplete answer to the question 'Which bullfrogs are protected?'

Completeness is the full achievement of some purpose. It seems that something can be complete only with respect to a purpose, and incompleteness is ordinarily a feature of explanations, reports, descriptions, and so on. So it may seem that it is not a feature of expressions at all, but an occasional

---

[13] 'Verifiability', n. 11 above, 120–3.

feature of (for example) speech acts. Perhaps we can call expressions 'incomplete' by association with the purposes for which they are used. So, for example, we can say that the description 'the tibia thereof is five cm or more in length' is incomplete, because its purpose is to classify bullfrogs as protected or not protected, but in some cases it is insufficient for that purpose.

Mark Sainsbury has shown that the importance of incompleteness is independent of imprecision. Suppose that someone makes a pearl-sized lump of pearl-stuff (call the lump P). Is P a pearl? We might say that the unclarity in the application of 'pearl' is different from that of 'bald'—it does not arise from imprecision, and does not involve the tolerance principle. Sainsbury sees the difference as important enough that we should not say that 'pearl' is vague. Like other philosophers of logic he uses 'vague' to mean 'imprecise', and 'pearl' does not seem to be imprecise: 'perhaps "pearl" has as its positive extension anything made of the correct material and formed in an oyster; as its negative extension anything not of the right material; and as its penumbra pearl-sized lumps of pearl-material synthesized outside of any oyster. I suggest we should see "pearl" not as vague, but as incomplete . . .'.[14] Sainsbury's proposal is potentially misleading, because it is important to see the ways in which 'pearl' is *similar* to 'bald': why they are both vague in the broad sense. Sainsbury's suggestion arises in the course of an argument that the 'supervaluational theory'[15] cannot give a good account of vagueness, because it treats a vague word as associated with three sets, its 'positive extension', its 'negative extension', and its 'penumbra'. Sainsbury points out that we could stipulate definitions of non-vague terms that are associated with such sets: his example is 'minor', subject to a stipulation that it applies to people under 17, and does not apply to people over 18 (I will call 'minor' in this stipulated sense 'minor+').[16] Seventeen-year-olds are in a 'penumbra'—the stipulation says nothing about them.

Sainsbury's suggestion is that 'pearl' is similar to 'minor+'. He claims that the meaning of 'pearl' does not 'speak to' P. The meaning of 'heap' (of, for example, sand), he claims, 'does say something about penumbral cases':

It says that as a competent user you must recognize borderline cases as borderline, and hence should not confidently and without a sense of stipulation apply or deny the predicate; and that your use remains governed by such principles as: if α is borderline for 'heap' and β is otherwise similar except that it has fewer grains, then β is not a clear case of a heap.[17]

---

[14] Sainsbury, 'Paradoxes', n. 1 above, 38. Grice gives an example of incompleteness as an illustration of vagueness in the brief discussion of vagueness from which I borrowed his definition of 'vague'. His example is uncertainty as to whether 'same person' would apply to Locke and Nestor, if Locke turned out to have Nestor's memories, but a different body (*Studies in the Way of Words*, n. 1 above, 178). [15] See Ch. 5.1 below.

[16] *Paradoxes*, n. 1 above, 37. [17] Ibid. 38.

I want to resist Sainsbury's suggestion, on the ground that, in a crucial respect, the meaning of 'pearl' is like the meaning of 'heap' or 'bald', and unlike the meaning of 'minor+'. It does make sense to call both 'pearl' and 'minor+' 'incomplete', but there is reason to say that the incompleteness of 'pearl' (and not of 'minor+') is a form of vagueness.

In Chapter 5.5 I will claim that recognizing that particular cases are borderline cases is *not* a requirement of linguistic competence—that there may be no clear borderline cases, and there are no paradigm borderline cases for the application of 'heap', in the sense that a clear case of a heap is a paradigm of the application of 'heap'. For present purposes it is enough to say that there is no reason to distinguish 'pearl' from 'heap' on the ground that only 'heap' has clear borderline cases. In fact, P seems a better example of a clear borderline case for 'pearl' than any particular collection of grains of sand would be for 'heap'. If P is not a borderline case, it is unclear what Sainsbury means by 'borderline case', and why he calls P 'penumbral'. He defines 'penumbra' so that an object is in the penumbra if it neither definitely has the relative property, nor definitely lacks it,[18] and that seems to be a good definition of a borderline case. P seems to be a good candidate for Grice's 'one just wouldn't know' test, and it is unclear why Sainsbury suggests that one could apply or withhold 'pearl' from P 'confidently and without a sense of stipulation'.

The point about α and β attracts a similar response: it does not distinguish 'pearl'. The meaning of 'pearl' does say something about P: for example, that if it is not a clear case of a pearl, then a pearl-sized lump of stuff slightly different from pearl-stuff is not a clear case. Just like the meaning of 'heap', the meaning of 'pearl' says that anything that resembles a paradigm better is a better candidate for the application of the expression. The meaning of 'pearl', like the meaning of 'heap', and *unlike* the meaning of 'minor+', can be explained by pointing to paradigms. It seems that the difference between 'heap' and 'pearl' is a difference in ways in which it may be unclear whether an object is sufficiently similar to paradigms. That is consistent with 'heap' and 'pearl' being similar in the important respect that their meaning can be explained ostensively—and in this respect both 'pearl' and 'heap' are different from 'minor+'.[19] P is like the disappearing chair: we are not equipped with rules for every possible application of 'pearl'. But the same is true of 'heap'.

What is more, there is reason to think that 'pearl' is imprecise in just the way that Sainsbury denies, when he claims that we should see it as incomplete and not as vague. The reason is that we could place P in a sorites series from

---

[18] *Paradoxes*, n. 1 above, 33.

[19] I do not mean that precise expressions cannot be explained by reference to paradigms ('metre' is a precise expression that can be explained using paradigms). The difference is the difference in what a speaker has to know about how the respective paradigms are to be used, in order to understand the difference between, for example 'that's a metre' and 'that's a child'.

clear cases of the positive extension of 'pearl' to clear cases of its negative extension.[20]

I do not want to deny a distinction between incompleteness and imprecision: 'minor+' is incomplete and imprecise, and it seems that *any* ordinary incomplete expression in a natural language must be imprecise. To come up with a formula that is incomplete and *not* imprecise, you need to create a precise demarcation between clear cases and penumbral cases—which can only be done with precise language. We could not make up a sorites series connecting a 17-year-old with clear cases of the application and non-application of 'minor+', or a sorites series connecting the bullfrog with different-length tibias with cases which the bullfrog regulation clearly does and does not protect. By contrast, every case with respect to which the application of an ordinary expression seems incomplete can be situated on a sorites series, in such a way that it is connected by a series of insignificant increments to clear cases of the positive and negative extension of the expression. It would not be rash to conclude that all incomplete expressions in natural languages are also imprecise. P is just a borderline case of 'pearl'.

For these reasons, I propose to treat incompleteness as an important form of vagueness in the broad sense. It is different from imprecision, but both incompleteness and imprecision can be thought of as puzzles about the ways in which objects must be similar to paradigms, in order for an expression to apply.

5. Incommensurability

Incommensurability is a relation that holds between X and Y, if and only if it is impossible to measure both X and Y on some common scale. Incommensurability is an important feature of practical decision-making, since options for action can be incommensurable with respect to the values that a choice can promote. Such incommensurabilities commonly arise from the fact that (i) options may have various attributes that contribute to their preferability, and (ii) option A may be preferable to option B in some respects, and option B may be preferable in others, and (iii) there may be no way of measuring options A and B on a single scale of preferability, because there is no way of commensurating the different attributes. Suppose that a good rope is strong

---

[20] Start with a paradigm pearl. Then imagine an almost fully developed pearl taken from an oyster and given a very thin coating of pearl material. Then imagine a very slightly less-developed pearl taken from an oyster and given a very slightly thicker coating of pearl material . . . That process can be continued until we reach P, and it can be continued past P by gradually altering the composition of the material, until we end up with something that is clearly not a pearl. We could create similar sorites series connecting other illustrations of incompleteness, such as Locke–Nestor.

and light. It may be possible to create a scale on which to evaluate ropes, using a formula that incorporates both weight, and a measure of strength. But if some rope is slightly stronger and slightly heavier than another, and if weight and strength are incommensurate, then the way in which the formula ranks the two ropes will be stipulative: there is no answer to the question that a good formula will reveal.

Consider Joseph Raz's example of a choice of careers, with a particular job as a teacher ('job A'), and a particular career as a lawyer ('job B') as options. Job A may be preferable to job B for some person in some respects (say, for convenience, just in respect of working hours), and less preferable in others (say, just in respect of pay). If there is no way to calibrate these two dimensions of working hours and pay (let alone all the other dimensions on which the options might have differed) in the same units, then there may be no answer to the question 'Which job is preferable in respect of both attributes considered together?' I will call such *options* 'incommensurable'. I will refer to the 'dimensions' that correspond to the attributes that cannot be measured in common units, and I will call such *dimensions* 'incommensurate'.[21]

Raz and John Finnis have appealed to incommensurability to make a general attack on moral theories that seek to maximize preferences or goods (I will call those theories 'consequentialist').[22] The attack rejects the notion of maximizing either preferences or goods as misconceived, on the ground that there may be no answer to the question, which of two options is preferable. If the dimensions on which a job may be evaluated are incommensurate, then the instruction 'take the best job' is senseless. I propose to accept their claim that options are often incommensurably valuable, and to consider its significance for vagueness.[23]

It is important to see that the incommensurability claim would be misguided if it were stated too generally—in the form, for example, of a claim

---

[21] We might say that working hours and pay are incommensurate dimensions partly because those considerations are, in turn, incommensurable with respect to importance.

[22] Finnis, *NLNR* 113, and *Fundamentals of Ethics* (Oxford: Clarendon Press, 1983), 119; Raz, *MF* ch. 13.

[23] The notion that options are generally commensurable with respect to value is not just a consequentialist notion—it is supported by, for example, Ronald Dworkin: see 'On Gaps in the Law', in Neil MacCormick and Paul Amselek (eds.), *Controversies about Law's Ontology* (Edinburgh: Edinburgh University Press, 1991), 84, and 'Objectivity and Truth: You'd Better Believe It' (1996) 25 *Philosophy and Public Affairs* 87. The obvious objection to claims of incommensurability is that people do in fact choose between allegedly incommensurable options, and that while they may find such decisions difficult, they do not have the sensation of choosing without a reason. But the fact that a person reasonably chooses A or B does not imply that reason requires A or requires B, even if reason requires that a choice be made. Finnis argues that the phenomenology of choice includes a tendency (presumably not an irrational tendency) to view the choices one has made as choices supported by reason. Raz responds to similar objections to the incommensurability claim at *MF* 335–40.

that no two careers can be compared with respect to value.[24] It is too easy to think of careers that would be unequivocally less preferable than either teaching or law, even for a person for whom neither teaching nor law is clearly preferable. Some such career (job X) is still *incommensurable* with job A and job B (they cannot be measured on the same scale), but job X is clearly less preferable. I will call A 'incomparable' with B, meaning that reason does not require a particular comparison; X is *comparable* but *incommensurable* with A and with B.

So the claim cannot be that careers cannot generally be compared — on the contrary, the claim has to be that careers *can* be compared, in such a variety of incommensurate ways that attention to the relevant considerations may not require that they be ranked in one way. If that is so, we can state the incommensurability claim in the very terms of the definition of vagueness that we borrowed from Grice: there are cases in which one just does not know whether to apply the expression 'preferable career' or to withhold it, and one's not knowing is not due to ignorance of the facts.

Because of their incommensurability, job A and job B are borderline cases for the comparatives 'preferable' and 'better'. So incommensuracy of dimensions is a form of vagueness of the comparatives of abstract evaluative expressions (such as 'good', 'beautiful', . . .).[25] Here an expression is 'abstract' if its application turns on plural, incommensurate dimensions.

This claim needs clarification and qualification. By calling incommensuracy of dimensions a form of vagueness, I seem to be saying that incommensurability is only a marginal phenomenon, and that is what Raz, for example, explicitly denies.

Consider Raz's 'mark of incommensurability': that neither of two options is better than the other, and it is possible to improve one without making it better than the other.[26] Now consider the choice of careers. Suppose that job A is a borderline case for application of the comparative expression 'preferable to job B': they bear the mark of incommensurability, because we can imagine a teaching job that pays a little bit more than job A, and is still not clearly preferable to job B. But if it paid as well as job B, job A would be clearly preferable to job B, because the working hours are better. We can imagine a sorites series of increments in pay: as the pay for job A increases, it gradually becomes more attractive, until it is clearly preferable to job B — but it seems that no single very small increment in pay would be enough in itself to make job A preferable, rather than a borderline case for 'preferable to B'.

---

[24] Cf. Raz: 'My point is not a skeptical one. There is no denying that some pursuits are more valuable than others.' *MF* 342.

[25] For an argument that what I call incommensuracy of dimensions leads to the same sort of indeterminacies as vagueness, see John Broome, 'Is Incommensurability Vagueness?', in Ruth Chang (ed.), *Incommensurability, Incomparability, and Practical Reason* (Cambridge, Mass.: Harvard University Press, 1997), 67.   [26] *MF* 325.

So there are clear cases of preferable jobs (jobs that pay more *and* have shorter working hours) and less preferable jobs (jobs that pay less *and* have longer working hours), and there are borderline cases in which one job pays more and the other has shorter working hours.

We can generalize this notion, and claim that, whatever the considerations are that go into evaluating a career, and however incommensurate they are, a job that is preferable on all the dimensions is unequivocally better, and a job that is less preferable on all the dimensions is unequivocally worse. If the dimensions are incommensurate, there are actual or possible borderline cases. The borderline cases do not necessarily begin just when it is no longer the case that one option is better on all dimensions. It may be perfectly clear that one option is better, even though it is worse in some respect than another option. There is no reason to expect a clear boundary to the borderline cases.

Incommensuracy of dimensions, it seems, is a form not only of vagueness in the broad sense, but specifically of imprecision (because it is a form of sorites susceptibility). It is important to point out that *not* all incommensuracy is a form of vagueness. There are various forms of incommensurability, and some have nothing to do with vagueness. Gradually increasing the pay for job A makes job A gradually more attractive, until it becomes more attractive than job B. But if you offer a mother increasing amounts of money to sell you her child, it would be reasonable for her to think that you are not even moving in the right *direction*. No borderline cases arise out of the incommensurability in value between keeping and selling your child. Raz calls such incommensurabilities 'constitutive', because a commitment not to weigh certain options (such as wealth, and keeping your child) is part of what constitutes the capacity to have certain relations (such as parenthood).[27]

It might seem that the options of keeping your child or selling it are *far* from incommensurable—that the reasonable parent weighs riches against keeping the child, and always finds the second option more valuable. There is nothing wrong with saying that the second option is better. Here the terminology that I have been using is useful: we can say that those options *are comparable*, but are still incommensurable. They are incommensurable simply because increasing the amount of money being offered does not make the sale option *more* attractive—so the two options are not being measured on a common scale.

Only incommensuracy of dimensions yields vagueness. In our jobs example the incommensurability in value of the two jobs means that we may face borderline cases for the application of 'better'. In the case of the sale of your child, there is no amount of money that would make it unclear whether

[27] *MF* 345 ff.

you would do better to make a deal. There could only be borderline cases if selling your child *could* be a good bargain.

If there are no borderline cases of constitutive incommensurabilities, we should not overstate the claim that incommensurabilities make abstract terms vague. But the more modest claim about jobs A and B is still very far-reaching: it extends to all cases of incommensurabilities in the application of abstract expressions like 'good rope'—to all cases of incommensuracy of dimensions. Note that the vagueness that arises from incommensuracy of dimensions is not just a feature of very abstract evaluative expressions such as 'good', but a feature of most abstract expressions. 'Crowd' is an example of an abstract expression: its application turns on the number of people in a gathering, but also on the density of the gathering. If gathering A is more numerous and less dense than gathering B, it may be unclear whether gathering A is more clearly a crowd. Most colour terms are examples too: because hue and saturation are incommensurate, some pinkish-reds may not be clearly redder than, less red than, or just as red as some purply-reds.

The application of some vague expressions involves little incommensurability (especially words that seem to refer to a single scale, such as 'heavy', 'old', 'slow', 'tall', 'wide' . . .)—and perhaps in some contexts there are no incommensurabilities in their application at all. But as with 'crowd' and 'red', there are obvious incommensuracies in dimensions of application of 'heap' and 'bald' (the philosophers' favourite examples of vague words), and the same is probably true of (for example) all terms for artefacts ('car', 'legal system'), and perhaps all terms for material objects ('mountain', 'galaxy').

Incommensuracy of dimensions entails vagueness of comparatives, and also entails that there is no precise answer to questions such as 'How good a novelist was Virginia Woolf?' or 'How bald is he?'

To sum up, incommensuracy of dimensions seems to be a pervasive feature of vague expressions. Does that mean that the incommensurability of, for example, jobs is a trivial, marginal problem? Chapter 7.3 will address that question, and argue on the contrary that incommensuracy of dimensions gives reason to conclude that indeterminacies in the application of vague expressions can be significant. It is true that the unclarity in the application of vague words always comes *in between* clear cases. But it is misleading to think of that unclarity as marginal, or a fringe, because those notions suggest that it is trivial—as if everyone were clearly tall or not tall, except for people between 177.3 and 177.4 cm in height (see Chapter 5.4). The implications of the incommensurability claim are reasons to think that indeterminacy is an *important* feature of the application of vague expressions. Within many domains from which someone has to choose, there may be *nothing but* borderline cases for the application of the words 'good' or 'better' (see Chapter 7.3).

6. Immensurability

Perhaps there is more to the problem of measuring options than incommensurability. Consider another example of Raz's: 'a good novelist, for example, might be judged by his humour, his insight, his imaginativeness and his ability to plot'.[28] Raz points out that these attributes are incommensurate. And while some novelists are clearly better than some others, many are incommensurably good, so that it is unclear which is better. This section and the next mention two further respects, besides incommensurability, in which it may be unclear how to evaluate a novelist.

First, there is no precise answer to the question 'How humorous (or imaginative ...) is this novelist?' There are no units of humour or imagination — those properties cannot be quantified. Perhaps that reflects the fact that there are, in turn, incommensurate dimensions of humour and of imaginativeness. But we have no reason to think that the impossibility of measuring imaginativeness is a superordinate phenomenon that necessarily results from incommensuracy of multiple dimensions. That view would need to suppose that there are measurable (albeit incommensurate) dimensions of imaginativeness, or else that there is a hierarchy of dimensions that will reach down to measurable dimensions at some lower level.

We can invent the term 'immensurate' to describe criteria of application that do not correspond to a scale. 'Immensurability' is the property that something has if and only if it can be assessed in some respect in which it cannot be measured.[29]

Immensurability entails incommensurability: if the imaginativeness of any one novelist cannot be quantified, then some novelists will be incommensurable with respect to imaginativeness. And if two dimensions are incommensurate, that entails that an abstract expression whose application turns on both dimensions is immensurate: if humour and imagination are attributes of a good novelist, and if they are incommensurate, then novelists are immensurable with respect to excellence.

Like incommensuracy, immensuracy entails vagueness of comparatives, and also that there is no precise answer to a question such as 'How imaginative is he?' Like incommensurability, immensurability is a common feature of the application of ordinary descriptive expressions. Examples are expressions for personality traits ('inquisitive', 'sensitive' ...). And terms for ordinary material objects tend to be immensurate with respect to their shape — not because they do not have characteristic shapes, and not because we cannot think of ways of quantifying shapes, but because there is some-

---

[28] *MF* 326.

[29] The claim that, for example, funniness cannot be measured presupposes a notion of measurement (and perhaps a notion of quantity); I address those notions briefly in the discussion of Griffin's views on incommensurability in Ch. 7.3 below.

times no answer to the question whether A is more heap-shaped, or more mountain-shaped, or more desk-shaped, than B.

7. Contestability

The application of an expression is 'contestable' if people who know all the facts can reasonably disagree about whether the expression applies to something. Contestability seems to be a form (or a feature) of vagueness: if it is reasonable to disagree about the application of an expression, it seems that someone might also reasonably be in doubt about whether to apply it. But Ronald Dworkin has long argued that 'contested concepts'[30] are not vague. His argument is that such reasonable disagreements are typically not about borderline cases, but about 'pivotal' cases—cases which *each* side in the dispute thinks are *clear*. So to the requirement of *reasonable* disagreement, we should add that for a concept to be contestable, it must be possible to have, as Dworkin might put it, a *substantive* disagreement—a disagreement that turns on different theoretical understandings of the term in question.

Dworkin's argument deserves attention because he claims, roughly, that vagueness in the law is inconsequential. The claim is an element in his complex argument that there is a right answer to virtually any legal dispute. That view deserves a close look, and it will be addressed in Chapter 4.3 and Chapters 8.1–8.3.

8. Family Resemblances

As part of his remarks on the application of words in *The Concept of Law*, Hart suggested that it was dogmatic to think that there must be one common feature or set of features that something must have if a term is to apply to it,[31] and he drew both on Wittgenstein's suggestive term and on his remark about games: 'if you look at them you will not see something that is common to *all*, but similarities, relationships, and a whole series of them at that. . . . we see a complicated network of similarities overlapping and criss-crossing: sometimes overall similarities, sometimes similarities of detail'.[32] Games vary widely in a wide variety of ways, but that does not mean that they have no common features. Some philosophers have suggested that there is no obstacle to stating common features of games, and Bede Rundle has suggested that the word would not be univocal if we could not do so.[33] Resolving the

---

[30] *TRS* 103; he also refers to such concepts as 'concepts that admit of different conceptions' (103) and 'abstract' concepts (103), and suggests that 'moral concepts' are contested concepts (136). He denies that they are vague at *TRS* 135–6 and *LE* 17.   [31] *CL* 15.

[32] *PI* 66; *CL* 280.

[33] Rundle, *Wittgenstein and Contemporary Philosophy of Language* (Oxford: Blackwell, 1990), 49–50; cf. Raz *PRN* 123.

question would mean asking what forms of multiplicity a good account of games has to incorporate, and what alternative to Wittgenstein's provocative metaphor would do justice to what he was trying to say. But we do not need to resolve those questions for present purposes. I claim that there is no better way to account for the application of vague expressions than in terms of resemblances to paradigm cases (see Chapter 7.4). That view does not entail (or need) a position on whether the objects to which a single unambiguous word applies can be linked only by 'overlapping' resemblances.

The understanding of vagueness proposed here does suggest, however, that if there are any family resemblance terms, they are vague. We could invent a term which applied precisely to *a*, *b*, and *c*, where *a* resembles *b* in some ways, *b* resembles *c* in others, and *a* resembles *c* in others. But there are no such terms in natural languages. If there are any family resemblance terms, they are all imprecise.

The reason is that resemblance is an *indefinite* requirement, which leaves it to language users to decide what counts as sufficient resemblance. There is no precise degree of resemblance that something must bear to any paradigm game in order to count as a game. The meaning of such a word seems to call on the user of a language to make an evaluative judgment: it seems to set a dummy standard. If there are any terms whose application turns on sufficiency of similarities (even if there are no family resemblance terms), we need to understand the application of dummy standards. In fact, the similarity model claims that the application of all vague expressions turns on sufficiency of similarities.

9. Dummy Standards

I am going to the store, and you ask me to bring home bananas. I ask how many I should buy, and you say 'enough'. Perhaps 'enough' means 'the right amount': you are declining to ask for any particular amount, but you are asking me to take into account the considerations relevant to deciding how many should be brought home. Is your request vague? We can say two things: (1) it does not seem to be a precise request—the considerations that bear on the rightness of an amount will not ordinarily require that you bring home a precise number of bananas (although we could easily imagine circumstances that require a precise number); (2) it is *different* from an ordinary vague request such as 'about half a dozen'—we might say that it does not request an amount (vague or otherwise), but requests you to choose an amount. Saying, 'enough' is like saying, 'you decide how many'. But it is different from saying, 'however many you wish'—the request itself requires you to consider what is appropriate.

In England the Supreme Court Act 1981 provides that people seeking judicial review of administrative action have standing only if the court considers that they have 'a sufficient interest in the matter'.[34] We might say that the Act sets a vague standard: it certainly does not say what precise interest gives an applicant standing. There are parties that clearly have a sufficient interest (e.g. a person who seeks to prevent a local authority from demolishing their home), and there are parties that clearly do not have a sufficient interest (e.g. a foreign national who seeks to overturn a defence procurement decision on the ground that it changes the balance of power with their home country). There may be many other clear cases, but somewhere in between there are borderline cases.

But perhaps it is better to say that the Act does not set a standard at all: that it calls on the courts to develop their own test of standing.

Let us call a provision that calls on a decision-maker to *set* a standard a 'dummy standard' (even if that is something of an oxymoron).[35] Dummy standards include provisions that prohibit excess, or require proportionality, or what is satisfactory, or due, or appropriate. Like the request for enough bananas, they presuppose a standard but do not lay down a standard.

It seems that vague standards bear a similarity to dummy standards, and that dummy standards bear a similarity to express grants of discretion. The Supreme Court Act might have been no different in effect if it had provided that applicants must have a 'substantial interest', or if it had provided that standing was 'in the discretion of the court'.[36] These three possibilities are *different*, because 'substantial interest' seems to *set* a standard (although it has no sharp boundaries), 'sufficient interest' seems to *presuppose* a standard but not to set one, and 'in the discretion of the court' seems to say that there *is no* standard. But they are similar in that the considerations that ought to go into a decision as to what to do in borderline cases of 'substantial' are the same considerations that ought to go into a decision as to how to exercise the express discretion. And they are the same considerations that ought to go into deciding what interest is 'sufficient'.

I do not think that there is any *specially* legal problem in sorting out the meaning of these different possible provisions. To understand all three — dummy standards, vague standards, and express grants of discretion — we have to understand pragmatic vagueness.

---

[34] Supreme Court Act 1981, s. 31(3).

[35] I do not mean that every piece of legislation that uses a term like 'sufficient' or 'satisfactory' sets a dummy standard. There may be rules of interpretation that give a particular (and possibly even a precise) content to such a standard. And if there is a doctrine of precedent, judicial decisions may give a particular content to a dummy standard.

[36] A provision conferring express discretion might well be treated differently: it might be taken to protect a decision at first instance from appeal to some extent, and it might insulate decisions to some extent from the doctrine of precedent. But it is also possible that courts would allow appeals (and take precedents to be binding) on the question of what principles ought to govern the exercise of the discretion.

10. Pragmatic Vagueness

I argued in Chapter 2.4 that context dependence is not a *form* of indeterminacy, so that the application of an expression is not generally indeterminate just because it depends on the context. But context dependence often seems to generate borderline cases.

Picture two different requests: (i) that you come to see me at 5 o'clock, and (ii) that you come to see me at about 5 o'clock. Now suppose that you come to see me at 5.05. Have you done what I asked you to do? We might be tempted to say that arriving at 5.05 would not comply with request (i), but would comply with request (ii). Request (i) is precise; request (ii) is vague.

But, of course, it may be perfectly *appropriate* to knock on my door at 5.05 when I asked you to come at 5 o'clock—and not because it is reasonable not to comply with my request, but because arriving at 5.05 counts as complying. You might be quite right to claim that you had done what I asked. In fact, we could imagine circumstances in which it would be rude to respond to request (i) by knocking on my door right at 5 (e.g. if it is conventional to be a little late). And we can imagine other circumstances in which request (ii) could only be properly met by knocking on my door within a few seconds of 5 o'clock ('about' might be a conventional politeness which is not to be taken advantage of). A puzzle seems to arise—it seems that no request is vague *or* precise, except with respect to circumstances.

We can resolve this puzzle if we can distinguish between the *meaning of the words* of the request, and *how the words are used*. We might say that this distinction is the distinction between what philosophers and linguists call 'semantics' and 'pragmatics'. If we draw that distinction, perhaps we can relegate the puzzle to pragmatics: we can say that request (i) is *semantically* precise and request (ii) is semantically vague. We can say that the requirements that arise from the two requests depend on the context, and that any vagueness in the requirements of request (i) is 'pragmatic vagueness', and that the requirements of request (ii), conversely, may be pragmatically precise. Does this distinction help?

One similarity between semantic and pragmatic vagueness is that we can devise forms of the tolerance principle to describe pragmatic vagueness. We might say that, when request (i) is used vaguely, a tiny difference in the time at which you arrive cannot make the difference between your meeting my request appropriately and your failing to do so. If arriving at 5.01 is appropriate, then arriving at 5.01.10 is appropriate. The sorites reasoning that arises from this pragmatic form of the tolerance principle has just the same structure as sorites reasoning with expressions such as 'heap' or 'bald' or 'about 5 o'clock' (expressions which we are calling 'semantically vague'). Indeed, we could describe pragmatic vagueness as the semantic vagueness of terms such as 'appropriate' or 'reasonable'.

Pragmatic vagueness can coincide with semantic vagueness. In some contexts, the only way to respond appropriately to the 'about 5' request may be to arrive within five minutes or so of 5 o'clock; *or* it may be quite appropriate to come at 6—all that will depend on our understandings, and the purposes of the visit, and other things that we have said, and so on. Note that the variability in the requirements of a request is not itself a form of vagueness; pragmatic vagueness arises from the fact that those variable requirements (the considerations that bear on how it is reasonable to take request (i) or request (ii)) will typically be *imprecise*.

There is an important reason for questioning the drawing of a sharp boundary between semantic and pragmatic vagueness: it is often impossible to isolate questions of the *truth* of statements, given a particular state of affairs (which we might call semantic questions) from pragmatic questions about what is appropriate or reasonable. Think of expressions such as 'useful', 'valuable', 'affordable'. We could say two things about their meaning:

(A) they apply only if something is *reasonably* useful, or valuable, or affordable (i.e. if it is useful *enough* to be adequate for a purpose, or is valuable *enough* to deserve pursuing etc., or is affordable *enough* to be a sensible purchase . . .).

or

(B) they are semantically precise but indefinite, so that they apply if something is of *any* use, or of *any* value, or can be bought *at all*. The fact that we only apply them when something is reasonably useful, or valuable, or affordable is a fact about pragmatics.

Here approach (B) seems to distance semantics fundamentally from the way people use words: as if it were *true* of *every* book (for example) that it is a valuable book, but we always use the term 'valuable' rhetorically, *as if* it were not true of books whose only value is for recycling.

The puzzle of whether to describe expressions as indefinite (and pragmatically vague) or as semantically vague is very far-reaching. Think of the expression 'violinist'. Does it apply truly to every person who has ever played, or even picked up a violin (but we *use* it as if it implied some standard of skill or at least persistence)? Or does it apply only to people who are reasonably skilful or at least persistent? Certainly the *use* of the word can implicate a very high standard—it makes sense to reserve it for virtuosi. We can identify such special uses of the word in special contexts as pragmatic. But what if its use in *all* contexts implicates *some* standard (lower or higher)? Then the semantics of 'violinist' cannot be isolated from the pragmatic factors that make particular standards appropriate in particular contexts of use: that is, we cannot say (as we are tempted to say with 'come at 5 o'clock') that 'he's a violinist' has a precise meaning that can be *used* vaguely.

Pragmatic Vagueness in Law

Pragmatic vagueness is important in law: it arises from pragmatic features in the application of legislative language—features that lawyers call 'interpretation'. A statute of Edward III prohibited giving alms to a 'valiant beggar', as a measure against the labour shortage after the Black Plague. What if someone should come on a valiant beggar 'in so cold a weather and so light apparel that if he have no clothes he . . . is likely to die by the way'?[37] The sixteenth-century scholar Christopher St German suggested that the *law* would punish someone who gave clothes to such a beggar, but that *equity* would exempt the alms-giver from the operation of the law. We could describe the result in equity as an interpretation of the statute (perhaps relying on an ascription of intention to the lawmaker, or on the purpose of the statute), or as a decision not to apply the statute (on grounds of conscience).

In carrying out that function, early English equity was a remarkable institutional response to the need for courts to do something reasonable with legal rules, including legislation. Courts sometimes fill that function without even mentioning equity (and English courts no longer mention equity when they interpret statutes). Courts can do so by appealing to the purpose of the statute, or to the intention of the lawmaker, or to analogies with other exemptions, or to public policy, or to the principles of the law, or by all of these techniques.[38]

We might say that, even if a beggar is clearly valiant, the statute does not apply in a blizzard. *Or* we might say that no beggar is valiant *in the relevant sense* or *for the purposes of the statute* in a blizzard. Because there is no sharp boundary to the circumstances in which equity (or the interpretive techniques of a court of law) will exempt someone from the statute, the statute is vague in a special respect which we can call 'pragmatic': we could say that it does not turn on the vagueness of any word, but on the imprecision of the court's interpretive techniques, or the imprecision of the reasons for not applying the rule, *or* we could say that it is a form of vagueness of 'valiant'.

Pragmatic features in the use of legislative language can be mistaken for a source of radical indeterminacy: a reason for rejecting Hart's notion of a core and a penumbra of application. Consider the question of whether an ambulance is prohibited from entering a park by a by-law prohibiting 'vehicles'. The question seems to debunk Hart's notion that there is a core and a penumbra to the application of a rule prohibiting vehicles in a park. Suppose that an ambulance enters a park to pick up someone who is seriously injured, and the driver is prosecuted for violating the rule, and a court acquits the driver. Hart

---

[37] *St. German's Doctor and Student*, ed. T. F. T. Plucknett and J. L. Barton (London: Selden Society, 1974), 99.

[38] In the much-discussed case of *Riggs* v. *Palmer* 115 N.Y. 506 (1889), for example, the court used all of the above.

seems committed to saying that the court has acted contrary to law, since it has not applied a rule to a core case (ambulances being clearly vehicles).

In fact, someone like Hart can respond simply to such a charge, although the simple response may generate complexities. Whether the court has acted contrary to law depends on what the law requires — on whether it requires that the rule be applied in such circumstances. It is conceivable that it *does*. Then the court has (perhaps wisely) not given effect to the law. But it is also conceivable that the court has a legal power (it may even have a legal duty) to change the law, or to depart from the law on grounds of conscience (equity). And it is conceivable that various interpretive techniques (such as those mentioned above) are themselves part of the law. If so, we can say that the law does not really prohibit vehicles from the park (but only vehicles that do not give rise to special exempting interpretive considerations). Or we can say that the law *does* prohibit vehicles, but that 'vehicle' in the relevant sense, or for the purposes of the prohibition, has to be understood in the light of those interpretive considerations. None of this poses a problem for Hart — he would face a problem only if it were *impossible* for the prohibition on vehicles to apply to ambulances. But the case of the ambulance in the park does show something important about the variety of ways in which it may be unclear what the law requires and permits. We could say that one such way is the indeterminacies that arise from the vagueness of legislative language, and another way is indeterminacies in the application of interpretive techniques.[39] In Chapter 7, I will argue that those two sorts of indeterminacy are fundamentally similar. It does not matter very much whether we distinguish them as semantic and pragmatic. What matters for present purposes is that both can be described as involving the same sort of reasoning, by reference to similarities — to clear cases of the correct application of a word (in the case of semantic vagueness), and to clear cases of appropriate use of an expression (in the case of pragmatic vagueness).

I do not propose to present anything like a theory of such reasoning; that would take a theory of the sufficiency of relevant considerations, and I expect that no such theory is possible. Relevance is not a theoretical notion, and if there is any less theoretical notion than relevance, it is the notion of sufficiency. I point out the parallel between semantic and pragmatic vagueness to show that we should expect nothing like a theory of semantic vagueness — that is, we should expect no good general explanatory account of when it is correct to apply a vague expression.[40] The similarity between semantic and pragmatic vagueness shows that, like analogical reasoning and unrestricted practical reasoning, the application of vague language can depend on the purposes for which the language is being applied, and can be a controversial,

---

[39] There may be a third, very important sort of indeterminacy, as to what interpretive techniques a court may (or must) use.

[40] I attack one such general account (claiming that the dispositions of speakers to apply or withhold an expression determine its correct application) in Chs. 6 and 7.

evaluative question. Decisions about the application of vague language in borderline cases cannot be isolated from evaluative considerations (see Chapter 6.4 below). These points do not entail that no difficult question has a right answer. Of course, they do not entail that there *is* a right answer to such a question, either. I will argue in Chapter 4 that there is no right answer to questions of the application of legislative language in some cases, and that that is shown by the fact that the evaluative considerations involved *cannot* generally be precise. But the claim has to be carefully qualified: it is not simply that when reasonable people disagree about the application of a vague word, there is no right answer.

11. Ambiguity

The contrast between vagueness and ambiguity is reasonably clear: 'painter' and 'rope' are both vague; only 'painter' is ambiguous. A vague word has one meaning (and its application is unclear in some cases); an ambiguous word has more than one meaning (and it may be unclear, in some cases, which is in use).[41] If a taxi driver asks if he should turn left, and you say 'right!', he may be in doubt as to whether you mean 'no, turn right!' or 'correct!'

Further distinctions are (i) syntax can create or resolve ambiguities ('turn right!' is unambiguous even though 'right' is ambiguous), but there is no such thing as syntactic vagueness; (ii) uncertainties arising from the use of ambiguous expressions can typically be resolved by finding out *which* meaning the speaker intended (if the speaker meant to play on words, or to create a puzzle, that is a fact about their intention too). Ambiguity is closer kin to homography ('lead'–'lead') and homophony ('hart'–'heart') than it is to vagueness. Ambiguity, homography, and homophony are all incidental features of language that, unlike vagueness, are only occasionally important (although they are occasionally very important) in law.

The relatively clear distinction between vagueness and ambiguity is not free from puzzles, however. We might say that some man with a little hair is bald *in a sense*, and that in another sense he is not bald. Then the unclarity is as to *which* sense of 'bald' is appropriate—and that sounds like a problem of ambiguity. The notion of different senses of vague words is discussed in Chapter 6.5, below;[42] it seems to be consistent with there being a fundamental difference between ambiguous and vague expressions.

---

[41] It might make more sense to use 'ambiguity' as a term for the occasional unclarities, and 'multiplicity of meaning' as a term for the property of words that may lead to unclarity; I think it is more conventional to use 'ambiguity' both for the property of words, and for the unclarities that may result from that property.

[42] And see the discussion in Ch. 5.1 of supervaluation theory, which portrays vagueness as a systematic form of ambiguity.

12. Beyond Words

Vagueness is not a self-contained problem. I may seem to be making it out as something much more *important* than it is supposed to be. I account for incommensuracy of dimensions as a form of vagueness; I claim that it is misleading to describe vagueness as a fringe or margin, that 'contestable concepts' are vague, and that questions about the application of ordinary vague words may include what Dworkin calls 'pivotal cases'. I claim that the vagueness of expressions is distinguishable but inseparable from its analogue, pragmatic vagueness, which is not a property of linguistic expressions at all, but purely a question of what it is appropriate to say and to do. And I propose that uncertainties in the application of evaluative expressions arise from their vagueness.

These consequences arise from an understanding of the notions of tolerance, and of borderline cases, and they call for a closer understanding of those notions. All non-artificial expressions discussed in this chapter appear to be susceptible to the tolerance principle, and they all yield borderline cases. It is true that borderline cases always *come between* clear 'positive' cases and clear 'negative' cases. That is, something is only a borderline case if we could identify or imagine cases to which the expression would clearly apply and cases to which it would clearly not apply. But the fact that borderline cases are always intermediate in that way does not tell us how widespread or how important the uncertainties are that arise in borderline cases.

It is ordinarily much more *important* whether someone has acted cruelly, or whether a job is good, than whether a collection of grains is a heap or whether a man is bald. But there is no fringe phenomenon in the use of expressions like 'heap' and 'bald' that can be coherently distinguished *as vagueness* from uncertainties in the application of 'cruel' or 'good'. No good account of borderline cases would treat 'bald' or 'middle-aged' as having borderline cases, and deny that there are borderline cases for the application of words like 'cruel' or 'good'.

The potential scope of the problem is unlimited. I do not propose to give a theory of everything, or even a theory of value, or a theory of meaning, although the arguments of Chapters 6 and 7 propose constraints that any theory of value or of meaning must meet. I propose to look at aspects of the sorites paradox—at higher-order vagueness, and at the obstacles to solving the paradox. The reason for doing so is to support some claims about the relevance of vagueness to an understanding of law; those claims follow in Chapter 4.

4

Vagueness and Legal Theory

VAGUENESS is a snare for legal theorists. They have grappled fitfully with an enigma it creates for legal theory—or, at least, for any theory that portrays courts as applying the law. If the law is formulated in vague language, what does a court do in a borderline case? If it is not clear what the law requires in such a case, how can a court apply the law? It almost seems as if there is no law for the case, and yet there is a legal provision that claims to tell people their rights and duties.

We can use the regulation of music in Britain to illustrate the problem. The Criminal Justice and Public Order Act empowers the police to direct organizers of 'raves' to shut down their sound equipment, and creates an offence of refusing to do so. The power applies to 'a gathering . . . at which amplified music is played during the night (with or without intermissions), and is such as, by reason of its loudness and duration and the time at which it is played, is likely to cause serious distress to the inhabitants of the locality'.[1] Perhaps 'music' did not sound lawyerly—the drafters persevered: ' "music" includes sounds wholly or predominantly characterised by the emission of a succession of repetitive beats'.[2] The definition of music is baffling, but it is still easy to imagine clear cases of a 'rave' as defined in the Act. It seems that there will also be borderline cases, chiefly because of the vagueness of 'serious distress'. Somewhere between the silent and the seismic, there is music to which the police power is not clearly applicable, and not clearly inapplicable.

Imagine one million rave organizers charged with disobeying a police order to shut down their music. All appear in the same court one after the other. The first defendant tormented most of Shropshire by emitting a succession of repetitive beats at a deafening volume, and he is convicted. All the defendants played the same music in the same way under the same conditions, except that each successive rave organizer played the music at an imperceptibly lower volume—until the one millionth rave organizer played it at a hush that undeniably caused no distress to anyone. He will be acquitted. But if the decrement in volume in each case is trivial, it seems that no particular conviction ought to be the last. Between any two successive defendants in the series, there is no difference that the inhabitants of the locality can perceive. Finding the organizer guilty in one case and not in the next case seems arbitrary, if there is no sharp boundary to the application of

---

[1] Criminal Justice and Public Order Act 1994, c. 33, s. 63(1).
[2] Section 63(1)(b).

the expression 'serious distress'. A court should be able to justify its decisions, and how can a trivial change in the music justify the difference between conviction and acquittal? If like cases should be treated alike, then the legal treatment of two cases should not be materially different when there is no material difference between them.

I will call that scenario the 'case of the million raves'. The court faces the task of dividing the defendants into two classes: the guilty and the not guilty. Yet there is no quietest rave. In this chapter and in Chapter 8 I will argue that that is not just a fact about the word 'rave', or the words of the Act. The law provides no technique for dividing the million defendants into guilty and not guilty, and yet the law would require the court to do so in the case of the million raves. If that is right, then the indeterminacy claim is supported. That claim threatens the cherished tenets of theories that take the standard view of adjudication: that the task of judges is to give effect to people's legal rights and duties, and to treat like cases alike.

1. Legal Theories

Legal theorists have argued about vagueness, but they have never come to grips with the paradox. Two opposed approaches to vagueness have been prominent in legal theory. One approach accepts the indeterminacy claim — that vagueness leads to legal indeterminacy in some cases. It takes the view that, in some cases, there is no right answer to the question of whether the expression applies. The indeterminacy claim is traditionally expressed by saying that a vague statement is 'neither true nor false' in a borderline case:[3] I will call that 'the traditional formulation'.

The other approach is to reject indeterminacy. This could be done by denying that the application of vague language is indeterminate in a borderline case. The epistemic theory of vagueness makes that denial; see Chapter 6. The second way of denying that vagueness leads to indeterminacy in the law, by contrast, has been popular with some legal philosophers. They concede linguistic indeterminacy (or take no view about it), but claim that law has special resources that eliminate any such indeterminacy — they claim,

---

[3] Joseph Raz formulated the 'indeterminacy thesis' in this way in a dispute with Ronald Dworkin about the nature of legal principles: 'if the content of the law is exclusively determined by social facts, then the law is gappy; that is, there are legal statements which are neither true nor false'. 'Legal Principles and the Limits of Law', in Marshall Cohen (ed.), *Ronald Dworkin and Contemporary Jurisprudence* (London: Duckworth, 1983), 73, 81. Raz uses the same formulation in a brief discussion of vagueness at *MF* 327. Cf. Jules Coleman: 'Philosophers generally agree that some sentences involving the application of vague predicates are neither true nor false.' 'Truth and Objectivity in Law' (1995) 1 *Legal Theory* 33, 49.

for example, that the plaintiff cannot succeed in a case in which the application of the law is indeterminate. David Lyons has recently expressed this view, in criticizing Hart's claim that the application of the law is indeterminate in a borderline case: 'It is unclear why the fuzzy boundaries of rules should cause gaps in the law. If a governing rule is not determinate enough to decide a case, it presumably cannot support a cause of action. A burden of proof cannot be sustained, and a defendant should presumably win.'[4] The 'presumablies' hint at unease. There seems to be something to the argument: in a borderline case, it is not clear that the plaintiff's case is made out. But that is all there is to it. It is not clear that the plaintiff's case is not made out, either. Lyons's approach ignores that fact, and concludes that cases in which the law does not clearly favour the plaintiff are cases in which the law does not favour the plaintiff.

The problem in a borderline case is precisely that it is unclear *whether* the plaintiff has a cause of action. The court cannot eliminate that problem by saying that, if it is unclear, then there is no cause of action. Suppose that a statute implies a term in a sales contract that the goods shall be 'of satisfactory quality', and suppose that the goods delivered under a particular contract are a borderline case for 'satisfactory quality'. If the matter is litigated, the court will have to decide whether the term was breached, and it cannot do so by applying Lyons's idea that the plaintiff's case cannot be made out. Whether the plaintiff is the seller (suing for the price) or the buyer (suing to recover the price) will depend on the accident of prepayment.

This example points out that being a plaintiff merely entails that you need to have a case. If yours is a borderline case, it will not be clear that you have a case, and it will not be clear that you do not, and the court will have to resolve the unclarity. Being a plaintiff does *not* entail that you will lose if yours is a borderline case. That is so not simply because it would be arbitrary for the buyer to lose as plaintiff and win as defendant, but because a legal system in which that happened would have *more* than just a statutory requirement of satisfactory quality; it would also have a rule that plaintiffs lose unless their case is clearly made out. Many legal systems have such rules in, for example, criminal law. Rules like that add something to the law. They do not repeat a principle that is implicit in the fact that a plaintiff must have a case.

Two important legal philosophers of this century have shared Lyons's view that law has resources that prevent gaps—Hans Kelsen and Ronald Dworkin. It is worth examining the very different approaches to vagueness

---

[4] Book review (1995) 111 *Law Quarterly Review* 519, 520, reviewing Hart, *The Concept of Law*, 2nd edn. (Oxford: Clarendon Press, 1994). It seems that the problem is not actually one of proof. What a plaintiff has to do is to prove facts that support a cause of action. In a borderline case, the plaintiff's problem is not that he or she cannot discharge the burden of proving facts, but that, as the second sentence of the quotation from Lyons suggests, it is unclear whether the facts support a cause of action.

that arise from their theories, not only because they are important theorists, but also because the difficulties that vagueness poses for their theories will enable us to identify the most important constraints that a good account of vague language imposes on legal theory.

This chapter sets out to identify those constraints by discussing Kelsen and Dworkin. I will try to support the following claims:

(1) The feature of vague language that is most difficult for legal theories to accommodate is higher-order vagueness: Dworkin's and Kelsen's theories cannot accommodate it.
(2) A legal theory should accept the indeterminacy claim.
(3) However, the traditional formulation of the indeterminacy claim, that a vague statement is 'neither true nor false' in a borderline case, is misconceived, and should be abandoned.

2. Kelsen: The Norm as a Frame

Hans Kelsen insisted that there are no genuine gaps in the law. The thesis survived all the complex transformations of his pure theory of law, from its classic formulation in 1934 until his death in 1973. In his zealous distrust of ideology masquerading as legal science, he suspected that any claim that the law does not give an answer to a legal dispute must cloak an attempt to evade the law. '[T]he principle that a positive legal order can always be applied to a concrete case', he wrote, 'is true of every positive legal order.'[5] This principle of completeness is based on a notion similar to Lyons's objection to Hart: in every legal dispute one party claims that the other is under a legal obligation. If that claim is not 'established',[6] the defendant has no legal obligation. A Kelsenian approach to vagueness would seem to side with Lyons against Hart. But the appearance is deceptive.

Kelsen's principle of completeness coexisted with a similarly durable doctrine of indeterminacy.[7] The law is indeterminate (*a*) when a valid norm confers an express discretion (e.g. a range of possible terms of imprisonment for an offence), or (*b*) when a general norm is ambiguous, or (*c*) when two purportedly valid norms conflict, or (*d*) when the linguistic expression of the norm is evidently contrary to the will of the authority that issued it.

---

[5] Hans Kelsen, *General Theory of Norms*, trans. Michael Hartney (Oxford: Clarendon Press, 1991) (hereafter *GTN*), 366; cf. *Introduction to the Problems of Legal Theory*, trans. Bonnie Litschewski Paulson and Stanley L. Paulson from the 1st, 1934 edn. of *Reine Rechtslehre* (Oxford: Clarendon Press, 1992) (hereafter *IPLT*), 84, and *The Pure Theory of Law*, trans. Max Knight from the 2nd, 1960 edn. of *Reine Rechtslehre* (Berkeley: University of California Press, 1967) (hereafter *PTL*), 245–6.　　　　　　　　　　　　　　　[6] *IPLT* 85.

[7] *Unbestimmtheit*, trans. as 'indeterminacy' in *IPLT* 78–9, 'indefiniteness' in *PTL* 349–50.

How can we resolve this tension between Kelsen's principle of completeness and his doctrine of indeterminacy? Kelsen himself set out to resolve it by claiming that a general norm is a 'frame'. Within the frame lie all the possibilities authorized by the lawmaker. A court will be applying the law if it gives effect to any of those possibilities. 'The fact that a judicial decision is based on a statute actually means only that it keeps inside the frame represented by the statute; it does not mean that it is *the* individual norm, but only that it is *one* of those individual norms which may be created within the frame of the general norm.'[8] Take the example of a law providing a range of sentences for an offence. Any sentence within the range will be legally valid, and any sentence outside the range will not. There is no gap in the law: every conceivable judicial disposition either is or is not provided for by the law. But there is indeterminacy, in the sense that there is more than one legally authorized disposition.

Now, Kelsen seems never to have discussed vagueness. But his treatment of ambiguity suggests that his doctrine of indeterminacy includes a doctrine of linguistic indeterminacy, and suggests a way to accommodate vagueness within that doctrine.[9] If a statute is ambiguous, and a defendant is liable on one reading but not on another, we might say that the application of the language of the statute is indeterminate, and Kelsen states that the law itself is indeterminate—that the court has discretion. We can construct a Kelsenian account of vagueness if we suppose that he would treat the application of a vague expression in a borderline case in the same way in which he treated the application of an ambiguous expression. If he did that, it would suddenly seem that Kelsen sides with Hart against Lyons.

Think of vagueness as ambiguity on a vast scale.[10] An ambiguous word like 'painter' has more than one meaning; a vague word, like 'tall', has an infinite range of meanings, as it could be sharpened in an infinite number of ways. An ambiguous norm is a frame, within which are the two or more meanings of the norm's expression. By using an ambiguous expression, a lawmaker confers discretion on a court to formulate an individual norm by choosing from those meanings. A vague norm is also a frame, within which are the infinite

---

[8] *PTL* 351; cf. *IPLT* 80.

[9] Claudio Luzzati has made a convincing argument that Kelsen's 'indeterminacy' is not linguistic in nature: 'Discretion and "Indeterminacy" in Kelsen's Theory of Legal Interpretation', in Letizia Gianformaggio (ed.), *Hans Kelsen's Legal Theory: A Diachronic Perspective* (Turin: Giapicchelli, 1990), 123. Kelsen's list of forms of indeterminacy ((*a*) to (*d*) in text above) supports that claim. Kelsen's notion of indeterminacy is an artefact of his preoccupations with the question of whether logic applies to norms, and with the relation between general and individual norms, which cannot be discussed here. It is sufficient for our purposes that Kelsen's doctrine of indeterminacy, though not a linguistic doctrine, gives his theory a potential device for accounting for linguistic indeterminacy. He used the device in that way when he discussed ambiguity; the discussion here proposes a way of using the same device to give an account of vagueness.

[10] 'Supervaluational' theories treat vagueness in this way; cf. Kit Fine: 'Vagueness is ambiguity on a grand and systematic scale.' 'Vagueness, Truth and Logic' (1975) 30 *Synthese* 265, 282. See Ch. 5.1 below. On ambiguity, see Ch. 3.11 above.

different ways of sharpening the vague expression of the norm. 'Tall', for example, could mean 'over six feet', or 'over five foot nine', or 'over five foot ten and a half' . . . By using a vague expression, a lawmaker confers discretion on a court to formulate an individual norm by choosing any of the sharpenings within the frame—any of the admissible sharpenings. This discretion is parallel to the discretion to apply one of the meanings of an ambiguous expression, and both are parallel to the discretion to impose a sentence within a range provided by law.

This Kelsenian account of vagueness escapes the objection to Lyons's account that I made earlier. It does not presume that a plaintiff can only win in clear cases. In a borderline case, it holds that the law authorizes the court to choose among sharpenings of the vague expression, on some of which the plaintiff would win and on some of which the plaintiff would lose. The account fails, however, for a reason that is also a (second) fatal objection to Lyons's view: it denies higher-order vagueness.

Vagueness is not, in fact, ambiguity on a vast scale, because there is no sharp boundary between admissible and inadmissible sharpenings of a vague expression. A decision-maker authorized to select tall candidates for a job has discretion, but not to adopt a reading of 'tall' as 'over four feet'. But what is the ambit of the discretion? We might say, it does not extend to candidates who are clearly not tall. But no sharp boundaries isolate the borderline cases from the clear cases. A norm, therefore, is not a frame, if by 'frame' we mean a sharp boundary demarcating the discretion of a court. Lyons's approach treats the borderline region as a sharply bounded area within which the plaintiff cannot win because he or she cannot make out a cause of action. The Kelsenian approach I have made up treats the borderline region as a sharply bounded area within which any decision the court makes is legally authorized. Neither approach succeeds, because it can be unclear whether a case is a clear case for the application of a vague expression.

The result is that Kelsen's principle of completeness fails. Perhaps there is no such thing as a minor flaw in a theory that sets out to be pure. This flaw is devastating. Without the principle of completeness, the theory can no longer portray courts as being able to act in every case on the authority of valid general norms—as applying the legal order to the concrete case. If the extent of the area of discretion is indeterminate, there will be cases in which it is indeterminate whether the lawmaker has authorized or forbidden a particular decision. Individual norms are not necessarily authorized by general norms. The dynamic, hierarchical structure of the pure theory cannot account for the application of the law.

It might seem that I have foisted a doomed account of vagueness on Kelsen, and that it would be more charitable to leave open the possibility that a Kelsenian could give an account of vagueness that would avoid this objection. To protect the principle of completeness, however, that account would have to eliminate higher-order vagueness. To ask whether that can be done, it will help to examine a sophisticated attempt — Ronald Dworkin's account of vagueness.

3. Dworkin: The Right Answer Thesis

Ronald Dworkin proposes that there is virtually always a single right answer to a legal dispute.[11] Jules Coleman has argued that 'Dworkin has abandoned the right answer thesis', replacing it in *Law's Empire* with a 'political theory of legitimate authority' which 'depends on associative communities exhibiting political virtues and ideals, not on the existence of right answers to legal disputes'.[12] But Dworkin keeps reasserting the right answer thesis,[13] and it seems that the continuing commitment is not accidental: his theory of legitimacy itself is bound to the right answer thesis by his view that the political virtues that legitimize the law are commensurable.

One possible objection to the right answer thesis is that if the language of a legal rule is vague, there is no right answer to a question of whether the rule applies in a borderline case. Dworkin responds that the objection fails 'to discriminate between the fact and the consequences of vagueness': rules of construction could eliminate the vagueness by, for example, requiring that the rule be applied only to cases in 'the indisputable core of the language'.[14]

Joseph Raz objected that Dworkin mistakenly characterizes vague terms as drawing two sharp lines instead of one: a sharp line between 'indisputable core' cases and disputable cases, and a sharp line between disputable cases and cases to which the term indisputably does not apply. Raz claimed that there are typically no lines between clear cases and unclear cases, and that, in the central type of vagueness, 'vagueness is "continuous"'.[15] Recently, Brian Bix has pressed the same objection, invoking Mark Sainsbury's argument that vagueness can best be characterized as boundarylessness.[16]

---

[11] For a defence of the thesis, see Ronald Dworkin, 'On Gaps in the Law', in Paul Amselek and Neil MacCormick (eds.), *Controversies about Law's Ontology* (Edinburgh: Edinburgh University Press, 1991), 84.

[12] 'Truth and Objectivity in Law', n. 3 above, 49–50; a similar argument is made in Jules Coleman and Brian Leiter, 'Determinacy, Objectivity, and Authority', in Andrei Marmor (ed.), *Law and Interpretation* (Oxford: Clarendon Press, 1995), 203, 214.

[13] See 'On Gaps in the Law', n. 11 above. Similarly, in a recent elaboration of his account of philosophical scepticism about morality and aesthetics, Dworkin proposes that the case for indeterminacy claims is weaker in law than in, for example, aesthetics: 'Objectivity and Truth: You'd Better Believe It' (1996) 25 *Philosophy and Public Affairs* 87, 136–8. But in those remarks he makes no categorical denial that there are any cases in which the law gives no single right answer.

[14] Ronald Dworkin, 'No Right Answer?', in P. M. S. Hacker and Joseph Raz (eds.), *Law, Morality and Society* (Oxford: Clarendon Press, 1977), 58, 67–9.

[15] Joseph Raz, *The Authority of Law* (Oxford: Clarendon Press, 1979), 73–4.

[16] Brian Bix, *Law, Language and Legal Determinacy* (Oxford: Clarendon Press, 1993), 31–2; see Mark Sainsbury, 'Is there Higher-Order Vagueness?' (1991) 41 *Philosophical Quarterly*

The objection to Dworkin's argument is that it ignores the problem of higher-order vagueness. The objection is valid. But it does not expressly deal with an elaborated version of the argument that Dworkin developed to defend his claim.[17] I will argue that the elaborated version fails. Examining the elaborated version, however, has an important consequence for philosophical accounts of vague language. Dworkin targets the traditional formulation of the indeterminacy claim: he characterizes the view that vagueness leads to indeterminacy as claiming that a vague statement is 'neither true nor false' in a borderline case. The 'neither true nor false' formulation is indeed the traditional way for philosophers to phrase the indeterminacy claim that Dworkin opposes. Examining the debate over Dworkin's argument suggests that the formulation should be abandoned. It is a garbled formulation of a valid claim.

Dworkin's Elaborated Argument

In Dworkin's formulation, V says that, if ϕ is vague, 'x is ϕ' may be true, false, or neither true nor false. V claims that, in the last of these three options, the use of ϕ in the formulation of a rule makes the law indeterminate. Dworkin says that indeterminacy in the law need not result: for example, a 'principle of legislation' could require that 'x is ϕ' be treated as false if it is not true.[18] When 'x is ϕ' is neither true nor false, it is not true. Therefore, the rule of construction (which I will call 'Dworkin's rule') appears to remove the indeterminacy that V alleges.

Now Dworkin's new opponent, R, claims that there is no sharp boundary between clear cases and borderline cases, so that, in V's terms, ' "x is ϕ" is true' may be neither true nor false. The crucial step in Dworkin's argument is to reject that claim: If 'x is ϕ' is neither true nor false, then ' "x is ϕ" is true' is false. Dworkin's rule still operates; there is no case in which ' "x is ϕ" is true' is neither true nor false.

The argument leaves the impression that V has made life difficult for R. Dworkin admits that R's predicament is unhappy, but he implies that R is stuck with V's view:

So R seems to be the victim of V's own formulation of his argument.[19]

The reader may feel that R has been cheated by this argument. After all, the circumstance that R called attention to might well arise, for all this complex argument. Someone told that if it is not true that a contract is sacrilegious he is to treat the contract as not sacrilegious may still find himself in the difficulty of being uncertain whether it is not true that the contract before him is sacrilegious. I agree. But that is a problem for V, not for my answer to R.[20]

---

167. Hilary Putnam makes a similar objection to Dworkin in 'Are Moral and Legal Values Made or Discovered?' (1995) 1 *Legal Theory* 5, 6.

[17] Ronald Dworkin, 'Is there Really No Right Answer in Hard Cases?', *AMP* 119.
[18] *AMP* 130.   [19] Ibid.   [20] Ibid. 405 n. 3.

R's problem is *V*'s assumption (which Dworkin points out[21]) that, whenever it is indeterminate whether '*x* is ϕ' is true, '*x* is ϕ' is not true. *V's* trivalent scheme (in which '*x* is ϕ' may be true, or false, or neither true nor false) presupposes bivalence for ' "*x* is ϕ" is true' (i.e. it presupposes that an utterance of the latter sentence must be either true or false). The trivalent characterization of vagueness frustrates the hapless *V* and the baffled *R*. The conclusion is that *R*'s problem is 'an embarrassment for *V*'s whole approach',[22] so that people should not say, as *V* says, that there is no right answer to a question of the application of vague language in a borderline case. As a result, Dworkin's argument against the indeterminacy claim is addressed only to *V*'s form of that claim. Dworkin's argument will be no objection to the indeterminacy claim, if it can be made without making *V*'s mistakes.

What's Wrong with V?

V's mistake is saying that, in a borderline case, '*x* is ϕ' is neither true nor false. Dworkin's mistake is his assumption that the claim that vagueness may lead to indeterminacy in a particular case must be framed in that way: that anyone who does not assert bivalence must assert trivalence. We can find a better way to formulate the indeterminacy claim, if we extract the kernel of good sense from *V*'s argument.

    V's claim is a negation. We can reformulate it in two ways, each giving a different scope to *V*'s negation. The first makes *V*'s negation external to the assertion that '*x* is ϕ' is true, and the second makes it internal to that assertion:

(1) *external negation*: in saying ' "*x* is ϕ" is neither true nor false', *V* is declining to assert that '*x* is ϕ' is true, and is declining to assert that it is false;

(2) *internal negation*: in saying ' "*x* is ϕ" is neither true nor false', *V* is both asserting that '*x* is ϕ' is not true, and asserting that it is not false.

The first option, external negation, is a figure of speech. It makes sense of *V*'s claim by not taking it in its literal meaning—by interpreting it as if *V* were saying, 'I wouldn't say "*x* is ϕ" is true, and I wouldn't say it's false'. Unless *V* is just being stubborn, the claim can be taken to mean that a borderline case is one in which a competent and informed speaker would not know whether to assert that *x* is ϕ. *V*'s claim is simply an idiomatic expression of doubt as to whether *x* is ϕ.

    If we take *V*'s claim in this way, Dworkin's rule does not eliminate vagueness. Reformulated in terms of external negation, Dworkin's rule is that '*x* is ϕ' is to be treated as false when a competent and informed speaker would be in doubt as to whether it is true. Dworkin's rule in this form would determine

---

[21] Ibid. 130.   [22] Ibid. 405 n. 3.

the outcome of cases in which a competent and informed speaker would hesitate to say that a contract is sacrilegious, and would hesitate to say that a contract is not sacrilegious. But this is a vague test for the validity of a contract, just as 'a contract is invalid if it is sacrilegious' is a vague test. There could be borderline cases for the application of a rule that a contract is invalid if a competent and informed speaker would say without hesitation that it is sacrilegious. That is so not simply because different competent and informed speakers might disagree, but also because any single competent and informed speaker will be uncertain about where his or her doubts begin.[23] Therefore, if we treat *V*'s claim as an external negation, *R* succeeds in showing that Dworkin's rule reduces indeterminacy, but does not eliminate it.

External negation is not a logical operation, but a rhetorical figure. Construing *V*'s claim as an external negation makes it into a rather misleading way of saying that it is not clear *whether x* is ø. It is misleading because it is easy to mistake for internal negation.

Internal negation is the negation familiar to classical logic. Logic countenances external negation of claims of knowledge and other modal operations, so that 'I do not know that she's at home' differs from 'I know that she's not at home' in the same way in modal logic as in ordinary speech. Similarly, logic discriminates between external and internal negation of quantifications, so that 'it is the case that all armadillos are not monogamous' differs from 'it is not the case that all armadillos are monogamous' in the familiar way in logic. But classical logic has no room for external negation of assertions. The only negation of the assertion $\vdash p$ is $\vdash \sim p$; there is no formula $\sim \vdash p$: the assertion sign belongs to the metalanguage, and the negation sign belongs to the object language.[24]

Dworkin has internal negation in mind in his argument against *V*. He defines *V*'s version of the no right answer thesis in terms of 'logical negation', explaining that $(\sim p)$ is the logical negation of (p), 'so that if (p) is false $(\sim p)$ is true, and if $(\sim p)$ is false (p) is true'.[25] And he states that *V*'s thesis 'holds that in some cases neither (p) nor $(\sim p)$ is true, that is, that in some cases bivalence does not hold'.[26]

But if *V*'s claim uses internal negation, *V* has worse problems than Dworkin's rule. First, Timothy Williamson has argued that claims such as *V*'s are absurd. *V* claims that in some cases, (p) is not true, and $(\sim p)$ is not true. If we accept the principle that truth is 'disquotational' (so that, for example, '*x* is ø' is true if and only if *x* is ø), then *V*'s claim leads to a contradiction:

---

[23] It is tempting to deny this claim; for reasons to accept it, see Ch. 5.2.

[24] This fact about conventional logic might be taken to indicate that we should make up a new logic, in which the external negation 'I do not assert that *p*' can be represented. That possibility would amount to inventing a three-valued logic, a strategy discussed below (n. 28).

[25] *AMP* 121.   [26] Ibid. 122.

(1) $\sim(T(p) \vee T(\sim p))$ (*V*'s denial of bivalence)
(2) $T(p) \leftrightarrow p$ (disquotational scheme for truth)
(3) $\sim(p \vee \sim p)$ (substitution in (1))
(4) $\sim p \mathbin{\&} \sim\sim p$ (De Morgan's Laws)
(5) $p \mathbin{\&} \sim p$ (elimination of negation)[27]

V's denial of bivalence entails the self-contradictory claim that x is and is not ϕ.[28]

V might reject some element of this argument.[29] Or *V* might accept the conclusion (that in a borderline case a contract is neither sacrilegious nor not sacrilegious, or is both sacrilegious and not sacrilegious)—and suffer the scorn of philosophers of logic, who value non-contradiction. After all, it makes a certain sort of sense to say, 'vagueness is genuinely paradoxical, so the only accurate way to describe what's going on is to contradict ourselves'.[30]

But there is a second, simpler argument that exposes the incoherence of *V*'s claim if it is taken at face value, as an internal negation. I propose that this simpler argument is actually a *worse* problem for *V* than the self-contradiction arising from the denial of bivalence.

The simpler, harder problem is that *V* cannot make either part of the claim. If it is not clear *whether* x is ϕ, it is not clear that 'x is ϕ' is not true, and it is not clear that it is not false. Not only are the two conjuncts of *V*'s claim logically inconsistent; *V* cannot even assert that either of them is the case.

---

[27] Here I have adapted the argument in Williamson, *Vagueness* (London: Routledge, 1994) (hereafter *Vagueness*), 187–9. As Williamson points out, the argument only works if the equivalent in his argument of *p* 'says something'. It does not work if we replace *p* with, for example, gibberish: nonsense cannot be true or false, and the conclusion (5) would not be a contradiction, but just meaningless. For Williamson's argument that a vague statement in a borderline case 'says something', see *Vagueness* 195–6.

[28] Note that three-valued logics can be constructed in which there is no contradiction in saying that a statement is neither true nor false: for discussion of examples dating back to C. S. Peirce, see *Vagueness*, ch. 4. A further example is G. H. von Wright's truth logic (Georg Henrik von Wright, 'Truth and Logic', in *Truth, Knowledge and Modalities* (Oxford: Blackwell, 1984), 26; I am grateful to José Juan Moreso and Pablo Navarro for pointing this out). Such logics yield a third option: instead of presenting *V*'s claim as an external negation with classical logic or an internal negation with classical logic, as I have proposed in the text, we could interpret *V*'s claim as an external negation, with a non-classical logic that countenances external negations (truth logic, for example, represents truth by means of a modal operator that has the effect of allowing external negation of assertions within the logic). Possible objections to using three-valued logics to deal with vagueness are that they replace the ordinary notions of 'true' and 'false' with artificial properties somewhat akin to the ordinary notions of 'clearly true' and 'clearly false', and that they ignore the reason given in the text below for not asserting that the utterance of a vague sentence in a borderline case is neither true nor false. Those objections cannot be developed here; it is enough for the present argument if *R* has available an alternative to *V*'s trivalence.

[29] The obvious stratagem would be to reject the disquotational principle (2). For Williamson's argument against rejecting disquotation, see *Vagueness* 190–2, and for a proposal that someone like *V* could reinterpret the principle, see Crispin Wright, 'The Epistemic Conception of Vagueness' (1994) 33 *Southern Journal of Philosophy (Supplement)* 133, 135–8.

[30] An approach with which Williamson has no patience: 'no attempt will be made to argue with those who think it acceptable to contradict oneself'. *Vagueness* 189.

There are utterances that *are* neither true nor false: examples are questions, commands, exclamations like 'Help!', and perhaps nonsense such as 'Tuesday is as pink as Thursday'. Vague statements in borderline cases are very different. We can imagine circumstances that would make a vague statement clearly true; no circumstances would make 'Help!' true. Moreover, an utterance like 'Help!' is *clearly* not true, and is clearly not false. It would be clearly wrong to say that it is either. In a borderline case, it is not clearly wrong to say that a vague statement is true, or to say that it is false: that is just what is in doubt. It makes sense to doubt whether a vague statement is true or false in a borderline case; it makes no sense to doubt whether 'Help!' is true or false.

If *V*'s claim is understood in terms of internal negation, then neither part can be made, and if both parts could be made it would arguably have the rhetorical function of a contradiction uttered for effect. If we construe *V*'s claim as a misformulated, self-contradicting internal negation that *V* is using rhetorically, we reach the same result as if we construe it as an external negation: *V*'s claim makes sense only if it is figurative. Perhaps the moral is that *V* should not formulate the indeterminacy claim by saying that a statement is neither true nor false in a borderline case, but by saying that it is unclear *whether* the statement is true.

What is the moral for Dworkin?

Because *V*'s claim, formulated as an internal negation, cannot be made and is contradictory, it gives Dworkin's rule nothing to work on. Dworkin's elaborated argument assumes that *V*'s alleged indeterminate category 'neither true nor false' is something that Dworkin's rule can treat as 'false'; in fact, it is absurd. Formulated as an external negation, on the other hand, *V*'s claim is not affected by Dworkin's rule, for the very reason Dworkin admits:[31] it may be unclear whether, for example, a contract is clearly sacrilegious, just as it may be unclear whether a contract is sacrilegious. That is a problem for Dworkin (and not just a problem for *V*), because it shows that Dworkin's rule cannot eliminate the unclarity.

It might be objected that Dworkin is right to think that *R* (along with anyone else who makes the indeterminacy claim) is stuck with *V*'s doomed formulation, *as long as R wants to assert that there is no right answer*. In saying that '*x* is *ø*' is neither true nor false, *V* was trying to say that there is no right answer to the question of whether *x* is *ø*. So arguing that *V* should not say that '*x* is *ø*' is neither true nor false seemingly amounts to arguing that *V* should not say that there is no right answer.[32] However, if it is indeterminate *whether*

---

[31] *AMP* 405 n. 3.

[32] This objection to my argument would be consistent with Dworkin's views: he treats the 'neither true nor false' formulation as characterizing the thesis that there are gaps in the law (i.e. the thesis that there is often no right answer to a legal dispute): 'the theory that says there are gaps

x is ∅, there is no right answer to the question 'is *x* ∅?' Does it make sense to say that it is indeterminate whether *x* is ∅, *without* saying that '*x* is ∅' is neither true nor false? I propose that it does: that we do not need to claim that there is a third truth value (or an infinity of truth values, or a lack of truth value) in order to claim that there is no right answer to the question 'is *x* ∅?'

As the sun goes down, *V* might say that it is indeterminate whether a particular moment is a moment of dusk or darkness, and that it is neither dusk nor darkness at that moment. Dworkin's rule could say, 'treat this third state of affairs as dusk'. It would be better to disagree with *V*, and to say, 'there is no third state of affairs; it's just unclear which of the two it is'. We do not need to assert trivalence in order to deny that there is a right answer in a borderline case, any more than, in order to claim that there is no last second of dusk in an evening, we must say that some third state of affairs intervenes between dusk and darkness.

Consider another example: When did the *Apollo 11* spacecraft leave the earth's atmosphere? To say that there was no last moment at which it was in the atmosphere (i.e. to say that it is indeterminate when it left the atmosphere), you do not have to say that the spacecraft went through a region that was neither in the atmosphere nor outside it.

Philosophers hanker to say that, if the truth of a statement is indeterminate, the statement is not true. There is no basis for this hankering. The sunset example and the atmosphere example show that there need be no third possibility, in order for it to be indeterminate which of two possibilities is the case.[33]

It seems that *V* should replace ' "*x* is ∅" is neither true nor false' with 'it is unclear whether *x* is ∅'. And then we reach the central theoretical problem with vagueness: how to characterize the unclarity in a borderline case. Chapters 5 and 6 defend a version of the popular view that we should call the unclarity 'indeterminacy', and say that, in at least some borderline cases, the meaning of the word does not determine whether the word applies.

Is Dworkin's Theory Affected?

How important is this argument to an assessment of Dworkin's theory of law? We need to ask whether the outcome of the debate can (1) advance or (2) impede Dworkin's thesis that there is virtually always a single right answer to a legal question.

in the law is the theory that says there are some, perhaps many, concrete propositions of law . . . which are neither true nor false'. 'On Gaps in the Law', n. 11 above, 84.

[33] Hilary Putnam says that a vague statement in a borderline case 'may have no determinate truth value' ('Are Moral and Legal Values Made or Discovered?', n. 16 above, 6). That shrewd formulation is consistent with the claim I make, as Putnam can be interpreted as saying not that the statement has some truth value other than 'true' or 'false', but that it is indeterminate which truth value the statement has. Crispin Wright tentatively rejects the notion of truth value gaps: 'The Epistemic Conception of Vagueness', n. 29 above, 138–9.

1. If Dworkin's rule did eliminate vagueness, Dworkin's argument would only establish that legal indeterminacy will not result from vagueness in the formulation of a legal rule *if such a rule of construction is used*. There may be no such rule. What is more, canons of construction tend to be formulated in vague language. Dworkin answers this objection by stating that 'we still leave open the question of how the law is affected by the fact that courts, in *these* canonical statements, have used vague terms'.[34] But Dworkin's argument that vagueness does not result in legal indeterminacy appeals to a rule for eliminating that vagueness. So vagueness in canonical formulations of canons of construction is outside the scope of that argument—unless, that is, there are rules for the application of the canons of construction that eliminate *their* vagueness. And either those third-order rules would have to be free of vagueness, or there would have to be rules for resolving their vagueness . . . Dworkin is reduced to asserting that the vagueness of a rule and the vagueness of rules of construction 'do not mean that our question has no right answer. . . . Nothing has yet been said, relying on the vagueness of the term "sacrilegious", to make us doubt that our question has an answer.'[35]

In fact, something can be said: the tolerance principle applies in just the same way both to 'sacrilegious' and to 'clearly sacrilegious'. When we face any single borderline case, this fact does *not* tell us that the law's application to the case is indeterminate. But it makes it perfectly clear that, unless the epistemic view is correct, there must be cases in which it is indeterminate whether a contract is sacrilegious or not.

2. Dworkin's right answer thesis is part of his theory of law as constructive interpretation of the legal practice of a community. It does not rely on the discussion of vagueness. Indeed, it might seem that Dworkin's discussion of vagueness is expendable, and that, by focusing on it, I have missed the point that the central elements of his theory leave the vagueness of language by the wayside.

It may well seem that the potent themes of Dworkin's theory of law are simply at odds with the argument that I have made. I may seem to have presumed that the requirements of the law are determined by the language in which the law is formulated, so that indeterminacies in that language mean that on some issues the law's requirements are *not* determined. Perhaps that view could be fleshed out with an explanation of what counts as a formulation of the law (i.e. with a theory of legal authority), and with an account of the systematic nature of law (of the circumstances in which you cannot understand what the law requires or permits simply by reading a formulation of the law, because you also need to understand rules of conflict, *vires*, repeal, precedent, and interpretation, and equitable doctrines, and so on). But no account of that kind—that is, no account which, even with important

---

[34] *AMP* 130.   [35] Ibid. 131.

qualifications, treats authoritative formulations as determining the requirements of the law—can be consistent with Dworkin's 'protestant' theory of
law. I claimed at the beginning of this chapter that vagueness creates an
enigma for any theory that portrays courts as applying the law: it could be
argued that Dworkin's theory simply is not such a theory, unless by 'applying'
we mean 'giving effect to the best constructive interpretation of'.

Throughout his work Dworkin has insisted that the law's requirements
cannot be identified (in clear *or* unclear cases) by asking how the language of
the authorities' purported formulations of law applies to a case. Thus,
Dworkin's discussion of legal principles in *Taking Rights Seriously* did not
simply add a new sort of standard to the legal toolbox; Dworkin claimed that
it is in the nature of law that people cannot identify legal rights and duties by
applying formulations of the law. *Rules*, he agrees, *are* 'applicable'—they
'provide' such-and-such, they 'stipulate' such-and-such; to state them is to
say how they apply.[36] *Principles*, on the other hand, 'state a reason', 'argue' in
a direction, are taken into account.[37] To state them is *not* to say how they
apply. Moreover, on Dworkin's view, someone who says that a rule is binding implies that principles support its application.[38] Therefore, no one can
state the requirements of the law merely by identifying the lawmaker, and
reporting what the lawmaker has required.

Similarly, in the theory of interpretation that *Law's Empire* expresses, purported formulations of the law go into the 'preinterpretive stage' with the
rest of the legal history of the community. Anyone who aims to state the
requirements of the law has only begun at that stage, and must go on to work
out what political virtues would justify the demands of the law, and then to
decide what set of requirements would portray the law as best exemplifying
those virtues. Stating the requirements of the law is never a matter of stating
the application of the words in which it is formulated.

Should we conclude that vagueness is neither here nor there in an interpretive theory of law? To address that question we need to focus on what is
really Dworkin's *main* argument about vagueness: he does not regard many
of the seemingly vague words used in formulating legal standards ('cruel',
'fair' . . .) as vague at all, but regards them as appeals to contestable concepts.[39] Vague words, in Dworkin's view, may present real (but uninterest-
ing) problems of *application*; concepts that admit of different conceptions, by
contrast, do not call for application at all, except in a special sense: they call
on people to participate in an interpretive practice of the kind described in
Law's Empire. So Dworkin warns against confusing 'the case in which a legislature uses a vague term, like "middle-aged" or "red", with the different

---

[36] *TRS* 24–5.   [37] Ibid. 26.   [38] Ibid. 38.
[39] See Ch. 3.7. Note that, when he makes the argument that indeterminacy arising from vagueness can be eliminated by a rule of construction, he expressly puts aside his account of concepts
that admit of different conceptions, for the purpose of argument: *AMP* 128.

case in which it lays down a concept that admits of different conceptions'.[40]
Law's Empire seems to maintain the same distinction: Dworkin calls vagueness a 'semantic defect'[41] and sees no semantic defect in words for concepts
that admit of different conceptions. Perhaps Dworkin could finesse vagueness by generalizing his claims about concepts that admit of different
conceptions to all concepts. After all, people have different conceptions of
middle age and redness.

But that approach would not eradicate vagueness. Words such as 'cruel'
and 'fair' and 'courtesy', which are Dworkin's examples of concepts that
admit of different conceptions, *are* vague in the characteristic sense identified in Chapter 3.2. They share with words like 'middle-aged' and 'red' the
susceptibility to the sorites paradox that leads to the claim that there are
indeterminacies in the application of vague words.[42] *That* problem is not an
artefact of a theory of law that suffers from a semantic sting: it is a problem
for an interpretive theory too.

Chapter 8 will address that problem further, by asking whether interpretation can eradicate vagueness. I will argue that, if we leave behind the 'application' view of law and adopt an interpretive theory, we will still have to
conclude that vagueness in the law leads to indeterminacies in people's legal
rights and duties.

4. Juridical Bivalence

It is a consistent feature of legal systems that legal institutions treat legal standards as if their application were bivalent. The potential content of court
orders is not bivalent, of course: penalties for offences and remedies in public and private law typically vary to correspond to variations in the seriousness of offences and in loss caused, and so on. But judgments are bivalent.
Lawyers talk as if everyone were either guilty or not guilty, either liable or
not liable. And courts yield one outcome or the other. We can call this way of
treating people's legal position 'juridical bivalence'.

To Dworkin, juridical bivalence is a reason to think that the requirements
of the law *are* bivalent.[43] John Finnis, by contrast, has called juridical bivalence 'a technical device for use within the framework of legal process'.[44] If
the indeterminacy claim succeeds, then juridical bivalence is, as Finnis

---

[40] *TRS* 128.   [41] *LE* 17; see also *LE* 351.
[42] Twenty-four-hour solitary confinement is cruel. So is 23-hour 59-minute solitary confinement. By a standard sorites series we can reach the conclusion that one minute of solitary confinement per day (or none at all) is cruel. Similar sorites series could be constructed for
'courteous', 'fair', 'reasonable', and so on.   [43] See *AMP* 120, and see Ch. 8.3.
[44] John Finnis, *NLNR* 280; see also 269, re the 'no gaps' postulate.

suggests, a device for coping with the complexity of affairs and the need for unequivocal outcomes.

It might seem that this device is a sham that should be abandoned: that the law should admit that there is a continuum of concerts, causing a continuum of distress to neighbours. Instead of forcing courts to divide the guilty rave organizers arbitrarily from the innocent, the law could respond with a continuum of degrees of guilt. This proposal promises to eliminate the indeterminacy arising from vagueness.

The promise fails. First, graded standards might be undesirable. Juridical bivalence radically simplifies some of the law's most difficult tasks. Often it seems to lead to injustice, when the court must give all or nothing to a plaintiff who, it seems, ought to get something in between. But in such cases it is generally the content of the law that is at fault, rather than juridical bivalence.[45] It is remarkably useful for the law to commit itself to saying that a will or a marriage or a contract is valid or invalid, rather than that it is somewhat valid. And although there are certainly degrees of culpability, it seems better for the court to respond with a finding of guilt or innocence (and with varying sentences), than to respond with a finding of some degree of guiltiness. The commitment to juridical bivalence enhances the court's claim to offer resolution (see Chapter 9.5 below, on the need for resolution). Perhaps we can even generalize and say that speaking unequivocally is vital to the self-respect that law cherishes.

Whether juridical bivalence is desirable or undesirable, though, we should see that the law cannot eliminate indeterminacy by abandoning it. The reason is that, just as there may be no right answer to the question 'Is this a rave?' (under the present law), there might be no right answer to the question 'How distressing is this concert?' (under a system that offered graded assessments instead of bivalent judgments). So, for example, measures of damages are often vague, even though they are graded: an injury leading to chronic backache does not call for any precise sum in compensation.[46]

Vagueness is much more complex than the simple linear reasoning of the

[45] For example, if a legal system suffers from all-or-nothing rules of negligence liability, it does not need to abandon juridical bivalence: it needs a sensible scheme of contributory negligence.

[46] So for many remedial decisions we could formulate sorites problems: if sum x_i is not sufficient compensation for *this* case of backache, then sum x_{i+1} is not ...; if six months' imprisonment is not a sufficient response to the seriousness of *this* assault, then six months and a day is not ... Not that all decisions about sentence and about general damages are sorites-susceptible: many are resolved by precise tariffs, or merely by the conventional use of round numbers. But sorites problems in remedies and sentences are important because unlike the the sorites problems that arise in the case of the million raves, they arise (and are resolved by stipulations) in many real cases. I have not found room in this book for a general examination of such sorites problems; I think that would need a close look at the nature of remedies and sentences, and a study of the extent to which they are available as of right (or are restricted by rights), and an account of the nature of the court's discretion, to the extent that they are discretionary.

sorites paradox suggests, because of incommensurabilities (see Chapter 7.3 below). There is more than one continuum of seriousness of distress. In regulating raves, the Criminal Justice and Public Order Act recognizes loudness and duration. If there is no right answer to the question of whether some very noisy, somewhat prolonged concert causes more serious distress than some rather noisy, very prolonged concert, then indeterminacies will remain in a scheme that gives an assessment of culpability that corresponds to the degree of seriousness of distress caused by a concert. With graded outcomes, just as with bivalent outcomes, a court has to give a precise answer in applying an imprecise standard.

5. Conclusion

Sorites reasoning has this ironic feature: it shows that the extent of the determinate is indeterminate. Because it is unclear whether some cases are in the core of application of a word, a rule of construction requiring that a rule be applied only in core cases cannot eliminate vagueness. I will argue in Chapter 7 that there are cases in which all the ample and complex resources of judicial interpretation of the requirements of vaguely formulated laws yield no right answer. The consequence of vagueness in formulations of legal rules is indeterminacy in the requirements of the law in some cases (and also indeterminacy in the answer to the judge's question 'How should I decide this case?' in some cases).[47] That conclusion seems to raise the unacceptable prospect of saying 'anything goes'. It seems mischievous to propose that there are cases in which there is no help for the conscientious judge who wants to do justice according to law—to propose that reason itself may have nothing to say about the outcome of important litigation. But that is the implication of the case of the million raves.

We can now return to the claims I have made:

(1) The feature of vague language that is most difficult for legal theories to accommodate is higher-order vagueness: Dworkin's and Kelsen's theories cannot accommodate it.
(2) A legal theory should accept the indeterminacy claim.
(3) However, the traditional formulation of the indeterminacy claim, that a vague statement is 'neither true nor false' in a borderline case, is misconceived, and should be abandoned.

The first point to notice is that claim (2) only holds up if vagueness leads to linguistic indeterminacy (Lyons and Dworkin accept, at least for the sake of

---

[47] That consequence will be avoided, however, if courts *replace* a vague standard with a precise standard, e.g. by specifying a period within which an action will be treated as having occurred 'within a reasonable time' for the purposes of an enactment using that phrase.

argument, that it does, and Kelsen could do so). Claim (2), therefore, relies on the rejection of the epistemic solution to the sorites paradox. In Chapter 6 I will propose reasons not to take the epistemic view.

The second point to notice is the importance of higher-order vagueness; in Chapter 5 I will take a closer look at that puzzle, by discussing the obstacles it poses to some proposed solutions to the sorites paradox.

The third point is that, even if we conclude that the facts of vagueness conflict with central claims of (to take the most important example) Dworkin's theory, nothing has yet been said as to whether the problem is trivial or enormous. If we conclude that, in the case of the million raves, the law does not identify a quietest rave, then we must conclude that there are some cases in which the law does not determine the parties' legal rights. But the question remains whether there are many such cases, or hardly any. By itself, the claim that there are no sharp boundaries to the application of vague expressions says nothing about how many cases there are in which the effect of the law is indeterminate—it only says that there are such cases. Chapter 5.4 suggests reasons for concluding that vagueness leads to significant indeterminacies: the same reasons that support the indeterminacy claim support the view that indeterminacies in the application of vague language are significant. The same elusive question is addressed further in the discussion of incommensurability in Chapter 7.3.

The final point to notice is the threat to the ideal of the rule of law. That ideal seems to forbid judges to decide cases otherwise than by giving the outcome determined by law. Theories adopting that view are popular. They make general theoretical tenets out of the standard view of adjudication: that it is the duty of judges to give effect to the law and to decide like cases alike. They take juridical bivalence not for the 'technical device' that Finnis takes it for, but as a picture of the structure of judicial duty. Chapter 9 faces up to the threat to the ideal of the rule of law that seems to result if we take a different view of the duties of judges.

But first we need to consider the efforts of philosophers of logic to solve the paradox of the heap. If those efforts succeed, they may rescue the standard view of adjudication. If, as I argue, they do not succeed, they may help us to reach a better understanding of the indeterminacy claim, and of its consequences for legal theory.

5

How Not to Solve the Paradox of the Heap

CAN the sorites paradox be solved? A solution might provide an alternative picture of the requirements of the law in borderline cases—a picture that would rescue the standard view of adjudication. Should we take it for granted that ordinary vague expressions are higher-order vague (as I did in Chapter 4)? What exactly is higher-order vagueness? A theory that shows that there is no such thing as higher-order vagueness, or that provides a technique for handling it, might rescue the standard view, by providing a model for the resolution of indeterminacies by the interpretive resources of the law. Finally, are the indeterminacies that arise from vagueness a trivial margin of fuzziness, or are they substantial? If they are trivial, perhaps the objections to the standard view can be ignored.

The questions about the sorites paradox and higher-order vagueness turn out to be connected. Like the theories of adjudication discussed in Chapter 4, various proposed solutions to the sorites paradox face problems with higher-order vagueness. In Section 1 I will give very brief accounts of three such solutions: supervaluation theory, degree theories, and the use of a 'definiteness' operator. We can generalize and say that theories of vagueness that seek to solve the sorites paradox, but also to postulate indeterminacy in borderline cases, face a problem of accounting for higher-order vagueness. They are at risk of swapping bivalence for trivalence, and denying one sharp boundary only to end up with two: (i) between cases in which an expression determinately applies, and cases in which its application is indeterminate, and (ii) between cases in which its application is indeterminate, and cases in which it determinately does not apply. Section 2 argues that no theory should deny higher-order vagueness, and offers the three theories mentioned an alternative: they can reiterate at higher orders the denial of a sharp boundary between truth and falsity that they made at the first order. Section 3 argues that such an approach is liable to run into a new form of pragmatic paradox which I will call the 'paradox of trivalence': denying sharp boundaries at all orders may lead to asserting sharp boundaries at an arbitrarily high order.

I conclude that higher-order vagueness is *truculent*: a theory should neither deny it, nor assert a particular number of orders of vagueness, nor even assert that ordinary vague expressions are vague at all orders.

Section 4 asks whether vagueness is trivial or substantial. The conclusions are (i) that there is no precise answer to the question 'How vague is a vague word?', and (ii) that although it is difficult to make general claims about the significance of vagueness, there are general reasons for rejecting the notion that it is trivial. Section 5 discusses the importance of a little-recognized fact about vagueness: that there may be no *clear* borderline cases of the application of a vague expression. Section 6 asks whether we can *dissolve* the paradox, in Wittgensteinian style, by not asking the question 'How big is the smallest heap?'

1. Semanticist Solutions

I propose that no theory should try to solve the sorites paradox. There are two general reasons for the proposal: the appeal of the familiar notion that vague words draw no sharp boundaries, and the fact that solutions to the paradox are bound to portray vague words as if they did draw sharp boundaries. The 'epistemic theory' expressly claims that there are sharp, unknowable boundaries between truth and falsity; I address it in Chapter 6. The potential solutions discussed in the present chapter are 'semanticist' theories: they claim that there are indeterminacies in the application of vague words.[1] My proposal is, of course, 'semanticist' in the sense that it claims that uncertainties in the application of vague expressions are not merely epistemic, because the meaning of vague expressions does not determine sharp boundaries to their application. But I will distinguish 'semanticist theories' as theories that assert indeterminacy *and also* propose a solution to the paradox.

The solutions to the paradox that I will discuss attack the tolerance principle. The epistemic theory claims that, in every sorites series, there is a counter-instance to the tolerance principle. The semanticist theories claim that the tolerance principle is false, or not altogether true, or that its truth is indeterminate, but they deny that there is generally any single counter-instance to the tolerance principle. I want to say that the tolerance principle can be true. Not that *any* tolerance claim is true, but that for the application of all ordinary vague expressions in most ordinary contexts, it is possible to come up with forms of the tolerance principle that are true. If we take that view, it leaves us in the predicament of what Crispin Wright calls a 'commonsensical indeterminist who essays to accept both the coherence of vague expressions—their possession of at least some determinate positive and negative instances—and their limited sensitivity [i.e. their tolerance]'.[2] The predicament is that we

---

[1] Note that philosophers of logic use the term 'indeterminacy' in various ways; in R. C. Koon's usage, for instance, the application of a vague expression is 'indeterminate' in an unclear case, and then the difference between epistemic and semantic theorists is a difference between those who think that indeterminacy is epistemic and those who think that it is semantic. See Koons, 'A New Solution to the Sorites Problem' (1994) 103 *Mind* 439.

[2] Wright, 'The Epistemic Conception of Vagueness' (1994) 33 *Southern Journal of Philosophy (Supplement)* 133, 141.

seem to be committed to the truth of the premises and to the falsity of the conclusion of a valid argument. That is an unbearably inconsistent set of commitments, not only for epistemic theorists but also for semanticists. It means going through life with an unsolved paradox. The most common approach of philosophers of logic who seek a solution is, as Wright points out, to try to draw 'a principled distinction between vagueness and tolerance'.[3]

My proposal needs a significant qualification. It is consistent with some solutions to the paradox, which are expressly presented as idealizations. Willard Quine, for example, solved the paradox by asserting bivalence, but admitted that to do so was to treat vague expressions *as if* they had sharp boundaries (see below, Chapter 6.6). Dorothy Edgington's theory of 'degrees of verity' is a degree-theoretical approach that treats people *as if* they bore a precise degree of closeness to certainty about the truth of a vague statement. Such theories give a precise account which bears a vague relation to the facts; they claim 'approximate truth'.[4] My claims are consistent with such idealized theories, although those theories *may* take a different view of how substantial vagueness is, depending on how approximate they are prepared to be.[5]

The point of this discussion is not to give a survey of proposed solutions to the paradox, nor even to do justice to the sophisticated elaborations of the theories discussed.[6] It is only to bring into focus the importance of higher-order vagueness. I will not discuss other objections to the theories, and I will not claim that higher-order vagueness necessarily defeats those theories; I only want to show the difficulty of a problem which, it seems, *any* semanticist theory would face. I expect that the only way for a proposed solution to surmount the problem is to idealize. But I will not prove that it is so.

Supervaluation Theory

The theory that I assigned to Kelsen is a supervaluational theory.[7] The idea is that a vague expression can be made more precise, and that its meaning gives

---

[3] Ibid. 142.

[4] Edgington, 'Vagueness by Degrees', in Rosanna Keefe and Peter Smith (eds.), *Vagueness: A Reader* (Cambridge, MIT Press, 1997), 294, 300, quoting Frank Ramsey.

[5] Solutions based on an idealization provide models of reasoning which may be useful for various purposes of logicians. A major concern of such theories (and of much recent work on vagueness) is to give an account of the truth-functionality of complex statements using vague expressions; I do not address that problem.

[6] In particular, I do not deal with what Stephen Schiffer calls 'unhappy face solutions', which claim that the tolerance principle is false but (unlike the epistemic theory) do not explain away its plausibility. See 'The Epistemic Theory of Vagueness' (1999) 13 *Philosophical Perspectives* 480, and 'Two Issues of Vagueness' (1998) 81 *The Monist* 193. Williamson argues that Schiffer's unhappy face solution is 'a new version of the old idea that vagueness involves irredeemable incoherence'. 'Schiffer on the Epistemic Theory of Vagueness' (1999) 13 *Philosophical Perspectives* 505, 515.

[7] A classic statement of supervaluation theory is Kit Fine, 'Vagueness, Truth and Logic' (1975) 30 *Synthese* 265. For discussions of the difficulty higher-order vagueness poses for

people a discretion to do so (a discretion like a judge's discretion to impose a sentence within a range). Speakers can 'sharpen' a vague expression in different ways by adopting different boundary points. Think of a vague statement as 'supertrue' if and only if it would be true no matter how you sharpened it (it is true on all sharpenings), and 'superfalse' if it is false on all sharpenings. Borderline cases are cases in which a statement is neither supertrue nor superfalse: it is true on some sharpenings and false on others. Supervaluation theory treats supertruth *as truth*, and superfalsity as falsity. It treats vague statements in borderline cases as neither true nor false.

The paradox is solved because a statement of the tolerance principle is false (i.e. superfalse, false on every sharpening). The principle of bivalence holds, but it is neither true nor false that any particular step on a sorites series is *the* step from truth to falsity (a statement that the boundary comes at a particular point is true on one sharpening, and is false on every other sharpening, so it is neither supertrue nor superfalse).

Higher-order vagueness is a threat because the theory needs a notion of 'admissible' sharpenings. The meaning of 'tall' does not allow you to sharpen it so that no one less than nine feet tall is tall. So the clearly tall people must be those who are tall on all *admissible* sharpenings. But 'admissible' seems to be vague, just as 'clearly tall' is vague. If there is no precise answer to the question 'Which sharpenings are admissible?' there is no precise answer to the question 'On which sharpenings must a statement be true in order to be supertrue?' We could formulate a new form of the sorites paradox for 'x is bald on all admissible sharpenings' (a sorites paradox for 'it is supertrue that x is bald'). It seems that the tolerance principle must apply in this series, unless there is a sharp second-order boundary between clear cases and borderline cases.

Degrees of Truth

Things can be more or less red, and a statement that something is red can be closer to or farther from clear truth; these notions can be taken to support the more controversial claim that statements can be more or less true. A vague statement is one which may be true to a degree. The simplest scheme of degrees presents 1 as clear truth, 0 as clear falsity, and uses the real numbers between 0 and 1 to represent the degrees between clear truth and clear falsity.[8]

The paradox is solved because the conditional premiss in a sorites

---

supervaluation theory, see Timothy Williamson, *Vagueness* (London: Routledge, 1994), 156–61, and R. M. Sainsbury and Timothy Williamson, 'Sorites', in Bob Hale and Crispin Wright (eds.), *A Companion to the Philosophy of Language* (Oxford: Blackwell, 1997), 458, 474.

[8] See e.g. Kenton F. Machina, 'Truth, Belief, and Vagueness' (1976) 5 *Journal of Philosophical Logic* 47, 60–1. See also Sainsbury and Williamson, 'Sorites', n. 7 above, 475–8.

argument is not true to degree 1. The tiny departures from clear truth add up with each step in the sorites argument, until it arrives at a clearly false conclusion.[9]

Higher-order vagueness is a threat because such a scheme of numbers presents a sharp boundary between clear cases and borderline cases. There is a sharp boundary between 1 and real numbers less than 1. If there is no sharp boundary to the cases in which it is clearly true to say that someone is bald, the scheme of numbers misdescribes the application of vague language.

Definiteness

Clear cases for 'tall' are people who are *definitely* tall. Crispin Wright proposes to use the notion of definiteness to allow indeterminacy and defuse the paradox, without 'any heavyweight—e.g. supervaluational or degree-theoretic—semantic apparatus'.[10] Instead of negating the claim that there is a sharp boundary,

(1) $\neg(\exists n)(Fx_n \,\&\, \neg Fx_{n+1})$,

we need to use 'the expressive resources afforded by an operator expressing *definiteness* or *determinacy*'.[11] The phenomena of vagueness should not be described by saying that any bald man will still be bald if he gains one hair, but by saying that no one who is definitely bald can become definitely not bald by gaining one hair.

(2) $\neg(\exists n)(Def[Fx_n] \,\&\, Def[\neg Fx_{n+1}])$.

Instead of saying that there is no sharp boundary between truth and falsity, (2) says that there is no sharp boundary between definite truth and definite falsity.[12] The paradox is solved because one instance of (2) does not yield a conclusion that can be substituted in another instance of (2): it does not reiterate.

---

[9] A degree theorist might say that the paradox is solved because *modus ponens* is invalid: it does not preserve degree of truth, because the statement at step i in a sorites series may be less true than either of the premises that, by *modus ponens*, support it (the conditional premiss will have a very high degree of truth, and the statement at step i – 1 will have a slightly higher degree of truth than the statement at step i). Edgington has argued that a degree theorist should avoid that 'Scare Story' about *modus ponens*, and consider an argument valid if and only if 'the unverity of the conclusion cannot exceed the sum of the unverities of its premisses.' 'Vagueness by Degrees', n. 4 above, 305. On that conception of validity, *modus ponens* is valid.

[10] Wright, 'The Epistemic Conception of Vagueness', n. 2 above, 142.

[11] Wright, 'Is Higher Order Vagueness Coherent?' (1992) 52 *Analysis* 129, 130.

[12] As Edgington has pointed out, it is not clear 'what is the fate of the offending [(1)], once it has been noted that [(2)] is innocent': 'Wright and Sainsbury on Higher-Order Vagueness' (1993) 53 *Analysis* 193, 193. Wright has recently suggested that the offending (1) needs to be abandoned—but in an unspecified way. 'The Epistemic Conception of Vagueness', n. 2 above, 142. It seems that Wright asserts neither (1), nor the straightforward epistemic claim that (1) negates: $(\exists n)(Fx_n \,\&\, \neg Fx_{n+1})$. Perhaps we should say that, on Wright's view, the truth of the tolerance principle is indeterminate.

Higher-order vagueness is a threat because there seems to be no sharp boundary between statements that are and are not definitely true. So the paradox can be reformulated at the second order:

(3) $\neg(\exists n)(\text{Def}[Fx_n] \,\&\, \neg\text{Def}[Fx_{n+1}])$.

(3) is as paradoxical as (1): it is a form of the tolerance principle for 'definitely F'.

2. Higher-Order Vagueness

These theories have at least two general options for dealing with the threat of higher-order vagueness: to deny that it exists, or to treat it in the same way as they treat first-order vagueness.

Denying Higher-Order Vagueness

Even if the application of words is indeterminate in some cases, it is tempting to think that it *must* be either determinate *or* indeterminate—if it is even indeterminate *whether* it is determinate, it seems that it is indeterminate. We can phrase the same puzzle with another expression that philosophers use to talk about indeterminacy: even if there is sometimes no fact of the matter, it seems impossible for there to be no fact of the matter as to whether there is a fact of the matter.

So it is tempting to think that there can be no such thing as higher-order vagueness. After all, someone who is in any shadow of a doubt is in doubt. Suppose that we show someone a sorites series of concerts, starting with a concert that clearly fits the definition of a rave, and moving by imperceptible reductions in volume to a concert that clearly does not fit the definition. Our subject will be in no doubt that the first concert is a rave, and at some point in the series there will presumably[13] be a single first concert about which he or she feels some doubt. So it may seem that any speaker will find three sharply bounded classes of case: cases in which *x* is undoubtedly F, cases in which *x* is undoubtedly not F, and cases in which there is some doubt.

This tempting view should be rejected. If there is a first case in which our subject experiences doubt, that does not mean that there is a sharp boundary to the doubtful cases, because there is no reason why he or she should not have started experiencing doubt at a different point in the series, and because a rational speaker will not say, 'I have no doubts whatever about *that* case,

---

[13] In fact, we should probably not even presume that much; I expect that 'she is in doubt' is a vague statement. But we do not need to come to a conclusion on the nature of doubt, for the reason given in the text below.

but I'm not sure about *this* immaterially different case'. Even if doubt were a precise psychological phenomenon, 'doubtful case' would still be vague.[14]

Wright has suggested that there is a sharp second-order boundary to clear cases of the application of, at least, words like 'red': the clear cases are those on which there is a consensus, and they end precisely where consensus ends: 'We have therefore to acknowledge, surprising as it may seem, that a Sorites series of indistinguishable colour patches can contain a last patch which is definitely red: it will be a patch about whose redness there is a consensus . . . and its immediate successor will be a patch about which the consensus breaks down.'[15] But this notion should be rejected for reasons that Sainsbury has pointed out: 'There is no requirement on you to align your usage with that of the maverick who first breaks ranks.'[16] There is just no reason to take any precise feature of the use of the word 'red' to mark a sharp boundary to its correct application.[17]

There is a further reason not to deny higher-order vagueness, if any comparatives are vague (see above, Chapter 3.2). The vagueness of 'balder' is itself a form of higher-order vagueness: if 'balder' is vague, then there cannot be a determinately last clearly bald person, because some other person might be neither clearly balder, nor clearly not balder. Chapter 7.3 argues that incommensurabilities provide a reason for thinking that comparatives of vague words are very commonly vague. If 'balder' is vague, 'clearly bald' must be vague. If 'clearly bald' is vague, then higher-order vagueness cannot be denied.

Reiterating the Denial of Sharp Boundaries

Anyone who wants to claim that there are no sharp boundaries at *any* order must escape the fate that Dworkin prepared for R: they must escape trivalence. That is *not* necessarily fatal to the three theories mentioned here. Each of them could say that there is no sharp boundary between clear and borderline cases:

> *Supervaluation theory*: 'this sharpening is admissible' is true if and only if it is true on every admissible sharpening of 'admissible'.[18]

---

[14] For a similar argument against the appearance that there can be no higher-order vagueness, see Williamson, *Vagueness*, n. 7 above, 161.

[15] 'Further Reflections on the Sorites Paradox' (1987) 15 *Philosophical Topics* 227, 245.

[16] Sainsbury, 'Is there Higher-Order Vagueness?' (1991) 41 *Philosophical Quarterly* 167, 177.

[17] This claim is elaborated below, in Sect. 4.

[18] Fine proposes two alternatives for supervaluation theory: 'Anything that smacks of being a borderline case is treated as a clear borderline case. The meta-languages become precise at some, but no pre-assigned, ordinal level. The only alternative to this is that the set of admissible specifications is itself intrinsically vague.' 'Vagueness, Truth and Logic', n. 7 above, 297. The first alternative is to deny higher-order vagueness (though not necessarily at the second order). The second alternative would seem to admit that supervaluation theory cannot give a precise account of vague language (but I am not sure what 'intrinsically' means).

Degree theory: 'this is the hairiest man of whom it is true to degree 1 that he is bald' (and other statements of degrees of truth) may be true to some degree less than 1 and greater than zero.

Definiteness: we should not say

(3) $\neg(\exists n)(\text{Def}[Fx_n] \& \neg\text{Def}[Fx_{n+1}])$,

but

(4) $\neg(\exists n)(\text{DefDef}[Fx_n] \& \text{Def}\neg\text{Def}[Fx_{n+1}])$.[19]

Each of the three theories denied bivalence, and it seems that they can deny trivalence too, by reiterating at the second order the denials of sharp boundaries they made at the first order. I think that all such attempts are doomed—doomed to generate sharp higher-order boundaries instead of sharp first-order boundaries, and to face a higher-order form of trivalence, which divides cases into the positive cases untouched by indeterminacy of any order, the cases that are indeterminate at some order, and the negative cases untouched by indeterminacy at any order.[20] If so, then semanticist theorists face a form of pragmatic paradox: the denial of sharp boundaries leads to the assertion of sharp boundaries. I will try to illustrate this puzzle by using a form of denial of sharp boundaries similar to Wright's approach, which Raz hinted at in his argument against Dworkin.

3. The Paradox of Trivalence

Recall R, Dworkin's opponent who wanted to defend the indeterminacy claim by reiterating V's denial of sharp boundaries to the application of vague words. I argued in Chapter 4.3 that R should abandon V's formulation of the problem. But it might seem that R's most straightforward response to Dworkin would be to *insist* on reiterating V's claim. Dworkin foresees this defence, and tries to forestall it. He characterizes V as distinguishing 'x is not ϕ' from 'it is not true that x is ϕ', and claims that the distinction makes sense only if there are 'independent criteria' for asserting that x is ϕ and that it is not ϕ. Even if V can make this distinction, Dworkin denies that R can make the corresponding second-order distinction (which R needs) between (1) 'p is

[19] Wright makes an assumption about the logic of 'Def' which, he claims, yields paradoxical conclusions from (4), with the result that higher-order vagueness (unlike first-order vagueness) is incoherent. 'Is Higher Order Vagueness Coherent?', n. 11 above, 131–2. Sainsbury ('Is there Higher-Order Vagueness?', n. 16 above, 174–6) and Edgington ('Wright and Sainsbury on Higher-Order Vagueness', n. 12 above, 193–6) have opposed that claim. I will not address that debate, because of the reasons offered in Sect. 3 for thinking that reiterating the use of a definiteness operator will still lead to a paradox.

[20] Thus Sainsbury claims that such theories end up drawing two sharp boundaries, between the 'unimpugnably definite' positive cases, the unimpugnably definite negative cases, and cases in between. 'Is there Higher-Order Vagueness?', n. 16 above, 169.

not true' and (2) 'it is not true that p is true'. '(1) says ... that the criteria for asserting (p) are not met. It does not say that the criteria for asserting $(\sim p)$ are met. But (2) seems to say nothing more than the same thing, that is, that the criteria for asserting (p) are not met. What more or less might it be taken to mean?'[21] The obvious answer to Dworkin's rhetorical question is this: 'it is not true that (p) is true' can be taken to mean that the criteria for asserting that (p) is true are not met. (It does not say that the criteria for asserting that it is not true that (p) are met.) V thinks that (p) is true (i.e. the criteria for asserting (p) are met) only in clear cases of (p). It is perfectly consistent with *that* for R to think that it is true that it is true that (p) (i.e. that the criteria for asserting that (p) is true are met) only in clear cases *of its being true that* (p). R simply needs to claim that calling an assertion 'true' adds something to that assertion, and V's scheme supports that claim — in fact, V relies on that claim.

Dworkin suggests that this answer to his rhetorical question would be absurd: it seems that he would claim that the criteria for asserting that (p) is true *just are* the criteria for asserting that (p). Yet he has already allowed V to distinguish between asserting that (p) and asserting that (p) is true. Against R, Dworkin deploys a powerful intuition about truth: that adding a claim of truth to another claim does not add anything to the claim. But that intuition is fatal to V, and not just to R. If we put that intuition aside long enough to allow V to distinguish the claim that (p) from the claim that it is true that (p), then we have given a substantive content to what philosophers call the 'truth predicate'. We have distinguished 'it is true that (p)' (in some unarticulated way[22]) from '(p)'. We have inserted a logical space between '(p)' and 'it is true that (p)'. And then there is no way to stop R from inserting the very same logical space between the claim that it is true that (p) and the claim that it is true that it is true that (p), and so on.

Dworkin allows V to distinguish between $T(p)$ and (p), but does not allow R to distinguish between $TT(p)$ and $T(p)$. He allows that adding the clause 'it is true that ...' can add something to a statement, but only once. So 'it is true that it is true that ...' is identical in meaning to 'it is true that ...'. That can only amount to stipulating that the truth of, for example, 'this is sacrilegious' can be indeterminate, but the truth of 'it is true that this is sacrilegious' cannot be indeterminate.

I propose that we have to allow the logical space that V alleges to both V and R, or else to neither. If we allow it to both, does R's claim succeed against Dworkin's defence?

---

[21] *AMP* 405 n. 3.

[22] Perhaps, as Dworkin suggests, we have presupposed that 'it is true that (p)' means 'the criteria for asserting that (p) are met'. Note that if we follow this reasoning (and characterize V as defining 'it is true that (p)' as equivalent to 'the criteria for asserting that (p) are met'), R can still pursue the scheme of denying that there are boundaries at any level: it makes perfect sense to distinguish between the two claims (1) 'the criteria for asserting that (p) are [or are not] met' and (2) 'the criteria for asserting that the criteria for asserting that (p) are met are [or are not] met'.

In his response to the original form of Dworkin's argument, Raz mentioned a technique by which denials of sharp boundaries might be reiterated (although he did not propose to adopt the technique). He suggested that, 'on some semantic theories', the view that vagueness is continuous 'entails the existence of an infinite number of truth values', generated as in Figure 5.1.[23]

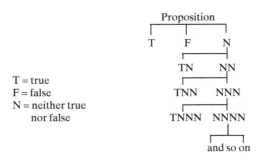

$$T = \text{true}$$
$$F = \text{false}$$
$$N = \text{neither true}$$
$$\text{nor false}$$

FIG. 5.1

The proposal is that someone like Dworkin's R might resolutely set about denying that there are sharp boundaries at each order in turn, and replacing each putative boundary between classifications at level n with a range of indeterminacy represented at level $n+1$ of the figure. I think that for R to follow this strategy would result in an even more elaborate scheme than Raz's (in fact, Raz's scheme is a fragment of such a scheme): see Figure 5.2.

Semantic theories that represent vagueness in this way face some problems. First, R should deny that there are sharp boundaries at *any* level, so that this figure can be continued to any number of levels. Because each level in the figure shows that purported boundaries at the previous level do not in fact exist, no finite level of the figure represents the facts about the truth value of (p) for all points on D. We would need to repeat the abolition of boundaries indefinitely to represent those facts. But looking at even the third level of the figure can make someone dizzy. It is no part of linguistic competence to be able to deal with the notion that the truth value of the statement that so-and-so is tall is, say, the twenty-seventh truth value from the left on the eighty-third level of the diagram. The notion is even less comprehensible than the notion that the statement has a truth value of 0.72681. If the hierarchy displayed in Figure 5.2 is a feature of the meaning of vague language, it is a feature that is hidden from the people who use the language. Doubtless, what would lead someone like R to deny that there are sharp boundaries is the instinct that the

---

[23] Raz, *AL* 74 n. 18.

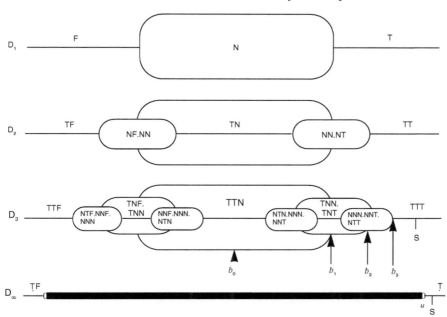

Fig. 5.2

Notes: *b* is a putative boundary between truth values of a statement applying a vague word. D is a dimension of comparison for objects to which the word might apply (the enumerations of D correspond to levels; at each level it is denied that *b* exists at the previous level). S is an arbitrary point at which it is certain that the word truly applies. *u* is a least upper bound for the range of borderline cases for the application of the word.

The diagram can be translated into English by reading F as 'it is false that', T as 'it is true that', N as 'it is neither true nor false that', by adding (*p*) at the end of every sequence of letters, and by reading '.' as 'and'. As Raz points out, F only appears at the end of sequences, because elsewhere it would simply amount to a disjunction of other sequences of the same level as the sequence which it commences. Only sequences beginning 'T . . .' are truth values (as Raz points out). The only completely determinate truth values are T and TF; any value with N is a borderline case of some order; any truth value with N is determinately a borderline case of a particular order. This diagram does not give the same representation as Raz's diagram, because I have not adopted his suggestion that $VTV = VV$.

meaning of words in a language is only what speakers of the language understand. Sharp boundaries would offend that instinct. But so would a hidden (infinite) hierarchy of border regions.

A second problem is that the scheme in Figure 5.2 will not, in fact, succeed in getting rid of sharp boundaries. The great attraction of the approach is that it *appears* not to present a higher-order form of trivalence. As we move along

D_∞ from left to right in Figure 5.2, there is no last case whose truth value includes N, and there is no first case which is Ṭ.[24] There seems to be no sharp dividing line between cases that are Ṭ (or ṬF) and the cases whose truth value includes N. That is just the result that R seeks.

But things are not so simple. I will call the hierarchy of truth values shown in Figure 5.2 'R's hierarchy'. We can describe R's hierarchy as a hierarchy of truth values, and of areas of indeterminacy. We can also describe it as a hierarchy of missing boundaries, marked b on Figure 5.2. b_n has the peculiar property that, although its location on D is indeterminate, we can make some assertions about it:

(1_b) for all n, $b_{n+1} > b_n$
(2_b) for all n, $b_n < S$.

Here, '>' and '<' mean 'to the right of' and 'to the left of' on D. (1_b) is R's proposition that there are no sharp boundaries at any level—that at level $n + 1$ there is a region within which the classifications diagrammed at level n are indeterminate. That is, the sequence (b_n) is an increasing ('monotonic') sequence.

(2_b) is a proposition that we can provisionally attribute to R: that there is some case S that is Ṭ (i.e. not a borderline case of any order). That is, S is an *upper bound* for the sequence (b_n). R's hierarchy spreads to the right (and to the left) as n increases, but it does not swallow up all of D_∞.

Now think of D as the real number line. It is an axiom of mathematical analysis that an increasing sequence of real numbers with an upper bound has a *least* upper bound. This is the axiom of 'completeness', which corresponds to the principle that there are no gaps in the real numbers. The least upper bound of the sequence (b_n), marked u on Figure 5.2, is a point such that, for an arbitrarily small number ε, there is a b_N such that $b_N > (u - \varepsilon)$. We can prove that the sequence (b_n) converges to a limit at u.[25] u, then, is *precisely* as unwelcome to R as any other sharp boundary would be. Borderline cases reach a limit at u: u is not a borderline case of any order; every point to the left of u is a borderline case of some order. Call the result the 'paradox of trivalence':

The project of denying that there are sharp boundaries of any order leads to positing sharp boundaries at an arbitrarily high order.

R wants to *deny* trivalence, but the technique of doing so itself leads to *asserting* higher-order trivalence. It is sometimes suggested that vague words are

---

[24] I am using 'case whose truth value is . . .' loosely, as a shorthand for 'case in which the truth value of the vague statement in question is . . .'.

[25] Let $\varepsilon > 0$. $u - \varepsilon$ is not an upper bound for (b_n), because u is the *least* upper bound. So there is a number N such that $b_N > u - \varepsilon$. For all $n > N$, $b_N < b_n$. $b_n < u$ for all n, so for all $n > N$, $(u - \varepsilon) < b_n < u$. So for an arbitrarily small number ε, $(u - \varepsilon) < b_n$. Therefore $\lim b_n = u$. I have borrowed this form of the proof from Kenneth A. Ross, *Elementary Analysis: The Theory of Calculus* (New York: Springer-Verlag, 1980), 42 (theorem 10.2: 'All bounded monotone sequences converge').

vague at all orders.[26] The paradox of trivalence suggests that the no sharp boundaries view should *not* make that claim—and it seems a good claim not to make. It is hard to make sense (let alone plausibility) out of the notion that 'tall' is 7th-order vague, or 4,166,332,096th-order vague). The no sharp boundaries view must deny that, for any n, there are sharp boundaries at n. Vagueness of order n should *not* be asserted for all n, but there is no order n at which there are sharp boundaries. These two claims seem paradoxical in themselves.

Ways of Escaping the Paradox of Trivalence

1. R could abandon proposition (2_b), above, and allow the hierarchy of borderline regions to swallow up all of D. It might seem relatively painless to do so: we simply allow that no vague statement is unequivocally true (T) or false (TF) in any case.[27]

There are two reasons for rejecting this escape route. The first is the initial consideration against the scheme in Figure 5.2: even if we abandon proposition (2_b) and the point u that it generates, we will still have an infinite hierarchy of regions of indeterminacy shimmering all over D—which offends R's healthy prejudice against semantic secrets. The second, related, reason is the pointlessness of theorizing that there is an indeterminacy at some level in the truth value of the statement that someone seven foot six inches tall is tall.

2. R could deny that the axiom of completeness applies. That might suit someone who is prepared to deny bivalence. It would not be necessary to deny that bivalence holds for propositions with which classically valid inferences can be formulated. R would claim that it is a feature of the meaning of vague words that their application behaves as if D were incomplete; perhaps we could say that this feature corresponds to the fact that the location of b_i is indeterminate. But I am not sure that it makes sense to do this: when the

---

[26] e.g. 'It is plausible that all natural languages are nth-order vague for all n.'. 'Glossary' to Bob Hale and Crispin Wright (eds.), *A Companion to the Philosophy of Language* (Oxford: Blackwell, 1997), 666, s.v. 'Higher-Order Vagueness'.

[27] Williamson adopts an epistemic analogue of this approach. In his theory, b_0 is the boundary between truth and falsity; it has a precise location on D. But the position of b_0 is unknowable, and it is knowable that (p) is true only to the right of b_1. b_1 also has a precise position, but we cannot know where it is either—we can only know that it is knowable that (p) is true at points to the right of b_2—and so on. So Williamson's theory presents a hierarchy similar to that shown in Fig. 5.2, but a hierarchy generated by iterations of a knowability operator, rather than by iterations of claims that there is no sharp boundary between two truth values. Williamson does not accept my (2), and as a result he reaches what he calls 'a mildly sceptical result': that 'for any proposition other than a logical truth there is a finite bound to the number of iterations of knowledge one can have of it' (*Vagueness*, n. 7 above, 229). For R a comparable conclusion would perhaps be unacceptably sceptical. It seems only mildly sceptical to suppose that no vague statement is knowably, knowably . . . true. It seems more sceptical to say that no vague statement is determinately true. I propose below that we should reject either form of scepticism.

sorites series runs along a number line (like a scale of height, for the application of 'tall'), denying completeness amounts to denying the completeness of the real numbers.

In any case, while the location of b_i is indeterminate, it appears that R would have to accept the proposition that, for each n, there is a line segment on D (with a length which, though indeterminate, is greater than zero) which represents the range within which there is an indeterminacy of order n in the truth value of a statement. We can accept analogues of (1_b) and (2_b) for a sequence of such line segments. That sequence will converge just as I alleged that the sequence (b_n) converges.

I propose that we should accept the following:

(A) R's distaste for sharp boundaries is a sound instinct.
(B) If we express that instinct by trying to deny at each order that there is a sharp boundary to the application of vague words, we end up with a new paradox: the project of eliminating sharp boundaries generates sharp boundaries.
(C) Moreover, accepting R's hierarchy as a representation of vagueness is in itself as unattractive as accepting sharp boundaries would be.
(D) The only way out of these difficulties is a conclusion that graphical representations of the truth values of vague statements are systematically misleading. I pursue that point in Chapter 7.

R needs some other approach than multiplying truth values. Note the consequence of the paradox of trivalence for Dworkin's elaborated argument. I have argued that, if he allows R to differentiate between '(p) is true' and '(p)', he cannot stop R from differentiating between 'it is true that (p) is true' and '(p) is true'. If that is right, R can come up with an infinite range of truth values. But a new version of Dworkin's rule *will* work: it can be reformulated to provide that a vague rule is only to be applied when it is Ṭ that the case fits the rule. So a modified form of Dworkin's rule, it seems, *would* succeed if V's 'neither true nor false' formulation were a good characterization of vagueness, even if Dworkin allowed R to reiterate the denial of sharp boundaries.

It seems that the paradox of trivalence will apply to supervaluation theory, to degrees of truth theory, and to the use of a definiteness operator. For any word whose application can be mapped on D, any theory that postulates a range of indeterminacy around putative boundaries (at all orders) will run into the same problem. And if a semanticist theory cannot escape the paradox of trivalence, it faces an objection: it cannot claim that there are no sharp boundaries in the application of vague expressions. It seems that an account of vagueness that wants to make that claim should abandon the *notion* of boundaries, instead of denying the existence of sharp boundaries at each order. Chapter 7 supports this proposal, and discusses objections to it.

Of course, there is one very simple way to respond to the paradox of trivalence: we could say that there are sharp boundaries to the area of indeterminacy. We cannot know where those boundaries are—so this proposal would offer an epistemic solution to the paradox of trivalence. The proposal tempts those who want to postulate indeterminacy in borderline cases and still solve the paradox.[28] But the idea that there are sharp boundaries to the application of phrases like 'definitely a heap' or even 'determinately a heap' faces the same objections as the idea that there are sharp boundaries to the application of the word 'heap'; I set out to articulate those objections in Chapter 6.

4. How Vague is a Vague Word?

Perhaps the standard view of adjudication is *roughly* correct: perhaps the application of vague language in the law is generally determinate (at least, once the resources of the law have been brought to bear), and cases in which there is no answer to a question of application are exceptional enough that they can be discounted. The standard view would substantially hold good, like a description of the movement of billiard balls that ignores wind resistance. A court would face a dilemma in the million raves case, but the defendants whose legal position is indeterminate would be only very few, and we can expect that real courts virtually never face cases in which the law does not answer the questions before the court.

We should not be hasty to reject this view. Assessing it means addressing a nebulous question: 'How vague are vague words?' What can we say about the extent of the indeterminacies in their application? If we can say nothing general, then there is nothing general to be said for or against this concessive vindication of the standard view of adjudication.

I think that there are reasons to conclude that the indeterminacy arising from vagueness can be substantial. It would be very odd to conclude that, although there are cases in which the application of the definition of a rave is indeterminate, they are limited to a tiny range of millidecibels, so that virtually every concert is either determinately a rave or determinately not a rave. The reasons to think that there are *any* such cases in the million raves case are

---

[28] Various philosophers have suggested such an approach; one particularly explicit example is Koons, who argues that there is 'semantic indeterminacy' in borderline cases, but writes, 'I am not embarrassed by a commitment to the existence of a sharp (but unknowable) boundary between those things that are definitely red (red under every permissible ordering) and those that are not definitely red. The desire to avoid sharp boundaries is no reason to postulate higher-order vagueness. I will not postulate such second- or higher-order vagueness unless some independent argument can be made for doing so.' 'A New Solution to the Sorites Problem', n. 1 above, 447. I propose that the independent argument is an argument against an epistemic account of the vagueness of Koons's terms 'definitely' and 'permissible', and gains support from a general argument against the epistemic theory (see Ch. 6).

also reasons to think that there are more than two or three. But whether there are tens or hundreds or hundreds of thousands may itself be unclear.

The vagueness of expressions varies greatly, and no doubt for some vague expressions indeterminacy is narrowly restricted. But perhaps vagueness can only be *trivial* if it is *pegged* to something precise. 'Roughly 177.3 cm tall' is trivially vague in a way that 'tall' is not. An understanding of vagueness should be able to say something about the difference between 'roughly 177.3 cm tall' and 'tall'. But both are sorites-susceptible. So an understanding of sorites reasoning itself would represent only a fragment of an understanding of vague words. To see this, imagine a semantic scenario: every person is either clearly tall or clearly not tall, *except* that clarity breaks down between 177.3 and 177.4 cm in height. Between those two heights, there are borderline cases, and any number of orders of vagueness, and, we might say, any number of degrees of truth of statements that a person is tall, or any number of admissible sharpenings of the word 'tall'. But someone 177.3 cm tall is definitely not tall, and someone 177.4 cm tall is definitely tall.

If all we know is that 'tall' is sorites-susceptible, then, for all we know, that scenario may be the case. In our scenario, we could formulate a sorites paradox—perhaps with steps in nanometres (though we could not formulate a paradox in millimetres: in our scenario it is not the case that anyone 1 mm shorter than a tall person is tall). And we could describe 'tall' as higher-order vague: the borderline cases are all taller than 177.3 cm and shorter than 177.4 cm, but it is not clear just where they begin.

If our scenario is absurd, there is more to vagueness than the sorites paradox. The fact that sorites reasoning seems to be possible tells us nothing about how vague a word is. To account for the vagueness of the word 'tall', it is tempting to think that we should be able to say *something* about how vague it is. We can say at least this: there is no *precise* answer to the question 'How vague is the word "tall"?'

Here is one way to approach that question: we could say that the extent of indeterminacy will be determined by the size of the increments with which a sorites series can be constructed. Consider two premises: 'any person who is 0.1 mm shorter than a tall person is tall' and 'any person who is 1 cm shorter than a tall person is tall'. We could construct a version of the sorites paradox with either premiss. If the latter is true, the word 'tall' is vaguer (there is more indeterminacy in its application) than if only the first is true. If not even the first is true, then the word 'tall' might as well be precise. It seems to be a necessary feature of vague words that there is no precise answer to the question 'What is the largest increment with which a sorites series can be constructed?' That means that the extent of the indeterminacy arising from vagueness is necessarily indeterminate.

We can call the step with which we can formulate a sorites paradox a 'tolerable step'. Consider three possible conditional premises:

(A) Anyone 1 mm shorter than a tall person is tall.
(B) Anyone 1 cm shorter than a tall person is tall.
(C) Anyone 1 m shorter than a tall person is tall.

(C) is false: 'tall person' is not *that* vague.[29] If (B) is true, 'tall' is much vaguer than if only (A) is true. If not even (A) is true, the vagueness of 'tall' is negligible, so that it might as well be precise, even if it is possible to formulate the paradox with a step of, say, a nanometre.

It might seem obviously true that, if the meaning of a word is tolerant at all, there is no largest tolerable step. It seems that if k is a tolerable step, then a step that is insignificantly larger than k must also be tolerable (in fact, if it is possible to *repeat* a tolerable step, it seems that twice any tolerable step must be tolerable, and three times . . .). This appearance is as obviously paradoxical as ordinary sorites reasoning: it leads to the absurd conclusion that any step is tolerable.

Roy Sorensen has formulated a 'meta-sorites' in which the categorical premiss is the proposition that 10,000 mm is not a tolerable step for 'short man', the inductive premiss is the proposition that a step 1 mm smaller than a step that is not tolerable must also be not tolerable, and the conclusion is that no step in millimetres is tolerable.[30] Sorensen argues that a proponent of the tolerance principle must accept the premisses, reasoning, and conclusion of the meta-sorites, which shows that the tolerance principle is inconsistent.

But it seems that the meta-sorites poses no new problem for a proponent of tolerance.[31] There are two reasons: (i) a proponent of tolerance who is not a nihilist seems already to be committed to the truth of the premisses, the validity of the reasoning, and the falsity of the conclusion of ordinary sorites arguments: such a person will just say that the conclusion of the meta-sorites is false too; it presents no new crisis. (ii) The proponent of tolerance is committed not only to Sorensen's meta-sorites, but also to a corresponding, reverse meta-sorites (of the sort I suggested in the text above), which starts from the premiss that, say, 1 mm *is* a tolerable step, and concludes that 1 m is a tolerable step. Sorensen's meta-sorites proves nothing, because it is reversible. The paradoxicality of meta-sorites adds nothing to the problems, if any, that an ordinary sorites series presents to a proponent of the tolerance principle.

But in any case, we do not need to engage in sorites reasoning to conclude that there is no precise largest tolerable step. The tolerance principle itself entails that conclusion. It is necessarily true that, if there is any tolerable step, there is no largest tolerable step.

---

[29] Although 'tall mountain' *is* that vague. See Ch. 6.5 on 'syncategorematic' terms.
[30] 'Vagueness, Measurement and Blurriness' (1988) 75 *Synthese* 45, 66.
[31] *Pace* Wright, who suggests that Sorensen's argument makes trouble for 'the commonsensical indeterminist'. 'The Epistemic Conception of Vagueness', n. 2 above, 141.

Suppose the contrary: suppose that 1 mm is the largest tolerable step. Then there would be some person $A_{(h = i)}$ (a person whose height is i), such that:

(1) $A_{(h = i)}$ is tall.
(2) $A_{(h = i - 1\,mm)}$ is tall.
(3) $A_{(h < i - 1\,mm)}$ is not tall.

(2) holds because we are supposing that 1 mm is a tolerable step, and for that to be the case is for it to be the case that anyone 1 mm shorter than a tall person is tall. (3) holds because we are supposing that there is no tolerable step greater than 1 mm, and if that is the case, there is a person who is tall, and is no more than 1 mm taller than someone who is not tall.

From (2) and (3) we conclude that 'tall' is precise. There is no tolerable step: you are tall if and only if your height is at least i – 1 mm. But that contradicts our supposition that anyone 1 mm shorter than a tall person is tall.

So it makes no sense to suppose that there is a precise largest step with which we can construct a sorites paradox. If the meaning of a word is tolerant, it follows necessarily that it is indeterminate how tolerant it is. Whether the sorites paradox can be formulated for 'tall' is a question of the meaning of 'tall'. But if it can be formulated, it follows necessarily that the largest tolerable step is indeterminate.

We can call this feature of vague words the vagueness of tolerance. The vagueness of tolerance is a form of higher-order vagueness. The familiar form of higher-order vagueness is the vagueness of phrases such as 'borderline tall' or 'definitely tall', or even 'determinately tall'. Those phrases are vague if and only if the magnitude of the range of borderline cases is indeterminate. If, as I have argued, tolerance is necessarily vague, then words whose meaning is tolerant are necessarily higher-order vague. If the tolerance principle holds, there is no precise answer to the question 'Where do the borderline cases start and stop?'

Noticing the vagueness of tolerance does not bring us very much closer to an account of the vagueness of 'tall', it seems, because we have got no closer to saying how vague 'tall' is. Indeed, the vagueness of tolerance itself, like the other features of sorites reasoning, could be illustrated even if someone 177.4 cm tall were definitely tall and someone 177.3 cm tall were definitely not tall. We still have not said how vague 'tall' is; we have only shown that it is indeterminate how vague it is. To understand the word 'tall', it seems that speakers need to understand something about how vague it is. The sorites paradox tells us nothing about that.

It seems difficult to say anything general about the extent of indeterminacy. But we can still say something significant: we have two pictures of trivial vagueness: 'roughly 177.3 cm tall', and a word similar to 'tall', for which we could formulate a sorites paradox in nanometres but not in millimetres. If the vagueness of 'tall' is different from the vagueness of such expressions, then it seems that we should reject the notion that vagueness is generally trivial.

5. No Clear Borderline Cases?

Inventing hypothetical borderline cases is a pervasive technique of philosophers of vagueness.[32] That is because it is not so easy to point to clear borderline cases.

In his argument that the supervaluational theory cannot account for higher-order vagueness, Sainsbury suggests that there are clear borderline cases: 'We intuitively contrast *clear* borderline cases and others. For example, one might think that a sixteen-year-old is a clear borderline case with respect to "child", whereas one might be unsure whether a fifteen-year-old is a borderline case with respect to "child".'[33] The way in which Sainsbury makes this claim *illustrates* the point that philosophers in search of an illustration of a borderline case typically need to hypothesize one. One might think that a 16-year-old is a clear borderline case, but then again one might not: one might be unsure whether a 16-year-old is a borderline case, or is clearly *not* a child. One might even be unsure whether to say that a 16-year-old is clearly a child, or to say that the same 16-year-old is clearly not a child. That distinguishes borderline cases from clear cases of the application of a vague expression: we do not need to say 'one might think' that a 4-year-old is a *clear* case with respect to 'child'. We might express this point by saying that there are no *paradigm* borderline cases: no cases which one must be able to identify as borderline cases of the application of 'child', if one is to display an understanding of the word.

A borderline case, it seems, is a case in which one is unable to say *either* that the statement is not true, *or* that it is not false. Or rather, one is uncertain whether to say one or the other. That uncertainty is consistent with there being a fact of the matter as to whether the statement is true or false, and it is consistent with uncertainty as to whether the application of the word is indeterminate. This is an insight of the epistemic theory that we should hold onto even if we reject the theory: uncertainty does not entail indeterminacy.

Remember 'minor+', defined so that it applies to people under 17, and not to people 18 and over (Chapter 3.4 above). If 17-year-olds are borderline cases, they are clear borderline cases. But that very fact seems to distinguish them fundamentally from borderline cases for the application of a vague

---

[32] For example, Kit Fine says that it is true that Yul Brynner is bald and false that Mick Jagger is bald, but he has to make up a 'Herbert' of whom it is neither true nor false that he is bald. 'Vagueness, Truth and Logic', n. 7 above, 268. Examples could be multiplied.

[33] Sainsbury, *Paradoxes*, 2nd edn. (Cambridge: Cambridge University Press, 1995), 38.

expression. Asked if a 17-year-old is a minor+, one would know just what to say—that the definition neither makes a 17-year-old a minor+, nor excludes a 17-year-old (it makes sense to say that it is neither true nor false that a 17-year-old is a minor+). And the definition leaves no room for reasonable disagreement about whether a 17-year-old is a minor+: there is nothing to disagree about, or to be unsure about. It *makes sense* for someone who speaks English to be unsure whether a 16-year-old is a clear case of a child, *or* is clearly not a child, *or* is clearly a borderline case. That distinguishes 'child' from 'minor+'. We might go so far as to say that, for example, 'clearly sacrilegious' is not *necessarily* even less vague than 'sacrilegious'.

I do not mean to claim that there are no borderline cases, and I do not even mean to claim that there are never any clear borderline cases for the application of any vague expression. No doubt, the task is to make a claim of the right level of generality. We have just no reason to claim that there are clear borderline cases for the application of all vague expressions in all contexts.

If there are no clear borderline cases for some expression, there seem to be two consequences. First, we have a reason to reject the 'neither true nor false' characterization of borderline cases (the 'traditional formulation' of the indeterminacy claim discussed in Chapter 4). The assumption that there must be clear borderline cases reflects the hankering to say that a statement whose truth value is indeterminate is not true. A theory should not assume that there must be clear borderline cases. We might put it that if there are no clear borderline cases, we should rule out theories that assimilate truth to clear truth.[34] The reason is that, in at least some borderline cases, it is not clear that a vague statement is not clearly true.

Secondly, a lack of clear borderline cases would play havoc with the ordinary conception of higher-order vagueness, which pictures second-order vagueness as unclarity in the distinction between clear cases and borderline cases. If there are no clear borderline cases, it seems that *all first-order borderline cases are also second-order borderline cases*: while there are some cases that are clearly clear cases, it is never clear that any case is *not* a clear case, and any uncertainty as to whether x is F coincides with uncertainty as to whether x is clearly F, or with uncertainty whether x is clearly not F, or both. But it seems implausible that there are sharp third-order boundaries between second-order borderline cases and clearly clear cases. If it is uncertain whether all first-order borderline cases are also second-order borderline cases, then it seems that they are third-order vague as well . . .

Higher-order vagueness is a destroyer of theories; the obvious response might be to seek a theory of higher-order vagueness, but we have seen some serious obstacles to theorizing about higher-order vagueness. If there are no

[34] As Fine's supervaluation theory does: '"A" is true ↔ It is definitely the case that A.' 'Vagueness, Truth and Logic', n. 7 above, 295. Perhaps something similar is done by all theories that use the term 'true' for one truth value in a scheme of more than two truth values.

clear borderline cases, and if speakers cannot handle orders of vagueness much higher than 2, then higher-order vagueness is an unstructured phenomenon that does not lend itself to any more theoretical pronouncement than the following:

A good theory should not postulate sharp boundaries at any order.

A good theory should not postulate an infinite number of orders of vagueness.

6. Conclusion: Can the Paradox be *Dissolved*?

If there are formidable obstacles to solving a paradox (i.e. obstacles to showing that a premiss is false, or that the reasoning is invalid), perhaps we should take Wittgenstein's advice, and seek a way to *dissolve* it, instead. That attitude seems to correspond to my suggestion that we should not try to solve the paradox, and the 'similarity model' is suggested by some of Wittgenstein's remarks (see Chapter 7.4 below). Yet, even if we decide not to try to solve the paradox, it is not a bit clear how to *dissolve* it, either.

Philosophical Investigations points out that expressions without sharp boundaries are *useful*,[35] and that may seem to be a promising start. The point was important to Wittgenstein, because he thought that it helped to clear away the demand for determinacy of sense that he attributed to Frege and to his own *Tractatus*. But many philosophers since Wittgenstein have made the same point about the usefulness of vague expressions, and have kept on trying to solve the paradox. The usefulness of vague expressions is consistent with many solutions (including those mentioned here, and including the epistemic theory), and does not in itself give any reason not to try to solve the paradox.

A more promising Wittgensteinian idea might be that the paradoxical question 'How big is the smallest heap?' is not a difficult philosophical question that calls for a theory, but a misformulated question. On this view, the sorites paradox is a flybottle—a trap for philosophers. Wittgenstein suggested that view in a brief discussion of the sorites paradox in *Philosophical Grammar*: ' "Make me a heap of sand here." — "Fine, that is certainly something he would call a heap." I was able to obey the command, so it was in order. But what about this command "Make me the smallest heap you would still call a heap"? I would say: that is nonsense.'[36] The notion is that philosophers should *stop asking* the nonsensical question. There are two problems with dismissing the paradox in this way. First, to ask the question 'What is the quietest rave?' is no *more* nonsensical than to ask 'Which of *these*

---

[35] *PI* 69, 71, 76, 79, 99.
[36] *Philosophical Grammar*, ed. Rush Rhees, trans. Anthony Kenny (Oxford: Blackwell, 1974), 240.

are raves?' with reference to the million concerts. Presumably Wittgenstein would not want to say that the question 'Is *this* a heap?' is nonsense — no matter how many times it is asked, and no matter what *this* is.

The second problem is that, like vague words, such questions have uses. It is common for clients to ask their lawyers such questions — 'What is the most our company can do in that jurisdiction without having to register?' 'What is the smallest proportion of chocolate we can use and still call it "chocolate"?' 'What is the earliest point at which we can arrest these bank robbers and still get a conviction for attempt?' If the law on these points is vague, then all these questions are like the paradoxical question 'How big is the smallest heap?'

Of course, it is not only lawyers that face such questions. A child asked to tidy a room may face the same form of question about the least tidy state of a room that counts as tidy. What is more, every practical question of the form 'How long should I wait for the bus before walking?' shares the paradoxical form of the question 'What is the smallest heap?'[37] Perhaps we can say that the expectation of a precise answer to such questions *would be* nonsensical, but the questions are not.

If we cannot just stop asking the paradoxical questions, it is not clear how to shake off the urge to solve the paradox. I will return to this question at the end of Chapter 6, after we have discussed the purest expression of the urge to solve the paradox: the epistemic theory.

---

[37] Edgington points out that, for example, dieters and procrastinators may have to ask themselves similar practical questions in the paradoxical form. 'Vagueness by Degrees', n. 4 above, 299. See also the discussion of sorites puzzles in evaluative reasoning in Ch. 6.4, below.

6

The Epistemic Theory of Vagueness

THERE is one simple way to solve the sorites paradox. It is to say that there *are* sharp boundaries to the application of vague words. In any sorites series there is some counter-instance to the tolerance principle—there is a sharp boundary. The most prominent form of this view holds that we do not or cannot know where those boundaries are; borderline cases are those that are too close to the unknown boundary for us to know which side of the boundary they are on. That is the epistemic theory of vagueness.

I have two purposes in discussing the epistemic theory. The first is to argue that it should be rejected. If it succeeds, then the indeterminacy claim is false, and there is a right answer to any question of the application of vague language used in law-making.

The second purpose is to support two related, controversial claims: that general evaluative and normative considerations are necessarily vague, and that the meaning of a word is (or is analogous to) a rule for its use. These claims support the indeterminacy claim: first, they underpin the notion that the application of vague linguistic expressions is indeterminate in some cases. Secondly, the two claims support the view that the interpretive resources of the law are themselves vague. The latter claim will prepare the ground for the account of the role of interpretation in law in Chapter 8. This argument supports the conclusion that the indeterminacy thesis is not just a point about legal *language*: vagueness is commonly a feature of legal rights and duties, and is a standard feature of the considerations on which judges ought to act.

I set out in this chapter to support those two claims, by examining and rejecting a type of theory of meaning. I do so by taking advantage of Timothy Williamson's sophisticated elaboration of the epistemic theory of vagueness. He proposes an account of the relation between meaning and use which supports the epistemic theory. In this chapter I give an opposed account of that relation, which supports and elaborates the similarity model of vagueness.

1. The Epistemic Theory

The epistemic theory has the attraction of simplicity. It also has the attractions of vindicating classical logic, of maintaining a simple relationship between classical logic and the meaning of words in a natural language, and of doing nothing obviously innovative with the notion of truth. Its problem is that it makes a bizarre claim about the correct application of vague words: it claims that their meanings determine sharp boundaries, which we cannot locate.

The epistemic theory has the consequence that you could lay a hair on the ground so that, all along its length, half of it is close to New York and half of it is not. Or you could, except that you have no way of knowing where the boundary is. The theory solves the paradox at the price of an apparently outlandish account of the meaning of words.

The most straightforward argument for the epistemic theory is to say that things just must be that way, because there is no other way to solve the sorites paradox. The acceptability of a bizarre truth about the meaning of vague words can be deduced from an acceptance of classical logic.[1] I will call this argument the 'logic argument' (see the discussion of Williamson's logic argument in Chapter 4.3 above).

Epistemic theorists do not restrict themselves to the logic argument.[2] They support it with arguments meant to dispel the appearance that their claims about meaning are bizarre. They offer explanations of the meanings of ordinary vague words aimed at unsettling the semanticist hunch that there can be no sharp boundaries to their application. I will call these arguments 'semantic arguments'.

I will address Williamson's work; he has given the most compelling statement of the logic argument, and the most systematic semantic arguments in favour of the epistemic theory.[3] I conclude that the theory is doomed to make untenable semantic claims, and that it can say nothing in defence of those claims but that they must be true as a matter of logic. That is, the epistemic theory must stake everything on the logic argument. Perhaps that conclusion is fatal for the epistemic theory, because it seems that the logic argument does not require us to assert bivalence for all vague utterances. As Williamson points out, it only requires us not to deny it for any vague utterance (193).

The fate of Williamson's semantic arguments is not only important for an assessment of the epistemic theory of vagueness. It is also important for an understanding of the relation between meaning and use. It is a familiar notion that the meaning of a word is determined by its use; Williamson interprets that notion as equivalent to the notion that the correct application of

---

[1] Cf. Mark Platts: the tolerance principle 'is false, since . . . paradoxes would be generated by its truth.' *Ways of Meaning* (London: Routledge & Kegan Paul, 1979), 230.

[2] Williamson suggests that they do not need to do so, and that it would not be helpful if they did: 'there is no need to insist, unconstructively, that there must be *something* wrong with the objections to bivalence in borderline cases'. *Vagueness* (London: Routledge, 1994), 186. In this chapter I will refer to Williamson's book by page numbers in parentheses.

[3] A third strand in Williamson's work has been to remove an objection he had seen to the epistemic theory, by explaining 'what makes us ignorant' (xi; Ch. 8 is his answer). I will not address that argument.

words supervenes on the dispositions of speakers. Scrutiny of this appeal to supervenience suggests that it gives an unsatisfactory account of meaning—an account that leaves the notion of correct application of words (and therefore the notion of a true statement) unintelligible.

2. Meaning and Use

Wittgenstein gave philosophy of language two slogans: 'the meaning of a word is its use in the language' and 'nothing is hidden'.[4] Williamson takes a view that many philosophers share: that the first slogan is sound if it is understood properly, and the second is misguided. He accepts the appeal of the notion that the use of (some) words determines their meaning; in his theory the use of those words also determines sharp boundaries to their correct application. Perhaps any semantic argument for the epistemic theory needs to take some similar approach, because it is hard to imagine what could determine whether a word like 'thin' applies to a given object in a given context, other than the use of the word. But it is also hard to imagine how the use of a word like 'thin' could determine *sharp boundaries* to its application, and this seems at a glance to be an objection to the epistemic theory. As Williamson puts it, the objection is that 'there is no line, for our use leaves not a line but a smear' (206). I will call this objection to the epistemic theory the 'use' objection.

To evaluate the use objection, we need to unpack the notions of determination, of use, and of meaning. In this section I will discuss Williamson's interpretation of those notions: he treats the view that use determines meaning as claiming that the correct application of words like 'thin' supervenes on the dispositions of speakers. I will claim that, if this supervenience account is correct, the use of words like 'thin' cannot be sharply bounded. On Williamson's view, that makes it impossible to give an account of vague statements as having a meaning in a natural language: it leads to nihilism about the meaning of vague expressions whose meaning is determined by their use. Section 4 proposes a different interpretation of the notion that use determines meaning—an interpretation that does not support the epistemic theory of vagueness. The account gives reason to think that understanding the vagueness of evaluative language is essential to understanding vagueness in general, and Section 5 addresses the vagueness of evaluative language. Section 6 gives an account of context dependence that is meant to support Sections 4 and 5.

[4] *Philosophical Investigations*, trans. G. E. M. Anscombe (Oxford: Blackwell, 1953), sects. 43, 435.

Determination

Williamson's response to the use objection offers an ingenious, austere account of determination: 'To say that use determines meaning is just to say that meaning *supervenes* on use' (206). And *that* is just to say that there cannot be a change in meaning, or a difference in meaning, without a change or a difference in use. Sameness of use entails sameness of meaning. That, Williamson implies, is all that we can make of the notion that use determines meaning.[5] An epistemic theorist can say that sameness of use entails sameness of meaning, so the fact that meaning is determined by use seems to give no reason to doubt that there are precise boundaries to the application of words such as 'thin'.[6]

Anyone who wants to reject the epistemic theory will feel an urge to make more of the notion that use determines meaning. It is important to Williamson to insist that nothing more can be made of the connection between meaning and use. He insists that there is no 'algorithm for calculating' meaning from use (206),[7] no 'recipe for extracting meaning from use' (207). But Williamson does not need to say that there *is* nothing more *to* the connection: the epistemic approach can say that the nature of the connection is unknowable, at least to humans. The conclusion is that the connection between meaning and use is a mystery. That connection poses no objection to the epistemic theory, because no opponent of that theory can give an account of the connection that shows that the application of vague words is determinate in clear cases, and indeterminate in borderline cases: 'The epistemic theory of vagueness makes the connection between meaning and use no harder to understand than it already is. At worst, there may be no account to be had, beyond a few vague salutary remarks. Meaning may supervene on use in an unsurveyably chaotic way' (209). I will argue that if meaning supervenes on use, then there cannot be sharp boundaries to the application of vague words (this section). I will also claim that, whatever difficulties there may be in giving a general philosophical account of the connection between meaning and use, no such difficulties stand in the way of an approach to meaning that is inconsistent with the epistemic theory of vagueness (Section 4). An account of meaning requires a notion of 'use' that is different from Williamson's.

---

[5] Cf. '"Meaning is use": that is, semantic facts concerning a language supervene on facts about the linguistic behaviour of masters of that language.' R. M. Sainsbury and Timothy Williamson, 'Sorites', in Bob Hale and Crispin Wright (eds.), *A Companion to the Philosophy of Language* (Oxford: Blackwell, 1997), 458, 480.

[6] Cf. Williamson, 'What Makes it a Heap?' (1996) 44 *Erkenntnis* 327, 331: 'The epistemic theorist can accept the . . . supervenience thesis and apply it to the borderline case.'

[7] Cf. 'algorithm for calculating reference'. Williamson, 'Wright on the Epistemic Conception of Vagueness' (1996) 56 *Analysis* 39, 42.

Use

For the purpose of stating the use objection, Williamson 'provisionally' identifies use with 'our dispositions to assent to and dissent from' a declarative sentence in varying circumstances (we will see that the theory needs to include some additional dispositions). We can call that notion of use 'use-as-dispositions'.

Williamson points out that we may be mistaken in (some of) our dispositions to assent to or dissent from the application of a vague word like 'thin'. We may even be systematically mistaken. These facts explain the appeal of the supervenience account: Williamson rightly insists that 'Truth-conditions cannot be reduced to statistics of assent and dissent' (206). Supervenience seems to allow Williamson to assert a necessary but non-reductionist connection between two sets of properties, without incurring an onus of explaining the way in which one phenomenon determines the other.

Meaning

Meaning and reference are interchangeable in Williamson's supervenience account of the connection between meaning and use. He characterizes the use objection as identifying the meaning of a declarative sentence with its truth conditions, and he sets out to show that the epistemic theory can assert that the use of words like 'thin' determines truth conditions that set unknowable sharp boundaries to correct application (205).[8] If use determines truth conditions, use thereby determines whether it is correct to apply a vague predicate to a given object in a given situation. So to state Williamson's supervenience claim, we can leave out the notion of meaning, and say that use determines the correct application (to given objects in given contexts) of some vague words.

To summarize, Williamson offers an interpretation of the notion that use determines meaning: *the correct application of vague expressions like 'thin' supervenes on the dispositions of speakers*. It is not quite clear which expressions this supervenience account applies to, although Williamson suggests that it is a general claim. He asserts that 'A slight shift along one axis of measurement in all our dispositions to use "thin" would slightly shift the meaning and extension of "thin",' and he suggests that the point applies generally, unless the meaning of words is 'stabilized by natural divisions' (231). Perhaps the claim extends, then, to all terms that are not terms for natural kinds. For the most part, I will leave aside the question of the scope of the supervenience account, and speak of 'words like "thin"'. But we should note that it

---

[8] However, meaning and truth conditions are not equivalent in the epistemic theory (a precise stipulative definition of 'thin' *would* change the meaning of 'thin', but *might not* change its extension (205, 214)).

is patently obvious that the account must apply to many terms (e.g. 'rave') used in formulating laws.

Note that the claim that a slight change in dispositions *would* slightly shift the extension of 'thin' is a significantly stronger claim than the supervenience claim. To say that correct application supervenes on dispositions is only to say that correct application *cannot change without* a change in dispositions. That says nothing about the consequences of any change in dispositions; it only states a consequence of identity of dispositions. There is an ambiguity in the claim that a slight shift in 'all our dispositions to use "thin"' would shift the correct application of 'thin'. Williamson may mean that *any* change in the base on which meaning supervenes (a base which includes all our dispositions) would shift the correct application of 'thin'. Or he may mean only to say that the correct application of 'thin' would change slightly if all speakers underwent a slight change in dispositions. Either claim would say more than merely that correct application supervenes on dispositions.

I will treat Williamson's supervenience account as including this stronger claim (in some form); when it is useful to distinguish it from the rest of the account, I will call it 'the correlation claim', since it seems to say that a difference (of some kind) in dispositions entails a difference in correct application.

The arguments in this section are all regress arguments. They allege indeterminacies in the base on which (in Williamson's account) meaning supervenes, and they rely on a claim that the supervenience account lacks resources to eradicate indeterminacies in the supervenience base. Their purpose is to show that Williamson's epistemic theory cannot maintain a connection between meaning and use. There are two alternative ways in which these arguments can succeed, and there is a third way in which the purpose might be achieved, independently of the regress arguments.

1. The regress arguments succeed if Williamson is committed to the correlation claim. They succeed because, on the correlation claim, if the supervenience base is not sharply bounded, then the correct application of a word like 'thin' will not be sharply bounded. If 'a slight shift along one axis of measurement in all our dispositions to use "thin" would slightly shift the meaning and extension of "thin"', then by the same token a slight indeterminacy in what counts as 'all our dispositions' would make the extension of 'thin' slightly indeterminate. It is not quite clear whether (or in what form) Williamson is committed to the correlation claim; perhaps an epistemic theorist should reject that claim as inconsistent with Williamson's view that 'Meaning may supervene on use in an unsurveyably chaotic way' (209).

2. Even without the correlation claim, the regress arguments succeed if correct application cannot be sharply bounded when the supervenience base is not sharply bounded. And that seems to be the case. Even if correct application supervenes on use in an unsurveyable way, it seems that it can be

sharply bounded only if it supervenes on a determinate base (i.e. everything must either be part of the base, or not be part of the base). The reason is as follows: if correct application supervenes on use, correct application can change only if use changes. If it is indeterminate whether something counts as use, then there may be two situations in which it is indeterminate whether use is the same in each. Then it will be indeterminate whether it is possible that correct application differs in the two situations. If it is indeterminate whether an expression may correctly apply in one situation and not in another, there is indeterminacy in meaning.

Compare another supervenience relation: the result of a fair election supervenes on the votes. If there is no answer to a question of the form 'Is *this* a vote?', then there is no guarantee of a determinate election result. The election will not give a result, if the result turns on the ballots whose status as votes is indeterminate. Supervenience of correct application of words on dispositions of speakers is similar, except that indeterminacy as to votes entails only the *possibility* that an election result will be indeterminate (the ballots whose status as votes is indeterminate may not make a difference). In the supervenience account of meaning and use, every indeterminacy in the supervenience base entails indeterminacy in the supervenient property. Elections answer yes/no questions, or select one or more alternatives from a list. If the epistemic theory is to use supervenience to maintain a connection between meaning and use, it needs the relation by which use supervenes on meaning to divide a continuum perfectly sharply (and, in fact, it needs that relation to divide a multiplicity of continua, corresponding to the grounds of application of words like 'thin').

3. Even if sharp boundaries *could* supervene on an indeterminate base, the supervenience account may not protect the epistemic theory against the use objection, if there is more to say about the way in which use determines meaning than merely that correct application supervenes on dispositions of speakers. A crucial aspect of Williamson's use of the supervenience account is his claim that no one can say more about the way in which use determines meaning than that correct application supervenes on dispositions. In Section 4 I will give an outline account of what more can be said. For the present, we should see that if nothing more can be said, then the notion that use determines meaning is unintelligible. That means that the epistemic theory cannot give an account of any intelligible connection between meaning and use. Its only option is to say that no one can give an account of any such intelligible connection.

Section 2 sets out the regress arguments. Section 3 aims to show the need for a different interpretation of the notion that use determines meaning from Williamson's. Rather than offering a competing interpretation of that notion, I argue that the supervenience account needs (contrary to some

suggestions of Williamson's) to treat some precise dispositional phenomenon as providing a norm for the application of the word, and that no such
phenomenon can do that job.

Dispositions Cannot Determine Sharp Boundaries

We can think of dispositions as properties (of speakers, in this case) that correspond to counterfactual propositions: a person has a disposition to behave
in a given way in a given situation if and only if he or she *would* behave in that
way in that situation. There may be fatal objections to the very notion that
people have such dispositions with regard to the application of words, or that
such dispositions have any precise connection with the correct application of
words. If we think of dispositions as lawlike generalizations as to what someone will do, there are ordinarily none that are borne out without exception. If
we think of dispositions as probabilities, then it is hard to see how sharp
boundaries could supervene on them. But I will set aside such potential objections, and accept for the purpose of argument that in any situation a person
has a disposition that corresponds to the fact that he or she either would or
would not say 'yes' to a question of the application of a vague expression in
any case. The result seems to be a sharply bounded set of facts on which, in the
epistemic theory, the application of words such as 'thin' supervenes. Those
facts are hidden from us (i) because we do not know precisely what people are
disposed to do, and (ii) even if we knew all that, we know of no algorithm that
would tell us whether it is correct to apply the word.

There are some good reasons for Williamson to adopt the notion of use-as-
dispositions. Suppose, instead, that we thought of use as speech events. That
would be fatal for the supervenience account: it would raise a question as to
which speech events count as the base on which meaning supervenes. How
recent would an utterance have to be for it to count as part of the base? The
answer to that question could not be determined by use, on pain of a vicious
regress. The supervenience account cannot treat use as a set of speech events,
because such a set would necessarily extend across time, and the supervenience account lacks the resources to account for a sharp boundary to the
dispositions that count as part of the base. Use-as-dispositions seems to avoid
this diachronic problem, because it seems that it can be treated as a purely
synchronic notion: the notion is that the application of an expression at any
moment supervenes on the dispositions of speakers *at that moment*. The
result is the view that boundaries are unstable: they change as dispositions
change. Williamson accepts instability as an insight of the epistemic theory,
and not as an objection.[9]

---

[9] But note that the instability that Williamson accepts (231) is not a consequence of adopting
a synchronic notion of dispositions: he appears to take the view that meaning continually

Imagine a speech community of just two people, who speak a language much like English. Suppose that one of them is disposed to say that it is dark at 8.30 one evening, and suppose that the other is not disposed to say so until 8.50. At 8.40 one of them says that it is dark, and the other says that it is not dark. On the supervenience account, this pattern of use determines that one of the two speakers is right (and also *which* of them is right)—in just the same way that their use of the word 'dark' determines whether either of them is right when they both say that it is not dark at noon. What is more, the pattern of dispositions determines a first nanosecond of dark.

If we thought only of the dispositions I have stated, it would seem particularly bizarre to say that the pattern of dispositions determines a first nanosecond of dark. In fact, it would be surveyably false. But there is any number of other facts about the dispositions of the two speakers, in addition to their dispositions to assent to or dissent from statements applying vague expressions—facts about the *strength* of their dispositions, and their dispositions to defer to each other, or not, etc. The supervenience account needs to appeal to such additional dispositions.

In summary, the supervenience account needs to treat speakers' dispositions (and not speech events) as use, and it cannot restrict itself to dispositions to assent to or dissent from assertions. It needs to appeal to additional dispositions.

Whose Dispositions? Speech Communities

On the supervenience account, correct application cannot change unless the dispositions of speakers change; if dispositions change, then correct application may (and, according to the correlation claim, *does*) change. This account implies that, when a speaker in Spokane dies, the truth conditions of statements applying the word 'thin' change, and a statement applying the word 'thin' in a borderline case in Bombay may switch from true to false. But this semantic butterfly effect is no more bizarre than the notion that there is a sharp boundary to the application of vague words, and it will not bother an epistemic theorist. Note, however, that it is a consequence that arises only if we think of the supervenience base as comprising the dispositions of (something like) all English speakers in the world. Does that make sense?

Williamson treats meaning as supervening on 'our use' (206). 'Our' is *unspecific*: 'we' could refer to you and me, or everyone, or some class in between. Until it is made specific, there is no sharply bounded supervenience base. The supervenience account needs a sharply bounded speech

changes as a diachronically extended pattern of use changes. As Williamson presents it, the supervenience account is vulnerable to the diachronic problem: he says, 'What you mean by "thin" does not depend solely on what you would say in your present circumstances and mood' (231).

community, and speech communities are not ordinarily sharply bounded. This is not only a geographical problem, but a problem of which foreign language speakers are also English speakers, which children count as competent, which speakers are too eccentric to count, and so on. The indeterminacy will remain whether the language community is simply 'speakers of English', or any subdivision. There is no way to define a language community that is non-arbitrary and precise. Perhaps the only viable criterion is mutual intelligibility, and that is extremely vague.

Moreover, use of a language within a community will include different ways of speaking corresponding to ethnic or local differences, social strata, women's talk, men's talk, written and spoken language and different genres of writing, formal and informal speech situations, different ways of speaking to grown-ups and children, conventions of exaggeration and understatement in particular situations, tendencies to self-consciousness in various situations, and so on and so on. To treat all the dispositions of members of the community as the supervenience base would be to distort the use of language within a community. But if we treat each of these innumerable ethnolinguistic varieties as a separate language, indeterminacy will arise as to which 'language' is being spoken on a particular occasion.

Suppose that there are two towns, Slough and Leighton Buzzard, in each of which people have varying dispositions to apply the word 'thin'. Suppose that there are precise facts about those dispositions, and that the dispositions of people in Slough are slightly different from the dispositions of people in Leighton Buzzard.

It might seem tempting to say that there are slightly different norms for the use of the word 'thin' in Slough and Leighton Buzzard (each of which differs, presumably slightly, from the norm for its use in English in general), and that in his or her idiolect each speaker has his or her own norm for the use of the word. Each of these 'languages' — English, or Leighton Buzzard English, or Slough English, or an individual speaker's idiolect — corresponds to a different set of dispositions to apply the word 'thin'.

Here lurks a problem for the epistemic theory: even if we can affirm the principle of bivalence for any *specified* 'language', a vague statement in a borderline case may be true in one 'language', and false in another. A speaker who utters a vague statement in a borderline case may say something that is true in their idiolect, and false in the English of their family, and true in the English of their town, and false in the English of their country, and true in English in general (and there are countless other 'languages' corresponding to countless other speech communities we could conceive of the speaker as belonging to). If meaning supervenes on use-as-dispositions, then the sharp boundaries to the application of vague words are not only unstable, they are also *relative* to a specification of whose dispositions count for the purpose of determining meaning. For any human language, the epistemic theory must postulate a large finite number of sharp extensions of vague words, corresponding to a large finite number of speech communities. It makes no sense to talk of *the* truth value of a statement, except in relation to one specification of the extent of the speech community whose dispositions determine its truth value (and one specification of which ethnolinguistic register is being used, and so on).

It would be simpler for the epistemic theory to say that all English speakers are members of *one* speech community, speaking one language — English. But the problem of membership is actually insurmountable for an epistemic theorist who wants to describe people simply as speaking *English*. To say that the dispositions of all and only English speakers count would be to give a vague specification of the base on which correct application supervenes: it may be unclear whether some young children, and eccentric adults, and students of English as a second language, count as English speakers. It is a specification that can only support the epistemic theory if there is a sharply bounded answer to the question 'Who counts as an English speaker?' The epistemic theory will say that every person either is or is not an English speaker, and that we cannot know whether to call some people 'English speakers'. But 'English speaker' and 'speech community' seem to be expressions like 'thin'—in Williamson's terms, their correct application is not 'stabilized' by natural divisions, and it seems that Williamson should say that their correct application supervenes on the dispositions of speakers. But the expression 'English speaker' cannot be explained as having a sharp boundary that supervenes on the dispositions of English speakers, because a regress would ensue:

(1) There are sharp boundaries to the correct application of 'thin'; they supervene on the dispositions of English speakers.
(2) There are sharp boundaries to the correct application of 'English speaker' (and, therefore, sharp boundaries to the base on which the correct application of 'thin' supervenes); they supervene on the dispositions of English speakers.
(3) There are sharp boundaries to the correct application of 'English speaker' (and, therefore, sharp boundaries to the base on which the correct application of 'English speaker' supervenes); they supervene on the dispositions of English speakers.

. . .

Is this regress vicious? It is not vicious merely in virtue of the fact that it generates an infinite number of unknowably true statements. That need not embarrass an epistemic theorist: if there is even one unknowably true statement, there is an infinite number of unknowably true conjunctive statements. It may seem that an epistemic theorist must simply say that there is an infinite number of unknowable answers to questions about membership in a speech community.

But the regress *is* vicious (at step 2, rather than at an arbitrarily high level), because the dispositions of English speakers may not determine sharp boundaries to the group of English speakers. Each step above step 1 asserts what it also presupposes: that the group of English speakers has sharp boundaries. To illustrate the problem with this regress of dispositions, consider the case of Elfi. I propose that an epistemic theorist who uses the supervenience account of meaning and use needs to admit that the following scenario is possible; the scenario shows that that account cannot portray use as determining sharp boundaries to the application of vague words.

Elfi the borderline English speaker

Imagine a woman called Elfi, who is a borderline case for the correct application of the term 'English speaker'. No one knows whether it is true or false to say that she is an English speaker. In fact (although no one can know it), her capacities place her so close to the hidden sharp boundary between English speakers and non-English speakers that if her own dispositions are included in the supervenience base, she counts as an English speaker, and if her dispositions are not included in the base, she does not count as an English speaker. *Are* Elfi's dispositions part of the supervenience base? They are if she is an English speaker, and they are not if she is not an English speaker. Either way, the dispositions of English speakers cannot answer the question whether Elfi is an English speaker. It is not just that no one can know the answer; it is that, if there is an unknowable answer, it is not supplied by the dispositions of English speakers.

On one interpretation of the correlation claim, Elfi is possible because adding any single speaker's dispositions to the supervenience base changes the truth conditions of a vague statement. And even on the pure supervenience claim, Elfi is possible because it is possible that those truth conditions will change if the supervenience base changes.

An epistemic theorist might say that, until we have an account of what *does* make someone an English speaker, there is no support for the notion that it is indeterminate in any case whether someone is an English speaker. And I have not shown that there is no hidden sharp boundary between people who are and are not English speakers. But the problem for the epistemic theory is that the dispositions of English speakers cannot determine whether it is true to say that Elfi is an English speaker. This is not a proof of indeterminacy, but it indicates that the epistemic theory cannot support the claim that it is *use* that determines the sharp boundaries that the theory postulates.

We should conclude that there is a constraint on the supervenience account: to the extent that use determines meaning, the principle of bivalence can only be affirmed *relative* to a precise specification of the speakers whose dispositions count as 'use'. Any such specification of the membership of any ordinary speech community (whether it is Leighton Buzzard English speakers or English speakers in general) would be a stipulation. If the truth of a vague statement supervenes on the dispositions of speakers, that statement may be true relative to some specifications of the class of speakers, and false relative to others. Sharp boundaries to membership in the class of speakers cannot supervene on dispositions of speakers. So the principle of bivalence can be affirmed only relative to a *stipulation*.

That is a dismal conclusion, because the goal of the theory was to apply classical logic to utterances in a natural language. It is impossible to use the supervenience account to do so, and in Williamson's theory the consequence is that, in natural languages, words whose meaning is determined by use are semantically defective. Those words are incoherent in a natural language.

To solve this problem of membership in a speech community, the epistemic theory could view *idiolects* alone as semantically adequate. If this works, the notion of a natural language would be rescued as a coherent notion *within an idiolect*: the extension of 'English speaker' within an idiolect would supervene on the dispositions of the individual speaker. But words like 'thin' would still have no meaning in a natural language. Think of each person as speaking their *own* language, and think of their statements as being true or false *in their idiolect*. Each speaker tries to achieve a rough match with the idiolects of others, but their statements have meaning only within their own idiolects. The problem of specifying membership in a speech community vanishes, at least if we are willing to take it for granted that any speaker has a *single* set of dispositions.

That approach is not Williamson's: he insists that 'linguistic meaning is socially determined', so that slight differences in dispositions among speakers do not generate multiple meanings (236).[10] That insight is patently sound, and it is an argument against the supervenience account.

Which Dispositions? Mistakes and Other Falsehoods

If we stick to idiolects, we have decided *whose* dispositions count. But a question remains as to *which* of a speaker's dispositions count. We saw that the supervenience base must include more than just dispositions to assent to or dissent from applications of a vague expression. Pertinent dispositions must include dispositions to defer to others, to hesitate and to hedge, to experience various psychological phenomena, and dispositions concerning the use of related expressions, and so on. But not all dispositions can be pertinent to the determination of meaning. If the correct application of 'thin' supervenes on

---

[10] Cf. 'what individual speakers mean by a word can be parasitic on its meaning in a public language' (211).

dispositions, it is plausible to think that it also supervenes on a base that does not include speakers' dispositions, e.g. to split infinitives. If it is true to say that sharp boundaries supervene on *all* dispositions of speakers, and some dispositions have nothing to do with the application of 'thin' (so that we can say that the application of 'thin' cannot change when there is no change except in *those* dispositions), then it is also true to say that (the same) sharp boundaries supervene on some proper subset of dispositions of speakers.[11]

The question for the supervenience account is how strong the supervenience claim should be. Does correct application supervene on all dispositions of speakers? on pertinent dispositions of speakers? on dispositions of speakers to assent–dissent? The first claim is too weak, and we have seen that supervenience on dispositions to assent to or dissent from declarative sentences applying the vague word would be too strong. The epistemic theorist needs to make a supervenience claim similar to the second listed above: that correct application supervenes on pertinent dispositions. But 'pertinent' is vague, and sharp boundaries to its application cannot supervene on pertinent dispositions of speakers, because a vicious regress would result. The epistemic theory will assert that the application of 'pertinent' *must* be sharply bounded, but it has no semantic argument to account for 'pertinent' as bivalent. Sharp boundaries to pertinent dispositions cannot be determined by pertinent dispositions: an account that made such a claim would end in a regress analogous to the regress that led to the Elfi scenario.

Perhaps a more serious problem for the epistemic theory is how to account for mistaken dispositions. Can we make sense of the notion that a person might be disposed to *misapply* a word? Williamson is, rightly, committed to doing so: he presents the possibility of mistakes as a reason why there is no 'recipe for extracting meaning from use' (193); his purpose is to absolve the epistemic theory from the obnoxious burden of having to say *how* use determines sharp boundaries. He insists that even the agreement of speakers in their dispositions to apply a word 'does not generally guarantee the correctness of that application. Whole societies can sometimes be mistaken.'[12] I have argued that the epistemic theory can only postulate a determinate base for the supervenience of meaning within an idiolect. But the possibility of mistake applies to idiolects too. Unless we abandon the notion of a mistake, and say that a word just applies to whatever a person is disposed to apply it to, we need to admit that a speaker might be disposed to misapply a word.

Williamson suggests that the problem is that someone's dispositions to apply the word 'thin' may be mistaken because a thin person may not look thin for some reason, and a speaker may not be familiar with the relevant

---

[11] Another way of putting the same objection is that the correlation claim, which says that a shift in dispositions would shift the meaning of an expression, needs an account of *which* dispositions it applies to.

[12] Williamson, 'What Makes it a Heap?', n. 6 above, 330.

comparison class (206). Those forms of mistake seem not to pose a basic problem for the epistemic theory: besides his or her disposition not to apply the word 'thin' to that person, the speaker will have other dispositions (to make a different judgment in different perceptual conditions or with greater familiarity with the comparison class, to decide that they had misapplied the word, to defer to better-placed speakers . . .). The correct application of 'thin' in the speaker's idiolect supervenes on *all* the speaker's (pertinent) dispositions. The complexity of dispositions might also account for dispositions to lie, or to be sarcastic, or generous: someone might be disposed to call someone who is not thin 'thin', but also to admit in the right circumstances that they were exaggerating.

But the problem of dispositions to misapply a word is more far-reaching: people may misjudge the application of the word 'thin', without having any other inconsistent disposition. They may not be thinking straight for a moment, or they may be systematically disposed to exaggerate in a way that is unreflective and thoroughly consistent. It seems that the supervenience account needs an account of dispositions to misjudge that do not arise from unfavourable perceptual conditions or lack of information. But the supervenience account cannot appeal to the dispositions of other speakers, on pain of the regress that would arise if the supervenience account appealed to use in a speech community. And it cannot appeal to dispositions across time, on pain of the same diachronic regress that would arise if a supervenience account tried to adopt the notion of use-as-speech-events.

This point about mistakes has more far-reaching consequences than the impossibility of a recipe or algorithm: it seems that it is not just beyond our capacities, but impossible *in principle*, to identify sharp boundaries to the application of the word 'thin' by reference to the dispositions of speakers. We could not do so without an account of which dispositions are mistaken, and we can have no such account unless we know the application of the word. This is not just an epistemic problem. No being with greater cognitive powers than ours could identify the correct application of a word *on the basis of the dispositions of speakers*, without already being able to distinguish mistaken dispositions from dispositions that count. So no such being could identify sharp boundaries to the correct application of a word merely on the basis of dispositions.

It seems that the epistemic theory must account for the word 'thin' as applying correctly, in a speaker's idiolect, while the speaker is disposed to do what others (or the speaker at other moments) would call 'misapplying' it. But that account is incoherent: it would eliminate the notion of mistaken dispositions, and would thereby eliminate the notion of the correctness of a speaker's dispositions (a notion which the account uses). 'Mistaken' would become a term that has meaning only at a moment within an idiolect, and could not apply to the consistent dispositions of the speaker.

How Use Determines Meaning: A Way of Supervening?

The general argument of this section has been that the supervenience account cannot help the epistemic theory, because it supposes that meaning is determined by a pattern of use, and 'pattern of use' is vague. It would beg the question against the epistemic theory to say that, because 'pattern of use' is vague, the extension of a pattern of use may be indeterminate. But a pattern of use of 'thin' cannot have sharp boundaries that are determined by a pattern of use of 'pattern of use'. The supervenience account has nothing to support the notion that there is a sharply bounded set of dispositions that are pertinent to the application of any vague word—except the logic argument.

Now we face a different and more basic problem: *if there were* a sharply bounded pattern of use of a word like 'thin', what would make it right or wrong to apply the word? As Williamson has pointed out, 'Our use determines many lines,'[13] such as the line between unanimity and lack of unanimity, or between majority assent and less than majority assent. But he points out that there is no reason to think that any such line is the line between truth and falsity (206). Williamson responds to these facts by renouncing reductionism[14]—implying that the supervenience account does not commit him to identifying any precise dispositional phenomenon as equivalent to the line between truth and falsity. Yet if supervenience is a relation of determination, it seems that Williamson must claim that something about the dispositions of speakers *makes* it right or wrong to apply a word like 'thin', so that some precise dispositional phenomenon *is* equivalent to the line between truth and falsity, but we cannot know which. And, on the correlation claim, a tiny change in dispositions brings about a tiny change in truth conditions, but we cannot know how.

The question that the supervenience account must face up to is '*How* does meaning supervene on use?' We cannot demand an *answer* to the question, but the proposition that there *is* an unknowable answer needs support. It is impossible in principle for the dispositions of speakers to determine the answer, because it is a question of *how* the dispositions of speakers determine anything. So this is a final regress argument against the supervenience account: it supposes that the use of a word supplies a norm for its application, but that very notion presupposes a *way* of supervening, a relation (though we have no algorithm for identifying it) between dispositions and correct application. That relation cannot itself be determined by dispositions. The

---

[13] 'Vagueness and Ignorance' (1992) 66 *Proceedings of the Aristotelian Society* (suppl.) 145, 155. In fact, if the argument so far presented succeeds, dispositions determine *no* lines such as unanimity or majority assent, unless there are sharp bounds to the speech community and to the pertinent dispositions of each speaker, and the problem of mistakes is solved, and so on.

[14] For Williamson's anti-reductionism, see (206) and 'What Makes it a Heap?', n. 6 above, 332.

epistemic theory does not need an account of the relation, but it does need to support the view that an unaccountable relation exists.

We might put this problem in the following way: the supervenience account is offered as an interpretation of the slogan that use determines meaning. But supervenience is not a *kind* of determination; to assert supervenience is only to raise the question 'What is the relation between the supervenient property and the base?'[15] That is an intelligible question, even if the answer is unknowable.

The epistemic response to this sort of objection can be summarized by saying that no one has come up with an account of what *makes* it correct to call someone 'thin' in a clear case (perhaps it is unknowable), and that whatever it is that makes an application (unknowably) correct in a borderline case is just the same as whatever it is that makes it correct in a clear case.[16]

The problem should not be rejected so quickly, however. The supervenience account is a way of saying that the agreement of speakers (or the consistency of an individual speaker) provides the norm for the use of a word like 'thin'. Granted that unanimity or majority assent do not make a word apply, it makes sense to ask how much agreement of what sort it takes to constitute the norm for the use of a word. The epistemic theory must say that *some* precise fact or set of facts about dispositions to apply the word 'thin' makes it correct to call one borderline-thin person 'thin', and makes it incorrect to call the next person in a sorites series 'thin'.

An epistemic theorist might say that this interpretation of the supervenience account demands an algorithm for calculating meaning from dispositions, where there is no algorithm. It is no objection to the epistemic theory that people do not have a technique for identifying how use determines sharp boundaries; that is just what the theory claims. But on the epistemic theory, there must be something that we have no technique for identifying—a *way* in which meaning supervenes on use. That is, a way in which a tiny shift in dispositions *can* (and, according to the correlation claim, *does*) make it the case that a word applies to an object that it would not otherwise apply to. Although the supervenience account does not have to explain the way in which dispositions do that, it does have to support the view that there is such a way.

---

[15] Cf. Jaegwon Kim, *Supervenience and Mind* (Cambridge: Cambridge University Press, 1993), 167: 'there is no single kind of dependence that underlies all cases in which supervenience holds'. Kim concludes that 'Mind–body supervenience . . . does not state a solution to the mind–body problem; rather it states the problem itself' (ibid. 168). On Kim's view, the task for a theory of mind is to explain what kind of dependence relates mind and body. My point here is that it makes sense to ask what kind of determination relates use and meaning, and that the epistemic theory has to claim that the question has an answer, although it will insist that no human being can know what the answer is.

[16] See 'What Makes it a Heap?', n. 6 above. And cf. Sainsbury and Williamson: 'Since no theorist of any kind . . . has given any such detailed account [of how meaning supervenes on use], the fact that the epistemic theorist has not should not count against the theory.' 'Sorites', n. 5 above, 480.

But that view is unsupportable. What is wrong with the notion that unanimity decides the application of vague words? Not that we do not know whether vague words apply just when a speech community is unanimous, but that we know that the fact of unanimity does not give anyone a reason to apply the word 'thin' in a case in which the phenomenon obtains, while withholding it in an immaterially different case in which the phenomenon does not obtain. This reason for denying that unanimity (or majority assent . . .) provides a norm for the use of a word would apply equally to *any* precise dispositional phenomenon.

Williamson has argued that it cannot be said that a community has not bothered to lay down a precise meaning for an expression, unless we can identify the sense in which speakers have bothered to lay down that the expression applies in clear cases.[17] But that is what speakers do in every situation in which they only happen to face clear cases of the application of an expression. We have a word for dogs, and a word for cats, and there is a clear sense in which speakers have bothered to distinguish between cats and dogs. But no one has bothered to provide for intermediate cases between cats and dogs, and if an intermediate case turned up, people would need to decide (i.e. determine) something that has not been decided. There is no ground to suppose that the application of 'cat' and 'dog' must be determinate in intermediate cases if it is determinate in clear cases: nothing in the practice of using those words bears on intermediate cases. In *this* regard there is nothing hard to understand about the connection between meaning and use: the *use* of the word 'cat' is in part to distinguish cats from dogs, and that use is fulfilled successfully without drawing a sharp boundary.

The case is similar with, for example, all artefact terms. People ordinarily deal with clear cases of cars, pianos, houses, and telephones. There is nothing bizarre or baffling about the borderline cases that are encountered in factories, building sites, or wrecking yards. A partly dismantled piano presents speakers with a manageable question of *whether to extend* the application of a term from the clear cases in which it is used; not with an unanswerable question as to *whether its application extends* to the new case.

Speakers bother to distinguish between cats and dogs without bothering to lay down a rule for intermediate cases. They bother to lay down the application of the word 'piano' to clear cases, without bothering about when the pieces in the factory become a piano, or when a piano stops existing. If that is the best way to describe those cases, it may be best to give a similar description of the use of words whose application lies on a natural spectrum, such as 'dark' and 'thin', in which there is nothing at all unusual about borderline cases. We bother to lay down a distinction between salient alternatives; why not say that we do not bother to lay down a rule for borderline cases? The

---

[17] *Identity and Discrimination* (Oxford: Blackwell, 1990), 107.

epistemic theory can reject that view by cleaving to the logic argument, but it cannot appeal to the unaccountable supervenience of meaning on use to reject that view. There is no defence of the epistemic theory on the ground that the connection between meaning and use is hard to explain.

I do not mean that there are no philosophical difficulties in giving an account of the relation between meaning and use. I mean that the use objection is not met by Williamson's account of use, because there is nothing mysterious about the proposition that the use of the word 'cat' lays down a rule for clear cases, and does not lay down a rule for cases intermediate between cats and dogs. The use of words for biological species and of words for artefact terms gives an answer to questions of application in clear cases. That use does not answer questions of the application of the expression in borderline cases. There is a clear and simple sense in which speakers have bothered to answer the question of the application of the words 'car', 'piano', and 'house' in clear cases, and have not bothered to do so in borderline cases. The dispositions that people no doubt have in borderline cases do not provide a complete guide to the correct application of the word.

We could put that very point in terms of the use objection, by saying that the use of vague words does not lay down a sharp boundary to their correct application. Properly understood, the use objection claims that the use of words provides a norm for their correct application, but rejects the notion that dispositions provide a sharply bounded norm. The added element that is needed in an account of the relation between the meaning of words and their use is the notion that use can provide a norm—a reason, on which a speaker could act, for applying or withholding a word. The tolerance principle is attractive because it seems that no trivial change in the grounds relevant to the application of a vague word could guide a speaker to apply the word in one case and withhold it in the other, in the way that norms are capable of guiding behaviour.

The obstacle to the notion that the dispositions of speakers determine a sharp boundary to the correct application of vague words is this: even if it made sense to say that the speakers in a community are (unknowably) disposed to withhold the word 'thin' from one borderline thin person, and to apply it to another person who is thinner in a trivial degree, that fact would not give any speaker a *reason* to apply and withhold the word in the same way.

The response that an epistemic theory could make to the objection in this form is obvious: it is to say that no one understands the relation between meaning and use well enough to make these claims about norms, and to challenge an opponent to explain the normativity of language use in a way that reveals indeterminacies in borderline cases of the application of vague words. So Section 4 explores some features of the ways in which use *can* provide a norm for the application of words.

3. Use as a Guide to Action

Two Senses of 'Norm'

Words such as 'rule', 'practice', and 'norm' share a familiar ambiguity between their descriptive and prescriptive senses. A fish may be bigger than the norm, and a person may violate a norm. This descriptive–prescriptive distinction is a distinction between what is normal and what is normative (between the way something is done, and the way to do something). So we can talk of what the police do *as a rule*, and of what a rule *requires* or *permits* the police to do.

I will differentiate the descriptive and prescriptive senses of such words by writing, for example, 'D-norm' and 'P-norm'. It makes sense to ask, 'what is the norm for the use of the word "thin" in Slough?' and to mean to ask either what is done in Slough, *or* what it is correct (from some point of view) to do in Slough—to ask for the D-norm or the P-norm. Of course, it also makes sense to ask such a question without differentiating; in fact, to differentiate between P-norms and D-norms is to raise questions about a relation that is ordinarily taken for granted.

The supervenience account has the advantage of offering a simple account of that relation. We can think of it as claiming that the meaning of a word like 'thin' is a P-norm for the use of the word, requiring that behaviour conform to the D-norm (use-as-dispositions) for the use of the word. On that account, when you use a word like 'thin', it *is correct to do* precisely what *is done*.

The supervenience account will not yield a precise P-norm if the argument of Section 3 is sound, because there is no precise D-norm for the use of a word like 'thin'. A D-norm is a regularity of conduct; in any pattern of conduct as complex as the use of the word 'thin', there is any number of regularities. The argument of Section 3 was that no such regularity counts as *the* D-norm for the use of a word like 'thin'. The phrase 'as a rule' is vague, and sharp boundaries to its application cannot supervene on dispositions. There would be a precise D-norm only if membership in the speech community were specified, and there were some sharply bounded set of pertinent dispositions. Most strikingly, there is no precise D-norm unless mistaken dispositions are counted out of the supervenience base. The notion of a mistake is itself a normative notion, and the possibility of mistakes upsets the notion that it is correct to do precisely what is done.

There are further reasons for thinking that there are no sharp, unknowable boundaries to the P-norm for the application of a word like 'thin'. Even if the notion of a precise D-norm for 'thin' made sense, there is a basic objection to the notion that a P-norm is a requirement that behaviour should conform precisely to the D-norm. It might be thought that that simple account of the relation between D-norms and P-norms does make sense: that people try to conform in their linguistic behaviour to the D-norm for their community. On this view, the D-norm is what they are aiming at, but because of their limited linguistic capacities, it is impossible for them to apply the P-norm reliably in borderline cases.

I propose that this view of vagueness should be replaced with a different account of the connection between meaning and use, based on a different understanding of the notion of 'use'. 'Use', too, has senses that are descriptive ('the use of heroin has increased') and prescriptive ('what's the use of that?'). We can talk of what use someone has made of a hammer (as a doorstop, paper-weight . . .) and also of the use, or point, or purpose of a hammer. The super-venience account employs the descriptive sense of 'use', when it claims that use-as-dispositions determines meaning. I will argue that the supervenience account cannot generate sharp boundaries because a precise D-norm, if there were one, could not supply the descriptive content of a precise P-norm. In broad terms, the claim is that the connection between meaning and use must be understood as a connection between meaning and the use that *is to be made* of words. It is a connection between meaning and the use that people *have made* of words just in so far as that gives a reason for the use of words.

Customary Rules

For a community to have a customary rule is for it to use a regularity of behaviour as a guide to behaviour. Anything that *is* used as a guide to behav-iour *can be* used as a guide to behaviour. This basic point about customary rules is an obstacle to an epistemic theory of the requirements of a vague cus-tomary rule.

Customary rules can be complex and subtle, and their requirements can depend on context in complex and subtle ways. Moreover, it can be difficult to distinguish between customary rules and the requirements of morality. There are all sorts of things that members of a community would never think of doing, and that would provoke hostility if someone were mad enough to try them—yet it may be unclear whether to say that those things are prohib-ited by a customary rule.

Is there a customary rule against shouting in an ordinary conversation? If the members of a community tend not to do so, perhaps they are not follow-ing a customary rule, but simply tend (in this respect) to act decently. Or per-haps they are following a customary rule that prohibits something which would be wrong even without the rule. Perhaps we can say that there is a cus-tomary rule when the regularity is itself a reason for the conduct in question (when the regularity defines good behaviour, rather than merely reflecting a tendency to behave well).[18] Suppose that in Singapore, and not in

---

[18] Cf. Hart (*CL* 255–6) and Dworkin (*TRS* 53ff.; *LE* 145), and Raz's distinction between acting on a general reason and following a rule (*PRN* 57).

Switzerland, people regularly take off their shoes when they enter someone else's house. Are Singaporeans simply more considerate (or fussier) than the Swiss? It may be better to say that acting considerately requires taking off your shoes in Singapore, but not in Switzerland (or that it is fussy to take off your shoes in Switzerland, but not in Singapore) — that taking off your shoes is required by a customary rule in Singapore.

The question is complicated in at least three ways:

1. The Singaporeans we have imagined might conceive of themselves as acting for background moral reasons. Perhaps a customary rule exists when, from the point of view of the members of the community, the regularity *is* a reason, even if the members of the community think of something else as a conclusive reason. The notion of something being a reason from the point of view of people who think they are acting on some other reason may seem puzzling. But to think of an example we only have to think of an instance of behaviour that is clearly governed by a customary rule, even if the participants in the custom think that they behave alike because they happen to concur in wisdom, or decency, or élan.[19]

2. It is the attitudes and responses of members of the community that make a regularity of behaviour into a customary rule; there is a vast multiplicity of forms and intensities of such attitudes and responses, and there is no clear answer to the question 'What form, intensity, and consistency of attitudes does it take to distinguish a customary rule from a mere regularity of behaviour with no normative force?' We might say, again, that all it takes is that the members of the community treat the regularity as a reason for conformity to the regularity. This account does nothing to diminish the unclarity. But that is a virtue, because the unclarity is a genuine feature of some rule-governed behaviour.

3. We can certainly say that there is a customary rule when there would be no reason to act in a certain way, if other people were not doing so; but what counts as a customary rule requiring you to do what you have other reasons (even conclusive reasons) for doing? The answer, again, seems to be the community's use of the regularity of behaviour as a reason in itself.

The use of a regularity as a reason for action is a feature of customary rules that survives the complications and uncertainties that accompany an attempt to give an account of customary rules. It may help us to understand vagueness.

Imagine a *precise* customary rule, requiring workers to stop work when the five o'clock bell rings. We can say that the requirements of the rule supervene on the behaviour of the members of the community. The requirements of the

---

[19] Picture any peculiar custom that has no point except to dramatize a distinction between people (such as lawyers wearing wigs), and you have an example of a customary rule — a practice in which the regularity functions as a reason for behaviour, even if participants in the practice think of themselves as acting on other reasons.

rule can change only if the behaviour changes. But we have not yet said enough about the connection between the behaviour of the members of the community, and the requirements of the rule. We can also say that the people treat the regularity of conduct in their community as a reason to stop work. We can put it that the rule consists in the way they treat that regularity. There is no customary rule if they all stop work at the same time merely for some other reason (e.g. if they do so to comply with an agreement with their employer, or because they want to work as long as they can and still catch a train that leaves just after five). The D-norm is the fact that they tend to stop work when the bell rings,[20] and the P-norm is the use of the D-norm as a reason to stop when the bell rings.

Imagine a *vague* customary rule: a rule governing how long people should stay at parties. Suppose that people tend not to stay too long at parties, and they tend to criticize people who stay too long. And they act in these ways not (or not only) for background moral reasons, but because staying too long at parties is not what people do.

How long is too long? That may depend on the type of party, and its size, and the sort of people who are there, and so on. Subject to such forms of context dependence, we might say that the requirements of the rule supervene on facts such as how long people actually stay at parties (and on what it takes to provoke criticism, and so on). But we can say more about the connection between the behaviour of the members of the community, and the requirements of the rule: no precise facts about how long people stay at parties make any precise difference to the requirements of the rule. The point is not simply that knowing such precise facts is unhelpful because we do not know how to calculate the rule's requirements from them. The point is that knowing precise facts is unhelpful because no one uses any precise facts about the community's behaviour as a precise guide to their behaviour, and the use of the community's behaviour as a guide *is* the rule (the P-norm is a *way to use* the D-norm).

The rule only requires what people use it as a guide to do. People's behaviour has a role in answering the question 'What is *correct*, what is *in accord with the rule*?' An action cannot go against the rule unless the regularity can be used to assess the action as wrong. And a person complies with the rule only if he or she uses the regularity as a guide to action. People *do not* use anything as a guide that they *cannot* use as a guide. So they do not use inaccessibly precise facts as a guide. Even if there were such a thing as the precise D-norm for staying at parties, the P-norm would not be precise. The difference between the vague customary rule and the precise customary rule is that

[20] It would be more complete to say that the D-norm is a complex variety of related regularities of behaviour including regularities of action, criticism, self-justification . . . That complexity takes nothing away from the precision of the rule being discussed: to describe all those forms of behaviour is to describe what is done with the precise phenomenon of the bell.

it is *possible to use* the D-norm of leaving when the bell rings as a precise guide to action.

The regularities of behaviour that people use as guides to conduct, and the ways they use them, vary widely within and among communities, and little can be said about them in general. As well as being vague or precise, customary rules can be very rigid or very flexible, and the potential variety of their content is unlimited. But we can make the general point that such normative practices presuppose the notion that the regularity is a justification for conduct, and people *do not* use anything to justify their conduct that they *cannot* use. The application of vague rules such as the one we have considered is subject to a built-in qualification of materiality: there is no such thing as an immaterial breach of such a rule. The precise rule makes sense of saying, 'he stopped work before he should have, but only by five seconds', but the vague rule does not make sense of saying, 'he stayed longer than he should have at the dinner party, but only for five seconds'.[21] The vague rule makes sense of deciding to leave a party, and it also makes sense of judging people as rude, or annoying, or overly scrupulous. But increments that *do not matter* cannot make the difference between action in accord with the rule and action contrary to the rule.

That claim leads to a sorites paradox for the requirements of vague customary rules. So an epistemic theorist has to say that the claim is incorrect, or else that the alleged customary rule is incoherent. There is a readily apparent epistemicist response to the claim: that it begs the question by relying on a tendentious definition of a rule. An epistemic theorist might say that the P-norm is a requirement of conformity to the D-norm; people are reliably right in identifying the D-norm (and therefore the P-norm) only in clear cases, because the behaviour is not all known, and is so complex, and because there is no algorithm for identifying the D-norm. It is possible to stay a second too long at a party, though no one can know that that is impolite, because no one can reliably identify it as too long.

The approach I have sketched can admit that people *may* be unreliable. But it denies that they are necessarily unreliable. And it claims that there is no sharp boundary to the requirements of a vague customary rule, because (i) there is no difference between what the customary rule requires, and what people use the rule to guide them to do, and (ii) people do not use the rule as a guide to do anything that they cannot use it as a guide to do. People will certainly be unreliable in identifying D-norms—e.g. in guessing at the answer to any question such as 'How many seconds did the average guest spend at dinner parties last year?' And individuals can also be unreliable in answering the

---

[21] No doubt it is possible to imagine circumstances in which someone leaves a dinner party five seconds later than they should have. I am claiming that it is not possible to imagine that they do so in virtue of violating a customary rule about how long to stay at parties, unless such a rule is pegged to a precise phenomenon (like the five o'clock bell rule).

P-question 'Is it time to go home yet?' That unreliability accounts for the possibility that someone might misbehave without meaning to misbehave. But the possibility of unreliability gives no reason to think that the rule has unknowable requirements.

To conceive of a P-norm as requiring conformity to a precise D-norm would ignore the role that the regularity (the D-norm) plays in the life of the community—its use. *If* (contrary to the claims of Section 3) any sharply bounded period of time counted as the D-norm, deviating very slightly from it could not count as going against the rule, because the D-norm could not be used as a standard by which to guide or evaluate conduct. And the use of a regularity to guide or to evaluate conduct is all that a customary rule is. There is nothing more to a customary rule, though there is more to questions such as whether it should be followed. A customary rule does not draw distinctions that the members of the community do not draw, and it cannot draw distinctions that they cannot draw.

We could say that customary rules provide a useful analogue with which to compare the meaning of a word like 'thin': both consist in the community's use of a regularity as a guide to conduct. Or we could say that *that* similarity is a reason to say that the meaning of an expression *is* a customary rule. The notion that the meaning of a word is a rule for its use sounds like an obviously false Wittgensteinian gesture, and several writers have argued against it.[22] When Wittgenstein says, 'we are not equipped with rules for every possible application' of a word (*PI* 80), and that 'the application of a word is not everywhere bounded by rules' (*PI* 84), he seems to imply that the application of a word is governed by rules in *some* cases. He seems to have thought, roughly, that the meaning of a word is a set of rules for its use—a set of rules that do not answer every possible question of its application.

The meaning of a word is certainly *not* a rule in Raz's sense of a protected reason for action:[23] there is nothing for it to be protected from. That distinguishes it from customary rules such as the rule against staying too long at parties, which *is* a reason not to act for certain other reasons. The fact that 'dark' applies to conditions sufficiently similar to pitch blackness does not exclude reasons to use the word differently, because there are no such reasons.[24] Moreover, the meaning of words carries none of the complex normative equipment that (other) rules carry: there are no duties or rights or

---

[22] A vehement example is Paul Ziff, *Semantic Analysis* (Ithaca, NY: Cornell University Press, 1960), 35: thinking of language as a rule-governed activity 'can produce, can be the product of, nothing but confusion'. A similar example, but without the exasperation, is Bede Rundle, *Wittgenstein and Contemporary Philosophy of Language* (Oxford: Blackwell, 1990), 5: rules are an 'overworked notion'.   [23] *PRN* 191.

[24] If there are ever reasons not to apply the word 'dark' when it is dark, they are reasons not to tell the truth (or reasons to speak figuratively . . .), and not reasons to diverge from the regularity that constitutes the D-norm for application of the word 'dark'. If they are excluded, they are excluded by reasons to speak the (literal) truth, and not by the P-norm for 'dark'.

powers. There is just one big, complex, remarkably pure coordination problem, to which a natural language is a complex solution.

We may view the meaning of a word as a customary rule, or only as sharing with customary rules a central normative feature: the use of a regularity of behaviour as a general guide to action. On either account, a theory of the practice of using a word must use the basic concept of normative theory, the concept of a guide to action. On either account, an epistemic theory of the application of words like 'thin' faces the same objections as an epistemic account of the requirements of a vague customary rule.

Use determines the correct application of a word just to the extent that it gives a reason to apply or not to apply the word. On this view, meaning is what you know when you know how to use a word.

Reasons

Remember the speech community of two speakers, one of whom was disposed to apply the word 'dark' at 8.30 p.m., and the other not until 8.50. That scenario was an attempt to concoct a surveyable pattern of dispositions to apply a word. The intuitive objection to the epistemic theory is that it is surveyably arbitrary to say that this pattern of dispositions determines a sharp boundary to the use of the word. It is arbitrary in the sense that the pattern of use gives no *reason* to say that one or the other speaker is incorrect when their dispositions disagree. By the same token, the facts that one speaker started applying the word at 8.30, and the other at 8.50 do not give either of them any reason to apply the word 'dark', or reason to withhold it, at 8.40.

The use objection cannot succeed in that simple form, because on the epistemic theory, something *is* hidden in this situation: each speaker's 'whole pattern' of the use of the word 'dark' is inaccessible, even to the speaker. So it is not surveyably arbitrary to say that sharp boundaries supervene on the dispositions of these two speakers to use the word 'dark', because their dispositions are not surveyable.

All that can be said in response is that, given the dispositions mentioned, there is no reason to think that any *other* fact about their use of the word would *justify* a claim that it is true to say 'it is dark' at 8.40, or that it is false. An epistemic theorist might say that no one has said what it would take to justify such a claim in a clear case (and might suggest that, whatever *that* is, it justifies making true statements (though it does so unknowably) in borderline cases too). But without saying what *would* justify the application of the word 'dark', we can say that it would take something intelligible to those speakers as justifying a distinction in the application of the word. An epistemic theorist can say that the reason is just *that it is dark*, and the property of darkness just must have sharp boundaries because of the logic argument. That approach would *abandon* the notion that use determines meaning.

What the epistemic theory cannot say is that the *reason* is that the light conditions fit the D-norm for 'dark'.

Summary

On the view that I have proposed, the notion that correct application supervenes on dispositions cannot support the epistemic claim that there are sharp boundaries to the correct application of words. Moreover, it cannot help to make sense of the notion that use determines meaning. Use determines meaning in the sense that a regularity of behaviour is treated as *a reason* for applying an expression. We should remodel the supervenience account's conception of use: dispositions matter just in so far as they *justify* applications of expressions, and they *can* justify applications of expressions only to the extent that they are intelligible to speakers as providing a justification. So an expression's D-use (*what is done with* an expression) determines meaning only in so far as it can show speakers *what to do with* an expression (its P-use).

It might seem that the argument presented here is verificationist, because it claims that there can be no unknowable truths about what statements mean. Williamson sees verificationism as a tacit prejudice against the epistemic theory, and he curtly rejects it.[25] But I do not think that the argument made here is verificationist in any objectionable sense.

Did the Earl of Orkney cross the Atlantic in 1398? There may be no way for people today to find out. For human beings, it is an unknowable truth or an unknowable falsehood that he did so. It would be a form of verificationism to say it cannot be true or false because we have no way of finding out.

But here it is a *fact* that is unknowable, and not a norm. Meaning is normative if it is the use of regularities as guides to behaviour. The notion of an unknowable norm makes no sense, if norms are capable of guiding behaviour. We can accept the notion of unknowable facts, without accepting the notion of unknowable norms.[26] It would make no sense to assert normative consequences for unknowable facts about the dispositions of speakers. The argument does not claim that a proposition is not true unless it is verifiable; it claims that a word does not apply to a known object unless it is intelligible to speakers that it should apply. It may be true, yet unknowable for people living today, that the Earl of Orkney was thin. But it cannot be true, yet unknowable for people who know TW, that TW is thin. It may be controversial, and

---

[25] See Sainsbury and Williamson, 'Sorites', n. 5 above, 480.

[26] Is a secret law purporting to create an offence an unknowable mandatory norm? No: it is intelligible, even if it is always false, to say that a secret law justifies an arrest and punishment. But it is unintelligible to say that the 'offender' had an unknowable *reason* not to commit the purported offence. (Except in the sense that the existence of the law might make it more likely that a sanction would be imposed on him—*that* is an unknown reason.) That is why publicity of laws is one of the requirements of the rule of law.

the controversy may be irresolvable, but the question is different in this respect from the question whether the Earl of Orkney was thin.

If there were a precise D-norm, it would be unknowable. As Williamson says, the whole pattern of a community's D-use is inaccessible to speakers (and in fact, the whole pattern of any one speaker's use is inaccessible to that speaker). But it would still be false that the P-norm can be unknowable. There is much that you cannot know about what you and others *have done* with the word 'thin', but none of that inaccessible information would help in deciding what *to do* with the word.

4. The Vagueness of Evaluation

General normative, aesthetic, and value terms are generally vague. We can construct sorites series for the application of 'right', 'good', 'beautiful', and gerundives such as 'to be done', and so on. Presumably most thick evaluative concepts ('brave', 'tolerant', 'rude' . . .) are vague too. This feature of evaluative expressions is not an accidental feature of human languages. 'Right' and 'wrong' are vague because they are abstract terms used to evaluate practical decisions, and the considerations relevant to practical decisions are very commonly susceptible to sorites paradoxes. There is no precise amount of time that you should spend with your children. There is no precise mean between being stingy and being profligate. On most mornings you have good reason to get out of bed, but only in special circumstances is there a first second at which you ought to get out of bed. The wise person will not brush his or her teeth all day, but will not ordinarily view any particular stroke as the last stroke of the toothbrush that reason requires.

Reasons for action are not necessarily vague: if you ought to watch all of a TV show that starts at 5 p.m., then you ought to be watching at 5 p.m. But basic reasons (e.g. that the show is gripping . . .) are vague. We might say that first-order reasons for action are precise only when they are *pegged* to some precise phenomenon.[27] And evaluative terms such as 'perfect' (and reasons to do something perfectly) may not be vague, depending on the context (e.g. on whether there are incommensurable requirements of perfection). But 'perfect' does not become meaningless when it is vague. So it is no exaggeration to say that vagueness is a characteristic feature of general evaluative language. Although there are some precise reasons for action, all the language in which we could conceivably talk in *general* terms about general

---

[27] Cf. Ch. 5.4 above. It would be rash to say that protected reasons are *typically* more than trivially vague. Whether they are vague or precise is a contingency that depends on the vagueness or precision of a directive, promise, etc. But protected reasons are often vague, and Ch. 9.2 argues that legal systems necessarily include vague rules.

reasons (and about rationality) is vague. For that reason I will talk of the vagueness of *evaluation*, and not just of evaluative language.

This is one of the most interesting aspects of vague language, but philosophers concerned with vagueness have had little to say about it. There are two reasons why the vagueness of evaluation is important for understanding vagueness in general: first, value terms can be used to formulate sorites paradoxes that stubbornly resist Williamson's anti-paradox techniques; secondly, evaluative presuppositions underlie context dependence, and perhaps all use of vague descriptive terms. The first of these considerations is an objection to the epistemic theory, and the second is a reason for thinking that the objection is fundamental and general.[28]

Evaluational Sorites Paradoxes

A good cook is making a batch of soup, and it needs salt. The quantity of salt matters: a good batch of soup this size will have more than a teaspoon and less than a tablespoon of salt. But however much salt is added, no marginal grain of salt makes the difference between a good batch of soup and a batch of soup that is not good. That is the case partly because tastes differ, but it is also because, whatever your taste, it will not be better or worse suited if one grain of salt is added to the soup. The cook knows that no single marginal grain of salt *matters*.

That reasoning leads to a sorites paradox for the application of the term 'good'. It is a stubborn paradox because of the role of knowledge in this situation: the point is that the conditional premiss in this form of the sorites paradox is known to be true. Consider the following propositions:

(1) The cook knows that it matters whether the soup is good or not.
(2) The cook knows that one grain of salt does not matter.
(3) Therefore, the cook knows that one grain of salt cannot make the material difference between good soup and soup that is not good.
(4) Therefore, the cook knows that, if the soup is good, it will still be good if one grain of salt is added to the pot.

There may be situations in which the cook does not know whether to say that the soup is good or not (cases that appear to the cook to be borderline cases for the application of 'good'); in such a situation, (4) is still true. The uncertainty is as to whether x_i is good (and it will also be unclear whether x_{i+1} is good). There is no uncertainty as to whether x_{i+1} is good if x_i is good.

[28] A potential puzzle that the vagueness of evaluation poses for Williamson is that it is false to say that the dispositions of speakers determine sharp boundaries to the application of a word like 'good', and it is not clear what could support a semantic argument that the epistemic theory applies to evaluative expressions. That puzzle cannot be explored here.

One grain of salt probably makes no perceptible difference to the soup at all. But that is not essential to this form of the paradox. The cook may find that adding an eighth of a teaspoon of salt makes a noticeable difference, but not a sufficient difference to *justify* drawing the significant distinction between soup that is good and soup that is not. Either way, the 'doesn't matter' paradox arises. So this paradox is stronger than forms of the sorites paradox that are based on indiscriminability, because it can apply when the inductive step makes a noticeable difference. This form of the paradox claims that a *discriminable* difference may not matter, and that if it does not matter, it cannot justify the distinction between good soup and soup that is not good (a distinction that does matter). If two batches of soup are not significantly different, one cannot be good if the other is not good, because that is a significant difference.

Williamson's strategy for resolving sorites paradoxes is to replace the paradoxical tolerance principle:

(TP) If x_i is F, then x_{i+1} is F

with the non-paradoxical 'margin for error principle':

(Ep) If x_i is known to be F, then x_{i+1} is F.[29]

That strategy fails if the above argument is sound, because the argument yields

(TP') It is known that if x_i is F, then x_{i+1} is F.

In this situation the tolerance principle is itself an evaluative proposition, which the cook knows to be true.

An epistemic theorist might respond (i) by pointing out that an evaluative judgment may be justified, without some agent knowing that it is justified, and (ii) by disputing the claim that there must be a material difference between soup that is good and soup that is not good. It may matter a *little* if the soup is a little too salty, and a great deal if the soup is much too salty.

These potential responses do not succeed:

(i) Since the epistemic theory must say that one batch of soup can be good, and another not good, when there is no difference that anyone could use to justify an evaluative distinction between them, the theory has to claim that justifications of evaluative judgments can be not just unknown to a particular agent, but unknowable to any agent. That would make evaluation unintelligible.

(ii) It is true that it might be a disaster if the soup is horrible, and no big problem if the soup is not good but not horrible. But it *typically* matters

---

[29] See proposition (6.6) in Williamson, *Identity and Discrimination*, n. 17 above, 105 (and 181, 232).

whether the soup is good, and it *never* matters whether an extra grain of salt has been added.

This evaluational form of the sorites paradox does not apply only to matters of taste. It is very far-reaching: similar claims could be made about almost any sort of practical decision about how much or how soon or how often . . . to do something unimportant or something vital. It is a form of the paradox that can be formulated using all the basic general terms of practical reason, such as 'reasonable', 'right', 'wrong', and so on.

The choices are stark for an epistemic theorist. I propose that we cannot make sense of the meaning of evaluative expressions if we attempt to assert bivalence for them. But the epistemic theorist is committed to saying that they are meaningless if we deny bivalence, and that a neutral attitude to bivalence is not an option.

Consequences of the Vagueness of Evaluation

The vagueness of evaluation has an important implication for pragmatic vagueness (above, Chapter 3.10). Because 'suitable', 'appropriate', 'reason-able', and all such terms are vague, the epistemic theory must extend to prag-matic vagueness. It must either assert bivalence for all phenomena of pragmatic vagueness, or claim that all the language in which we describe those phenomena (and all the general language in which they could conceiv-ably be described) is incoherent.

A related ramification of the role of evaluation in pragmatic vagueness is that evaluative considerations are needed to account for context depend-ence, as I will claim in Section 6.

Finally, the vagueness of evaluation has *general* importance for under-standing vague language, because evaluative presuppositions underlie the use of vague *descriptive* terms as well as terms like 'good'. Such a conclusion is inescapable if we accept the view proposed in Section 4, that the meaning of a word shares normative features with customary rules. We could formu-late a 'good soup' paradox for the requirements of the customary rule against staying too long at parties. By the same token, we could formulate a good soup paradox for the correct application of 'thin' or 'red'. Words such as 'thin' and 'red' are *useful* (good) for drawing significant distinctions. The *purpose* of drawing a distinction using the word 'red' cannot be accomplished via a trivial step. Drawing the distinction has a point that it would not have if x_i were red and x_{i+1} were not red. It may *matter* whether something is distinguished as red, in a way that demands justification. Something that reflects light only at 6562 Ångstroms can be trivially different in colour from something that reflects light only at 6563 Ångstroms. But if 'red' is used to draw material distinctions that may require justification, then something that is red cannot be trivially different in colour from something that is not red.

It might be objected that what *matters* depends on the situation, and that it might matter (it might matter enormously) whether something reflects light at 6562 or 6563 Ångstroms. Yet the difference in colour is trivial. So the fact that it may matter whether something is red does not mean that the difference between something that is red and something that is not red cannot be a trivial difference in colour.

One difference between 'reflecting light at 6562 Ångstroms' and 'red' is the generality of 'red'. It applies generally not only by applying to a range of hues, but also by applying to a range of intensities and saturations, so that there are various grounds of application. But it might be objected that we could construct precise general predicates such as 'between 6500 and 6600 Ångstroms'. We could also construct precise *compound* predicates with saturation and intensity components. Let us call some such predicate 'red+'. The epistemic theory claims that 'red' is like 'red+', except that the boundaries of its application are determined by dispositions rather than by stipulation. It might matter whether something is red+, so the fact that it may matter whether something is red does not mean that the good soup paradox applies to 'red'.

The difference between 'red' and 'red+' is that we can explain the meaning of 'red' by pointing to paradigms and saying that it applies to them, and to things that are sufficiently similar in relevant respects. Even if the same objects that serve as paradigms of 'red' are also red+, we could not explain the meaning of 'red+' in the same way: things must resemble the paradigms *in a particular way* to be red+. In fact, there *are no* paradigm red+ objects (no objects that are useful for explaining the meaning of 'red+'). 'Red' is different because knowing its meaning involves knowing how to make judgments of similarities to paradigms. Its meaning cannot be explained more completely than by saying that it applies to things that are sufficiently similar in relevant respects to paradigm cases. The requirements of relevance and sufficiency are evaluative considerations. 'Red' is not ordinarily an evaluative term, but its use presupposes the evaluative considerations involved in judgments of relevance and sufficiency. To say that 'red' is like 'red+' (except that its sharp boundaries of application are determined by dispositions) is to make the use of the word inexplicable.

So we could formulate a paradox just like the good soup paradox, using 'red' instead of 'good'. And like the good soup paradox, it would be stronger than the indiscriminability paradoxes that writers have formulated using 'red'. Perhaps we can make the good soup paradox entirely general, by applying it to the notion of truth, as Dorothy Edgington has suggested: 'The difference between a true and a false judgment is meant to be a difference that *matters*. Yet for any putative line, there will be no significant difference—no difference which matters—between things just either side of it.'[30] In summary, there is no value-free understanding of language, because of (i) pragmatic vagueness of purposes for which words are used and (ii) context dependence and (iii) the role of evaluative considerations in the use of descriptive language. The intractability of evaluational sorites paradoxes is not only an argument against applying the epistemic theory to evaluative expressions; it is an argument against the epistemic theory. This book offers no theory either of value or of morality, and it is not the place to refute moral theories that allege that there is no such thing as the correct application of moral expressions (as moral truth). But we can say something about a moral theory: no theory should claim that there are sharp boundaries in all contexts to the correct application of general evaluative expressions.

5. Context Dependence and Vagueness

An account of vagueness needs to deal with the fact that people apply the same vague expression differently in different contexts (see Chapter 3.10 above). The complexities of context dependence are unlimited, but we can simplify matters by focusing on three forms. First, vague words are often 'syncategorematic': a sandcastle may be large even if it is smaller than a house that is not large. Secondly, the application of vague words may depend on the *comparison class*. A large house in Stow-on-the-Wold may be smaller than a house in San José that is not large. Thirdly, the application of vague words depends on the *purposes* of the people who are communicating: it may be true to call a house 'large' if you are talking about living in it by yourself, and false if you are talking about living with six children.[31]

For these three reasons and others, a vague expression can apply *and* fail to apply to the same object in different contexts. That fact points out a similarity between vague and ambiguous expressions: both vague words like 'large' and ambiguous words like 'hot' have multiple senses. It might be thought that context dependence is simply a *form* of ambiguity, distinct from and irrelevant to vagueness. Proponents of bivalence can offer a neat account of ambiguity: bivalence is maintained, because an ambiguous statement can be both true *and* false, as long as it is true in a different sense from the sense in which it is false. So it might seem that the epistemic theory can

---

[30] 'Vagueness by Degrees', in Rosanna Keefe and Peter Smith (eds.), *Vagueness: A Reader* (Cambridge, Mass.: MIT Press, 1997), 299.
[31] The second and third forms of context dependence mentioned here can be thought of as forms of syncategorematic meaning, the question being 'What is the category to which the object must be taken to belong for the purpose of a statement describing it?' That question is answered partly by comparison class and purpose (that's big *for* a house, *for* a house in Stow-on-the-Wold, *for* a family of seven . . .).

treat context dependence as ambiguity, and claim that vagueness is only a feature of *fully disambiguated* context-dependent expressions.

Williamson suggests such an approach. He discusses arguments that vagueness *is* context dependence and rejects them, pointing out that a knowledge of the context in which a vague statement is uttered will not enable anyone to identify the truth of the statement in a borderline case (215). His conclusion is that the epistemic account is needed to preserve bivalence: that vagueness is 'reduced but not eliminated by context' (281). In Williamson's view, 'Vagueness and context dependence are separate phenomena' (215). The implication is that context dependence is a form of relativity, which poses no more threat to the principle of bivalence than ambiguity poses. Once the context is fixed, vagueness remains. I will claim that the problem is worse than this view suggests, because ordinarily nothing will count as fixing the context *precisely*.

On the epistemic theory, it seems that a context-dependent expression has as many senses — and there are as many sharp boundaries to its application — as there are contexts. How many contexts are there? How many senses and sharp boundaries are there for, for example, the word 'thin'? Comparison classes and the purposes of speakers vary along a multitude of continua. The number must be infinite. The notion of an infinite number of sharp boundaries to the application of 'thin' or 'small' might sound bizarre and objectionable in itself, but an epistemic theorist will insist that it is neither: *any* account of the application of a word like 'small' or 'thin' will have to account for its varying as the context varies. If the context can vary infinitely, then the application of the word must vary infinitely. Any account of the application of vague words needs to account for the relativity of context dependence, and there is nothing objectionable in this regard in the epistemic account.

But in fact there is reason to conclude that context dependence does not just impose a trivial requirement of relativity, but presents a fundamental problem for the epistemic theory. The problem is that contexts are typically *unspecific*. If you say that you have found a small house, you may do so without specifying the standard (the sense in which you are using 'small'). You may not specify the comparison class, and you may not specify the purposes that you have in mind. And although the context may be a guide to the relevant standard, there may be nothing in the context to supply a fully specific standard. The context may or may not be a guide to the truth of the statement. Even on the epistemic theory, the truth of your statement will depend on a standard that is not supplied. If the sense of 'small' is unspecified, then your statement has no specific truth value. What you say will, in a borderline case, be true on some standards and false on others, and there will be no precise answer to the question 'What is the standard?'

The epistemic theory could treat context-dependent expressions as semantically incomplete, and conclude that statements using them are semantically defective unless their sense is specified. But that approach would defeat the epistemic project of 'applying' classical logic to natural languages. In fact, it would even defeat the fall-back epistemic project I suggested earlier, of applying classical logic to idiolects. Context dependence is a characteristic feature of vague words, and we commonly make statements using vague words without specifying the sense in which we are using them. When we do specify a sense, respects typically remain in which that sense is unspecific: 'small for a family of seven' is more specific than 'small', but it is still unspecific. An indefinite variety of further qualifications could be added to the specification. It would be impossible to add all those qualifications, and no one talking about houses needs to do so. But without them, the correct application of vague words like 'large' and 'small' depends on something that has not been specified. Yet for an epistemic theorist to view those statements as lacking truth value would mean concluding that much vague discourse is semantically defective.

The alternative is for the epistemic theory to claim that the context on which the application of vague expressions depends *is* always (or at least characteristically) fully specific. An epistemic theorist might say that every vague statement has a truth value that depends on the context, and that to make a vague statement without specifying a fully specific purpose, and comparison class, and so on, is to speak indexically, appealing to the *salient* standard—the standard appropriate to the context of utterance.

It might sound odd to suggest that the *truth* of a statement depends on what amounts to a conversational maxim (a maxim that the statement means, for example, 'large with respect to the comparison class that is salient in *this* context'). But we can keep that maxim in its place by saying that the truth of a statement depends on its sense, that a vague context-dependent statement may have a multitude of senses, and that the salient sense is the sense which *ought* (by conversational convention) to be ascribed to a speaker's utterance.

But that approach will not solve the problem of unspecificity: the salient sense of a statement—the sense it has in the context of the utterance—is *itself* characteristically unspecific. First, the comparison class is typically unspecific: it will generally include the house next door, and it may not include every house in the world. What determines the extension of the comparison class? It may be determined by an express stipulation, but ordinarily it is limited just by *relevance*. To judge what comes within the comparison class is not to answer a question of fact whose precise answer is unknowable, but to make an evaluative judgment concerning what *matters* for the purpose in question. This fact ties the unspecificity of context dependence to the vagueness of evaluation (see above).

Secondly, on the epistemic approach suggested here, the truth of a statement that a house is large may depend partly on the *purposes* for which someone is calling it 'large'.[32] There may be no specific answer, in a context, to the question 'Large for what purpose?' The context of utterance will typically rule out some purposes, and may make some purpose or purposes salient (such as 'for a home for a family of seven'). But ordinarily no such purpose made salient by the context will be fully specific. Perhaps there is ordinarily nothing that *would count as* a fully specific purpose, when the purposes concern people's general needs and complex activities. The purpose of living with six children certainly makes a difference, and will often be all that is needed to determine whether a particular house counts as large for that purpose. But that purpose leaves a great deal unspecified, and not merely unknown. The conclusion must be that context-dependent expressions are not fully disambiguated by context. To the extent that that is the case, the principle of bivalence cannot be asserted for context-dependent expressions. It would be like asserting bivalence for statements reporting the length of periods of time in heartbeats.

It is possible to succeed (or to fail) in some cases in finding a large house in spite of the unspecificity in the standard—just as a year *really is* longer than 10 million heartbeats. What is not possible is to conceive of the application of the expression 'large house' as bivalent, when the context does not supply a standard. If the epistemic theory admits that conclusion, and asserts the principle of bivalence only for specified standards, then it faces the objection that most vague utterances (specifically, all context-dependent utterances, when the context is not fully specific) are semantically incomplete.

6. Conclusion: Putting a Price on Bivalence

> If one abandons bivalence for vague utterances, one pays a high price.
>
> (Williamson, *Vagueness*, 186)

> We stalwarts of two-valued logic buy its sweet simplicity at no small price in respect of the harboring of undecidables.
>
> (Quine, 'What Price Bivalence?' (1981) 78 *Journal of Philosophy* 90, 91)

> ... how can [logic] lose its rigour? Of course not by our bargaining any of its rigour out of it.
>
> (Wittgenstein, *Philosophical Investigations*, 108)

Williamson and Quine both see themselves as stalwarts of bivalence. Yet to Williamson, Quine's approach is 'close to global nihilism' (298 n. 2). There

---

[32] As examples of features of context on which the extension of 'thin' might depend, Williamson cites 'the purpose at hand, the salient comparison classes, previous uses of it in conversation, and so on' (214).

seem to be two issues: (i) whether it is even coherent to refuse to assert bivalence — to buy or sell two-valued logic, and (ii) how to drive a good bargain. I do not know how to address issue (i); perhaps the best approach for an epistemic theorist is to claim (unlike Williamson) that a coherent theory of semantics *must* assert bivalence.

As regards issue (ii), Williamson and Quine agree that the cost of abandoning bivalence is to lose its 'sweet simplicity', 'simplicity of theory' (Quine[33]), or 'simplicity, power, past success, and integration with theories in other domains' (Williamson 186).

Their disagreement is that Williamson denies that there is a cost to be paid for asserting bivalence. If Williamson is right, then there is nothing to count against the elegance of bivalence. Quine says that the cost of asserting bivalence is disregarding the facts, and treating ordinary expressions *as if* their application were bivalent.[34] If the argument of this chapter is right, Quine is right about the cost of asserting bivalence: it means ignoring the reasons to deny that there are sharp boundaries to the application of ordinary vague expressions. I have argued that Williamson's supervenience account of meaning and use cannot dispel that view.

If there are costs to be paid both for asserting and for denying bivalence, it is unclear what would decide the question. It is beyond the scope of this book to try to assess the *value* of applying classical logic to natural languages, and if there is any such value, it is undoubtedly incommensurable with the cost of asserting bivalence.[35] Both Quine and Williamson view the question as *theoretical*, and Quine explicitly compares the question to questions of theoretical physics. But classical logic does not have the form of a scientific theory, and if it is falsified by vagueness, it is not falsified in the way that, for example, the steady state theory of the universe was falsified by the discovery of the cosmic background radiation. So I do not know how to address this aspect of issue (ii) either — except to say that the reasons for denying that there are sharp boundaries to the application of vague expressions are cogent, and to leave logic to take care of itself.

So I propose to take a neutral attitude to bivalence (and neither to assert it nor to deny it in particular borderline cases). If there are frequently no *clear* borderline cases of the application of vague expressions (see Chapter 5.5), a neutral attitude is appropriate in individual borderline cases, and consistent with the denial of sharp boundaries.

To avoid the paradox of trivalence, this neutral attitude should not picture

[33] 'What Price Bivalence?' (1981) 78 *Journal of Philosophy* 90, 91.
[34] 'Bivalence requires us . . . to view each general term, e.g. "table", as true or false of objects even in the absence of what we in our bivalent way are prepared to recognise as objective fact.' Ibid. 94.
[35] As Quine asserts: 'The values that we thus trade off one against the other — evidential value and systematic value — are incommensurable.' Ibid. 90.

indeterminacy as an area within which neutrality is appropriate. This approach should deny that there is any gap between true and false statements, and also that there is a sharp boundary between them. If we represent the application of words spatially (as a segment on a line, or an area on a plane, or a solid in a space), this conjunction of denials seems nonsensical: it is like trying to picture two geometrical figures on a plane that do not overlap, do not share a boundary, and are not separated by a space. So the approach I propose cannot take spatial metaphors too seriously as a description of the application of vague words: it needs to abandon the notion of boundaries, instead of saying that it is indeterminate where the boundaries are. Chapter 7 discusses that approach.

For law, the consequences of this chapter are three: first, we have seen reasons to support the indeterminacy claim against the strongest challenge that philosophers of logic have mounted against it. I do not propose that champions of classical logic such as Williamson have failed in providing classical logic with a defence that it needs. Whether classical logic needs defence is a question outside the scope of this book. Secondly, we have seen reason to think that the general evaluative and normative linguistic expressions that the law uses are necessarily vague. Not only that, but because any conceivable expressions of that kind would be vague, we have reason to think that general evaluative and normative *considerations* are necessarily vague. This claim will play an important part in the discussion of the role of interpretation in law in Chapter 8 of *Vagueness*. Finally, we have seen that the context dependence of legal language supports the indeterminacy claim.

7

Vagueness and Similarity

WITTGENSTEIN remarked that the words 'rule' and 'same' are interwoven.[1] A vague rule is one for which, in some cases, it is not clear what is 'the same'. We will better understand vagueness in legal rules if we understand the role of similarities in the cases to which a vague rule applies. This approach corresponds to Mark Sainsbury's proposal to replace what he terms the 'classical conception' of vagueness with a model of similarity to paradigms.[2]

This chapter discusses two models of vagueness, the 'boundary model' and the 'similarity model'. The boundary model is the framework of classical conceptions of vagueness. It represents the extension of a word as a geometrical figure, and represents vagueness either as a failure of language to draw a boundary to the figure, or as ignorance of the boundary that language draws. In the similarity model, vagueness is flexibility in the normative use of paradigms. The associated indeterminacy is not a deficiency or incoherence in the social facts that determine meaning, but is a feature of the creativity of language use.

The two models take contrasting approaches to the question 'What objects does a vague word apply to?' Section 1 outlines the boundary model; that model claims that the meaning of a vague word is a function of the actions or dispositions of individuals, and a vague word applies to objects picked out by that function. Section 2 borrows the apparatus of social choice theory from welfare economics to argue that the dispositions of individuals cannot determine the application of vague words—that a language is not an aggregate of idiolects. A potential objection to that conclusion is that a model that pictures the determination of the application of vague words as a social choice can use resources ('distancings') that are unavailable in welfare economics. Addressing that objection leads in Section 3 to a discussion of incommensurabilities in the application of vague words, addressed by means of a critique of James Griffin's suggestion that options of incomparable value are roughly equal in value. Section 4 discusses the similarity model, which claims that there is no more complete answer to the question 'What objects does a vague word apply to?' than 'objects that speakers treat as paradigms, and objects that are sufficiently similar to the paradigms'.

---

[1] *PI* 225; cf. *Remarks on the Foundations of Mathematics*, 3rd edn., trans. G. E. M. Anscombe (Oxford: Blackwell, 1978), 418–21.

[2] 'Is there Higher-Order Vagueness?' (1991) 41 *Philosophical Quarterly* 167; Sainsbury argues that 'the idea of thinking of vagueness in terms of boundaries' is a bad idea (178). Sainsbury seems to think that the model he proposes can be shown to be free of paradox; as suggested in Ch. 5, I do not propose that that is the case.

1. The Boundary Model

Some terms and concepts need to be introduced for the description of the boundary model, particularly the concept of an ordering and its role in the sorites paradox. The rest of Section 1 presents the boundary model, and argues that it characterizes vagueness as unclarity in the location of a boundary, when in fact the notion of a location of a boundary does not make sense.

Imagine a vague predicate F, whose applicability can be represented as a function of the position of an object on a dimension of comparison[3] D:

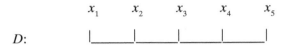

$$D:$$

The variable x ranges over objects to which F may apply (using 'object' as a shorthand for whatever a word may apply to). x_1, x_2, x_3, x_4, and x_5 are names for values of x on D. Fx_5 is clearly true; Fx_1 is clearly false. x_5 and x_1 are *clear cases* of F and ~F. It is not clear whether Fx_3 is true; that is, x_3 is a *borderline case*. $x_?$ is the left-most x which is F.

This apparatus is meant to make it easy to describe the ordering relations that are needed for both the sorites paradox and the boundary model. We can set out some notions that will be useful in this description as follows: $x\text{R}y$ means 'x is at the same point as y or to the right of y on D'. ~$x\text{R}y$ means 'x is to the left of y on D'. The *consistency principle* is the proposition $x\text{R}y \leftrightarrow (Fy \rightarrow Fx)$ (e.g. if Horace is as tall as or taller than Percival, then if Percival is tall, so is Horace). By the consistency principle, $(\forall x)(x\text{R}x_? \leftrightarrow Fx)$.

The following properties of relations will be important:

Completeness: $(\forall x)(\forall y)(x\text{R}y \lor {\sim}x\text{R}y)$

Transitivity: $(x\text{R}y \mathbin{\&} y\text{R}z) \rightarrow x\text{R}z$

Reflexivity: $x\text{R}x$.

An *ordering* (sometimes called a 'weak ordering') is a binary relation that is complete, transitive, and reflexive (e.g. 'greater than or equal to' applied to real numbers). R is an ordering of x on D. A *strong ordering* is a binary relation that is complete, transitive, and not reflexive (e.g. 'greater than' applied to real numbers). R is a weak ordering, because it is reflexive.

We can now describe the boundary model as the view that vagueness is either ignorance as to the position of $x_?$ on D (in the epistemic theory), or indeterminacy in the position of $x_?$ on D (in some semantic theories). All objects are ordered on D, and F applies to the borderline object x_3 if and only

---

[3] Sainsbury used this term in 'Concepts without Boundaries', inaugural lecture, King's College, London, 1990, 12.

if $x_3 R x_7$. I will argue that the boundary model should be rejected, because vague words are typically unlike F: the application of a vague word may not be ordered, so that a boundary will be lacking not because its precise location is indeterminate, but because the idea of a precise location does not make sense.

The Sorites Paradox

The tolerance principle is the proposition that, for some increment on D,

$$(\forall x)(Fx_n \rightarrow Fx_{n-1}),$$

where $x_n R x_{n-1}$, and n is the number of iterations of the increment. We can stipulate that the tolerance principle applies to the increments between successive objects marked on D. That stipulation generates the sorites paradox, which has the following form:

(1) $\sim Fx_1$
(2) Fx_5
(3) $Fx_n \rightarrow Fx_{n-1}$
(4) $\therefore Fx_1 \,\&\, \sim Fx_1$.

Sorites reasoning is essentially scalar. To construct a sorites series, we need the denumerable increment that the tolerance principle requires. All sorites series are ordered; they need the ordering that a scale provides. But that does not mean that sorites series require a cardinal scale: the ordinal relation provided by any ordering is enough. So scales can be created ad lib: we do not need to come up with a scalar ground of application of an expression in order to formulate a sorites paradox. Sorites reasoning can be applied to words whose applicability depends on immensurable criteria. We can construct sorites series even for words as hopelessly vague as 'nice' or 'pretty', based on change across time, for instance (where units of time would give the increments required to formulate the tolerance principle). For any vague predicate F and any object x, it is possible to construct an ordered sorites series, with clear cases of applicability at one end, clear cases of inapplicability at the other, and with x occurring at some point on the series. We may also accept that it is possible to construct a series of objects, distinguished each from the next by tiny increments, with clear cases of applicability at one end and clear cases of inapplicability at the other, on which any two given objects x and y appear. But I will argue that it is not necessarily possible to do so on an *ordered* sorites series. It is not necessarily true that xRy or true that $\sim xRy$ for all objects x and y (i.e. there is not necessarily a complete ordering of the applicability of vague words). In fact, objects are *typically* incompletely ordered for applicability of ordinary vague words.

If the boundary model succeeded in fixing sharp boundaries, the epistemic view of vagueness would succeed. The argument that follows is not simply that the model fails to generate such boundaries, but that the ways in which it fails suggest that vagueness is better described by the similarity model.

Answering Questions

We can answer some legal questions by citing rules: to the question 'What concerts can the police lawfully shut down?' part of the answer might be, 'the police can lawfully shut down raves'. Vagueness in the rule is a potential for difficulty in answering particular questions within the scope of the general rule ('Is *this* assembly prohibited?'), even when we know all useful facts about the situation.

The questions typically thought of as posing problems of vagueness are sentence-questions (questions that can be answered 'yes' or 'no') as to whether a predicate is true for an object: 'F*x*?' Hart considered that most vagueness in law is associated with this sort of question: 'The crucial question presented to a court in all such cases is always one of *classification* of some presented particular.'[4] The boundary model treats such a question as asking whether the point that *x* occupies on *D* is to be classified as F or ~F. On the boundary model, vagueness in F makes it unclear, in some cases, how that point is to be classified.

But vagueness is a potential obstacle not only to solving problems of classification, but also to answering *wh-* questions of the form 'How F is *x*?' By treating objects as having a location on *D*, the boundary model presumes that there is a precise answer to the *wh-* question, so that the indeterminacy of vagueness is just indeterminacy in classification of points on *D*. In fact, there are indeterminacies that are not apparent if we consider only sentence-questions.

The vagueness that is an obstacle to answering a *wh-* question corresponds to the vagueness of comparative adjectives. Vagueness in the positive 'competent' is an obstacle to answering the question 'Is that person competent?' in a borderline case. Vagueness in the comparative 'more competent' is an obstacle to answering both questions of comparison like 'Who is more competent, Horace or Percival?' and the *wh-* question 'How competent is Horace?' It is an obstacle to answering *every wh-* question of that form. It is not an obstacle to answering every question of comparison (Horace may be clearly more competent than Percival), but for every object, it is an obstacle to answering some questions of comparison.[5] Because of vagueness of comparison, Horace can be a borderline case for 'is more competent than Percival', even when both are clearly competent or clearly not competent.

---

[4] 'Theory and Definition in Jurisprudence' (1955) 29 *Proceedings of the Aristotelian Society* (suppl.) 239, 259. [5] See Ch. 3.2.

There are legal sentence-questions and legal *wh-* questions. A legal *wh-* question need not be vague: there may be a precise answer to 'What is the tariff on corn?' But far from having the precise answers the boundary model presupposes, legal *wh-* questions are often exceptionally vague: they are the questions a court asks when sentencing, or assessing general damages, or determining the quantum of spousal maintenance.[6] These issues too *can* be governed by tariffs, but they are typically governed by vague rules that require the court to ask questions such as 'How serious was this assault?' or 'What is this person's need?' or 'How much is this person able to pay?'

It might seem that we could translate sentence-questions and *wh-* questions into each other: a sentence-question into a question of deduction (via the consistency principle) from the answers to the two *wh-* questions 'How F is x?' and 'How F is $x_?$?', and a *wh-* question into a disjunction of sentence-questions ('Is $x_?$ x_1, or x_2, or x_3, or x_4, or x_5?'). These translations fail if the vague expression in question does not generate an ordering. In such a case, there is no such thing as $x_?$, and x may be neither x_1 nor x_2 nor x_3 nor x_4 nor x_5. Similarly, it is impossible to precisify a vague expression whose application is not ordered, except by replacing it with an expression whose application *is* ordered. Replacing 'competent' with 'at least as competent as Hector' does not eradicate vagueness, if people are not ordered for competence. And, if the applicability of a vague expression is not ordered, there may be no precise answer to the question 'What is the degree of truth of this statement?'

This claim seems to be at odds with philosophers' understanding both of the penumbra of application of vague positive adjectives, and of the application of comparative adjectives. Dorothy Edgington writes that 'the ordering of the penumbra is an essential part of the correct use of vague terms'.[7] And Michael Dummett writes that 'it is a feature of our use of comparative adjectives that they always express transitive relations'.[8] I propose that these claims are right if they are understood in a certain way (and we could extend Edgington's claim to clear cases too). The statement that Hector is more competent than Percival implies (i) that, if Percival is competent, then Hector is too, and (ii) that, if Percival is more competent than Horace, then Hector is more competent than Horace too. To use vague terms correctly we need to understand these things.

But the truth of the statement that Hector is more competent than Percival may be indeterminate. The ordering of the penumbra is a part of the correct use of vague terms in the same way that it is part of the correct use of vague terms to understand that if Hector is competent, then it is not the case that Hector is not competent. Yet it may be indeterminate whether Hector is

---

[6] See above, Ch. 4 n. 46.
[7] 'Wright and Sainsbury on Higher-Order Vagueness' (1993) 53 *Analysis* 193, 198.
[8] 'Wang's Paradox', in *Truth and other Enigmas* (London: Duckworth, 1978), 262.

competent, and it may even be indeterminate whether he is more competent than Percival.

By the same token, I propose that the transitivity that Dummett refers to is a tautology. Recall the definition of transitivity: if Hector is more competent than Horace, and Horace more competent than Percival, then Hector must be more competent than Percival (even though 'competent' is vague). Transitivity is a feature of our use of comparative adjectives only in the same way that classification of objects is a feature of our use of positive adjectives. The transitivity of comparatives is as tautologous as the proposition that if Hector is competent, then it is not the case that Hector is not competent. Transitivity follows on comparison just as the law of excluded middle follows on classification. Both classification and comparison are affected by vagueness.

If we think of all vague words as having corresponding comparatives, and all comparatives as describing strong orderings (so that vagueness is only an obstacle to answering sentence-questions), a framework is prepared for the boundary model.

The Boundary Model

> If we represent concepts in extension by areas on a plane, this is admittedly a picture that may be used only with caution, but here it can do us good service. To a concept without a sharp boundary there would correspond an area that had not a sharp boundary-line all round, but in places just vaguely faded away into the background. This would not really be an area at all, and likewise a concept that is not sharply defined is wrongly termed a concept.

> (Gottlob Frege, *Grundgesetze der Arithmetik*, vol. ii, sect. 56)

Frege's spatial metaphor is attractive, and it pervades discussions of vagueness. In jurisprudence the metaphor is at least as old as the title of John Austin's *The Province of Jurisprudence Determined.*[9] The metaphor is commonplace in talk of 'line-drawing' in legal argument, and it gives the etymology of 'define' and 'determine'. Boundaries, areas of indeterminacy, and borderline cases are irresistible terms in discussions of vagueness.

Spatial metaphors can be misleading, but they are not false, and there is no reason to try to expunge them. But we can expose the misleading potential of the metaphors by accentuating them. The overgrown metaphor that results is the boundary model. It is the natural habitat of the sorites paradox, because it provides the ordered scales that the tolerance principle needs. Abandoning the boundary model in favour of the similarity model does not

---

[9] In Lecture VI, Austin expressed his purpose to 'distinguish completely the appropriate province of jurisprudence, from the regions which lie upon its confines, and by which it is encircled'. *The Province of Jurisprudence Determined*, Hart edn. (London: Weidenfeld & Nicolson, 1954), 193.

solve the sorites paradox: even if objects are not ordered for the applicability of an expression, it is still possible to concoct sorites series—it is just impossible to place every object on such a series.

In the boundary model, the meaning of a word is like a segment on a line, or an area on a plane, or an n-dimensional solid in an n-dimensional space. On these terms, the problem of vagueness is an inability to mark end-points on a line segment, or to draw a boundary around an area, or to identify the surface enclosing an n-dimensional solid. When we view vagueness in this way, Frege's quandary is compelling: a line segment would not really be a line segment at all if it had no end-points.

What could decide where boundaries are? Various possibilities might manifest themselves with different words. One class of possibilities is that something (such as original acts of naming, or intentions to refer to natural kinds, or Platonic forms) causes words to apply or not to apply. If the meaning of words corresponds rigidly to such causes, and the causes are determinate for all possible applications, then boundaries exist in conceptual space independently of (at least part of) the way people apply them. If they are hard to locate, that is because people have limited access to the real conceptual space in which they exist.

To reject such a theory, at least for some words, is to accept that use of words determines their meaning. Chapter 6 argued that there are no sharp boundaries to the application of vague words, because there is no sharply bounded body of use on which sharp boundaries might supervene, and because, if there were, it could not play the normative role that use plays. Here I will put those problems aside, and argue that the boundary model is unable to account for sharp boundaries as an aggregate of the dispositions of speakers. If that argument succeeds, it may seem that the boundary model gives a faithful picture of indeterminacies in the application of vague words. But I will make the further claim that semantic theorists should not adopt the boundary model.

Let us assume, in favour of the boundary model, a sharply bounded set of speakers and a determinate set of individual dispositions. Let us further assume a *rich* set of facts about such dispositions: that every speaker has a determinate $x_?$, and also a determinate ranking of all points on D for closeness to $x_?$ (their own $x_?$ is at the top of their ranking of objects). Can we picture the meaning of F as an aggregate of these individual rankings?

2. Vagueness as a Problem of Social Choice

We can represent the aggregation of individual rankings into a social choice of the location of $x_?$ in the way that social choice theory represents the aggregation of other sorts of individual judgments. Social choice theory postulates that a social choice ought to respond in some way to the judgments or interests of individuals. That postulate corresponds to the principle that (at least for some words) use determines meaning.

The early utilitarians presumed that the utility of different individuals could in principle be compared, and therefore measured on a common scale. They pictured the social utility of an alternative as a sum of individual utilities. Kenneth Arrow initiated modern social choice theory by claiming that interpersonal comparisons of utility are meaningless, and that a study of social choices should refer instead simply to individuals' preference rankings of alternatives.[10] He postulated that, for each individual, there is a determinate preference ordering of all alternatives. This second postulate of social choice theory corresponds to the simplifying assumption we have made, that each speaker has a ranking of all points on D for closeness to $x_?$ at any instant. Arrow represented social choice as a function aggregating individuals' orderings.

Societies make choices in a variety of ways—by fulfilling the preferences of a dictator, for example, or by more or less irrational voting mechanisms, or through markets, or by imposed standards that have no regard for the preferences of individuals. Arrow proposed conditions on social choice functions so minimal that it seemed that any acceptable function must meet them. Then he proved that no function can meet them. Arrow's conditions are as follows:

> I ('independence of irrelevant alternatives'): the social choice between any two alternatives must be determined solely by individuals' rankings of those two alternatives, and not by their rankings of other alternatives.
>
> P ('the Pareto principle'): if every person prefers x to y, so does the society.
>
> U ('unrestricted domain'): the function must give a social ordering for any possible set of individual orderings.
>
> D ('non-dictatorship'): no single individual ordering can imply the social ordering.[11]

Now consider society's choice of $x_?$ as a function aggregating individuals' rankings of points on D for closeness to $x_?$. It is reasonable to insist that a function aggregating those rankings must meet Arrow's conditions, with an exception which will be discussed:

[10] '... the behaviour of an individual in making choices is describable by means of a preference scale without any cardinal significance, either individual or interpersonal'. K. J. Arrow, *Social Choice and Individual Values*, 2nd edn. (New York: Wiley, 1963) (hereafter *Social Choice*), 11; see p. 9 re meaninglessness of interpersonal comparisons of utility.

[11] This is a paraphrase of the revised conditions discussed in the 2nd edn. of *Social Choice* 26–7, 30–1, 96–7. The conditions are summarized and the proof is stated in Arrow's article on 'Arrow's Theorem' in *The New Palgrave: A Dictionary of Economics*, ed. John Eatwell *et al.*

D is reasonable because the location of $x_?$ cannot depend on one person's judgment: there may be prestigious speakers, but there is no dictator.

P in our context is the rejection of essentialism: if F names an essence, then even a unanimous judgment as to $x_?$ may not decide where $x_?$ is.

U requires that the social function be able to define $x_?$ for any set rankings. It might be reasonable to restrict this condition in some way: we do not need a function that will define a boundary for a set of judgments in which someone ranks a seven-foot-tall person as closer to the boundary between 'tall' and 'not tall' than a six-foot-tall person. Restrictions on U are discussed below.

I requires that whether x is closer to $x_?$ than y is depends solely on speakers' *rankings of those two objects*. So if object x is ranked above object y when objects x_1 and x_2 are also ranked, x must rank above y when x_1 and x_2 are not considered. And the relative rankings of x and y do not depend on the *distance* that speakers would place between x and y. The possibility of rejecting I is discussed below.

If it is reasonable to apply conditions I, P, U, and D, Arrow has proved the impossibility of an acceptable social judgment as to the location of $x_?$ on D. But, in fact, Arrow's impossibility proof does not apply to *that* judgment. Along with his general impossibility result, Arrow proved that a social choice *can* satisfy conditions I, P, and D if condition U is restricted by an assumption of 'single-peaked preferences'.[12] It must be possible to plot the alternatives on a line, and each individual must rank the alternatives so that no alternative lies between two higher-ranked alternatives on the line. In our case, we supposed that an individual may rank x_2, x_3, or x_4 highest in choosing $x_?$, but cannot rank x_3 lower than both x_2 and x_4. The rankings are single-peaked.

This significant restriction on Arrow's condition U fits some social choice situations,[13] and is plainly appropriate for a function aggregating judgments as to the location of $x_?$. Choice of $x_?$, both individual and social, must be single-peaked. That is, ranking of alternatives must decrease continuously in both directions from the alternative ranked first. For x_2, x_3, and x_4 to be ranked 1, 3, 2 would violate transitivity: since Fx_4 is more clearly true than

---

(London: Macmillan, 1987); see also Amartya Sen's article 'Social Choice', in *Palgrave* (I use Sen's abbreviations).

[12] *Social Choice* 75–80; Arrow built on an argument by Duncan Black that majority voting yields determinate results given single-peaked preferences.

[13] It would apply, for example, if all political parties in an election lay on a spectrum from left to right, and if, in any choice between two parties, voters always preferred the party that was closer on the spectrum to their first choice. If any voter ranked, for example, a far-right party first and a far-left party second, preferences would not be single-peaked.

Fx_3, for example, when x_2 is ranked first in a choice of $x_?$, x_3 must be ranked higher than x_4.

Majority voting is one social choice function that would generate a determinate $x_?$ among individuals with single-peaked preferences. Arrow's theorem does not rule out the possibility of a function aggregating individuals' applications of F (or dispositions to apply F). The social determination of $x_?$ for F shows how the boundary model works. But now we can show that most vague words are crucially unlike F.

Incompleteness of Social Orderings

The problem with many real vague expressions is that their applicability cannot be plotted along a line. 'Crowd', for example, does not automatically apply with increasing strength as numbers of people increase, but also depends on density of people. The boundary model approaches that problem by treating such words as multi-dimensional, so that, for example, 'crowd' describes an area on a plane, and colour words describe a solid in the three dimensions of hue, saturation, and intensity.

Even if the dimensions can be aggregated so as to arrive at individual orderings, those orderings will not be single-peaked. For F, speakers cannot rank x_2, x_3, and x_4 in the order $x_2x_4x_3$. But if we must allow that three speakers could rank three objects for, for example, 'green' in the orders xyz, yzx, and zxy, then a condition similar to U returns to the set of conditions on an acceptable social choice function. The aggregation of individual orderings is impossible.

Individual rankings of objects for closeness to the least crowdlike crowd (that is, for closeness to the analogue of $x_?$ for 'crowd') will not be single-peaked, and therefore cannot provide a social ordering. Think of a group of 1000 people scattered here and there in Hyde Park ('group A'), and an angry knot of six people shouting outside a government building (group B). Suppose that both groups are borderline crowds, and suppose that group C is like B but includes one more person. The consistency principle will require a speaker to rank C above B in a ranking for applicability of 'crowd'. But C need not be more truly a crowd than A, even if B is ranked equally with A. That is, there is something wrong with the notion of 'equally truly a crowd' applied to A and B: the relation 'more truly a crowd' is incomplete.

Words whose application is immensurable (see Chapter 3.6) cannot be plotted on a dimension like D: sometimes we can say that one person is balder than another, but there is no measure of baldness. There are various scalar qualities associated with baldness (number of hairs, length of hairs . . .), but they cannot be combined to generate an ordering. And other grounds of application of 'bald', such as arrangement of hairs, are not scalar at all. Immensurate criteria of application are common and important. It makes sense in some cases to say that one person is nicer than another, but it

does not make sense to set out to measure niceness. There is no scale of niceness on which people could be plotted, in the way that they could be plotted
on a scale of height.[14] Arrow's system was designed to analyse something
immensurable (utility) by a purely ordinal method. But if niceness is immensurable, and 'nicer' is vague, then there are two problems: (i) because we cannot say that rankings will be single-peaked, we cannot deny a form of U
which leads to the impossibility theorem; (ii) we see that the assumption we
started with, that individuals have determinate rankings, is not only false but
necessarily false in the case of expressions like 'nice'. If we gave speakers a
long list of their acquaintances, and asked them to rank the acquaintances for
closeness to the least nice nice person, no doubt they might put numbers
beside names. But if 'nicer' is vague, the precision of those numbers would
misrepresent the facts about the correct application of either 'nicer' or 'nice'.
The ordered individual rankings of the boundary model are pseudo-
orderings produced by a theoretical requirement of determinacy.

Distancings?

Arrow abstracted away from the *intensity* of preferences. He needed to do so,
to avoid the problem he saw of the meaninglessness of interpersonal comparisons of utility. But in considering the correct application of words as a
question of social choice, perhaps we can abandon Arrow's abstemious focus
on rankings. We could add to our hypothetical base of facts not only rankings, but also distancings. Speakers are not only capable of ranking one
object as farther from $x_?$ than another; they are also capable of (at least
rough) judgments as to *how far apart* on D different objects are. If we treat
such judgments (distancings) as part of the argument of a social choice function, we escape Arrow's impossibility theorem—by rejecting condition I.[15]

Such an approach would have a deal of work to do, to explain why it does
not face the problems that made condition I attractive to Arrow: first, cardi-
nality (what is a person's measure of crowdness or niceness?), and secondly,
interpersonal comparability (can your measure of niceness be stated in the
same units as mine? and should your dispositions count for more than mine?
for less? just the same?). These problems are not the same in social welfare
theory as in the social determination of meaning, and I do not know how to
show that interpersonal comparison should be avoided in the latter for the
same reasons as in the former. If we cannot show *that*, then perhaps we should
not be too quick to conclude that Arrow's impossibility theorem applies.

If we abandon condition I, we should not exaggerate the prospects for

---

[14] But see the brief discussion of measurement in Sect. 3, below.
[15] Cf. Amartya Sen, *Collective Choice and Social Welfare* (San Francisco: Holden-Day, 1970),
90. Sen shows how admitting cardinal utility judgments would violate condition I.

making sense of social choice as to the application of words. The direct effect is only that an impossibility theorem does not apply; we have not even shown that a determinate social choice of boundaries is possible. And we have not yet faced up to another problem that arises from the difference between social welfare and social determination of meaning. There may be a variety of possible social welfare functions, and they may be open to criticism on various grounds (and perhaps none will be the best). But with respect to social choice functions determining application of words, we face a question that welfare economics need not face: which possible function *is* the function that *does* determine meaning? The notion of aggregation seems to lack resources to answer that question, even if we add distancings to the base. The problem is analogous to the supervenience account's lack of resources to say that there is a *way in which* sharp boundaries supervene on use.

That is a very broad objection; there is a simpler objection that arises if we stay within the social choice approach, rather than questioning its point. The objection is that *distancings will necessarily be rough* when comparatives are vague. Recall that vagueness in the comparative 'more competent than' entails that there is no precise answer to the question 'How competent is Hector?' and, I argued, there is no complete ranking of people for competence. By the same token, there is no precise answer to a distancing question, like 'How much more competent is Hector than Percival?' The upshot is that, even if we can escape Arrow's impossibility theorem by abandoning condition I, we have no reason to think that a *precise* location of $x_?$ is possible, and every reason to think that it is impossible. No function that meets conditions U, P, I, and D can yield complete aggregates of non-single-peaked rankings; no function that meets conditions U, P, and D can be expected to yield *precise* aggregates of rough distancings.

But this proposal raises an important possibility: that because we have rough distancings, a *rough* social aggregate is possible.

I think that making sense of this possibility requires a closer look at the problem that (i) ruled out complete social orderings based on rankings, and (ii) leads to the conclusion that distancings cannot be precise. That problem is incommensurability in the application of words such as 'nice' and 'competent' (and 'heap' and 'crowd' and so on . . .). As proposed in Chapter 3.5, we can use the debate over value incommensurability to illustrate the structure of incommensurability in the application of abstract terms in general.

3. Incommensurability and Boundaries

> . . . values seem to present a case of a *vague* ordering, which is a sort that is not well understood.
>
> (James Griffin, *Well-Being*, 81)

If there are multiple, incommensurate grounds of application of 'competent' or 'bald', then people are not completely ordered for the application of those words (and the comparatives 'balder' and 'more competent' are vague). We can draw a parallel between incommensurabilities in the application of such ordinary vague expressions, and the incommensurabilities in the application of very abstract evaluative expressions ('good' and so on), which Raz and Finnis (among others) have alleged.

But this suggestion will meet with resistance from people who have denied or discounted value incommensurability. If the argument of this chapter is successful, it seems that those writers need to claim that options are completely ordered for value: that 'better' is not vague. But perhaps they can retreat to the notion of roughly complete orderings of options.

James Griffin has used the notion of orderings to make a sustained (though equivocal) defence of the commensurability of options with respect to value. He admits that 'The absence of a complete ranking would indeed upset the policy of maximising (though upset and incompleteness come in degrees).'[16] But he says that it is difficult to find convincing examples of incomparability, and he suggests that the notion that there are such examples arises from a misunderstanding of the notion of quantity. He concludes, ' "Well-being" is certainly a quantitative attribute, in the sense that we sometimes say that one thing makes us better off, or at least as well off, or exactly as well off, as another.'[17] That turns out to be a very weak sense of 'quantitative'. In Griffin's sense, an attribute is quantitative with respect to a domain if *any two* members of the domain can be compared with each other with respect to that attribute. Quantities of value arise from the 'possibility of ranking items on the basis of their nature'.[18] How generally must it be possible to rank alternatives, in order for an attribute to be quantitative? Griffin says that this is partly a matter for stipulation, and that his requirements are 'relatively undemanding—merely that $(\exists A)(\exists B)(A>_a B \lor B<_a A \lor A=_a B)\ldots$'.[19]

Recall the job in teaching (job A) and the job in law (job B), from Chapter 3.5. We know everything we could want to know about the jobs, but it is not clear whether A or B is better (they are 'incomparable'); both are clearly better than job X. In Griffin's terms, these facts make the value of jobs quantitative, in virtue of the fact that job X is clearly not as good as job B or job A.

Corresponding to the claim that well-being is a quantitative attribute is Griffin's claim that it can be measured. But this is a weak claim, too. Griffin starts with Stevens's liberating definition of measurement as 'the assignment of numerals to objects or events according to rule—any rule'.[20] But that is too

---

[16] James Griffin, *Well-Being* (Oxford: Clarendon Press, 1986) (hereafter *Well-Being*), 90.
[17] Ibid. 95.   [18] Ibid. 90.
[19] Ibid. 344 n. 6; '$>_a$,' '$<_a$' and '$=_a$' mean 'has more/less/same amount of an attribute'.
[20] Ibid. 93, quoting S. S. Stevens, 'Measurement, Psychophysics, and Utility', in C. W. Churchman and P. Ratoosh (eds.), *Measurement: Definition and Theories* (New York: Wiley, 1959).

liberating: there is no sense in which we *have measured* a group of people if we assign the numeral 0 or 1 to each of them according to a rule requiring the toss of a coin (although we may have *created* a measure by which to treat them in some way). The added requirement to make sense of the notion of measurement must be that the rule for assigning numbers gives some significance to comparisons between the numbers for some purpose of assessment (a stronger requirement would be that the rule gives significance to arithmetical operations on the numbers — then the scale would be cardinal).

Griffin agrees that the liberating definition is too wide, and he suggests that 'it seems better to restrict the term "measurement" to attributes that are in some sense quantitative'.[21] That restriction is very weak, because of Griffin's weak sense of 'quantitative'.

Consider jobs A, B, and X. They are quantitative with respect to value in Griffin's sense, because it is possible to rank some of them: A is better than X, and B is better than X. We can also assign numbers by a rule, such as 'rank the available jobs with respect to value'. So, in Griffin's terms, the value of jobs is measurable on a single scale: jobs are commensurable with respect to value. Yet the only job to which we can assign a number is job X, which gets '3'. And if we add job Y, which is not clearly better or worse than X, it becomes impossible to assign numbers to any of the jobs. We can say that both A and B are better than either X or Y. But we cannot claim to have measured the jobs in any stronger sense than that we can make such statements.

Griffin's tendency is to minimize incommensurability of value; Raz claims that it is significant.[22] It is a delicate matter to find anything more than hunches on which to choose between such claims. When some option can be identified as better than some other option, Griffin draws general conclusions such as 'well-being is ordinally measurable',[23] and 'we are able to compare mixed-value goods'.[24] Yet he admits that there are *some* incompletenesses in ranking.[25] Griffin and Raz accept and, I think, we should accept that both Griffin's test of commensurability *and* a similar test of incommensurability are generally met for evaluation of options. Some options can be ranked, and some options cannot be ranked.[26]

Those two bare claims tell us nothing about how to judge between the competing hunches that value incommensurability is significant and that it is marginal. Each bare claim is consistent with either conclusion about the significance of incommensurability. Can we say *anything* general in favour of a conclusion?

---

[21] *Well-Being* 343 n. 4.

[22] '. . . both values and valuables are to a large degree incommensurable'. *MF* 321.

[23] *Well-Being* 96.

[24] 'Mixing Values' (1991) 65 *Proceedings of the Aristotelian Society* (suppl.) 101 (hereafter 'Mixing Values'), 109.   [25] *Well-Being* 96.

[26] Griffin *denies* incommensurability because on his view of measurement, the possibility of ranking any options is sufficient for options to be measurable. I have *asserted* incommensurability

It seems that Griffin claims that the cases in which two alternatives cannot be ranked are sufficiently restricted that we can treat any two such alternatives as *roughly equal*. He says that 'rough equality is a long way from incomparability'.[27] The difference seems to be that, if options are roughly equal, it is reasonable to *rank* them as equal. It is right to be indifferent between them.

Two items are incommensurable, in the strict sense of the word, if and only if they cannot be ranked at all. One might call this relation 'incomparability'. I think that, in the domain of prudential values, it is hard to find cases of strict incomparability. Up to a point, one can rank novels ... Admittedly, when the balance starts to level off, one often can no longer tell precisely how they are ranked. Indeed, there may be many cases in which, for this reason, precise comparison is defeated. But that is not incomparability.[28]

This conclusion is puzzling: Griffin seems first to stipulate that A and B are incomparable if they cannot be ranked (I have followed him in this), then to admit that there may be no *precise* comparison between A and B, and then to deny that A and B are incomparable. I think that the answer to the puzzle is that, in Griffin's view, when 'precise comparison is defeated', we can reasonably (perhaps we *should* (prudentially)) be indifferent between A and B. He writes, 'Where we have rough equality, we treat the items, when it comes to choice, simply as equals.'[29]

It seems that, in Griffin's view, *rough* comparability is *never* defeated: 'better than or equal to' is a roughly complete relation—it determines a vague ordering.[30] And he appeals to one of the spatial metaphors of the boundary model, suggesting that there is an 'area of indistinctness'[31] which does not disturb the claim that well-being is measurable.

Does Griffin's account of rough equality show that incommensurabilities are insignificant? One challenge to that view arises from the account of rough equality that Raz had given in *The Morality of Freedom*. Raz agrees that A and B are roughly equal if and only if it would be right to be indifferent between A and B. But he claims that indifference is not necessarily appropriate when neither option is clearly better. The choice between A and B is important even if neither is clearly better, whenever the reasons in favour of preferring each option are weighty reasons.[32]

It seems that incommensurabilities in Griffin's 'area of indistinctness' may

because I have been using a more demanding notion of measurement, according to which commensurability would require that *all* options could be ranked.

[27] *Well-Being* 81.   [28] 'Mixing Values' 111.   [29] *Well-Being* 97.

[30] Cf. 'We seem, therefore, to have not so much a partial [i.e. incomplete] ordering, as something new and little understood, namely a *vague ordering*.' Ibid. The suggestion seems to be that a vague ordering should not really be called incomplete—it is roughly complete.

[31] Ibid. 96.

[32] *MF* 332. Another factor that is important to Raz is whether the reasons for A and for B are very different reasons. I think that that is an additional reason not to be indifferent about the decision, and that the importance of the competing reasons is sufficient to make the decision one that matters.

be significant incommensurabilities, even if the 'area' is tiny. We can translate the argument so as to apply to our simple sorites series of concerts, to make the point more vivid: a court's choice of a last guilty defendant in the case of the million raves is a very important decision, because for some defendants it means the difference between conviction and acquittal. Even if all but two or three of the million defendants were clear cases, the court's resolution of the unclear cases would still be important decisions. Calling x_i and x_{i+1} roughly equal would not solve the problem.

So it seems that resolutions of incommensurabilites can be significant decisions even if incommensurability is as marginal as Griffin suggests. But of course, the merits of the cases of x_i and x_{i+1} *are* roughly equal: the million raves case is a convincing illustration of the problem of indeterminacy because the increments in the sorites series are tiny. If each adjacent pair in a sorites series were not roughly equal, we might say, the tolerance principle would not be attractive. But if incommensuracy of dimensions is a form of vagueness (see Chapter 3.5), it might seem that it *must* be a fringe phenomenon: that two objects that are *significantly different* cannot be incomparable, even if x_i and x_{i+1} are incomparable.

There is something more we can say about rough equality—something inconsistent with the conclusion that two incomparable options must be roughly equal. It seems that if A and B are roughly equal, then a tiny improvement in A will not make A clearly better than B. But a significant improvement *will* necessarily make A better than B. If A and B are incomparable, no trivial improvement will make A clearly better. Where A+ is clearly but only slightly better than A, if A and B are incommensurable, then A+ and B are also incommensurable.

Notice that this is a form of the tolerance principle for the comparative form of the sorites paradox (Chapter 3.2). And the question of whether incommensurabilities of dimensions can be significant is like the question of how large the increment in a sorites series can be. Recall that Chapter 5.4 concluded that (i) there is no precise answer to that question, and (ii) the reasons for rejecting the epistemic theory are reasons for saying that the tolerance principle is not generally restricted to trivial increments. Vagueness is trivial only when pegged to precise expressions.

By the same token, we can argue (i) that when A and B are incomparable, there is no precise answer to the question 'How much better does A have to be in order to be clearly better than B?', and (ii) that incomparability is never trivial. To conclude that A really is incomparable with B is to conclude that there is *some* improvement in A that would not make A clearly better than B. It would not actually be contradictory to conclude at the same time that there is some slightly greater but still trivial improvement in A that *would* make it clearly better. But it would be a bizarre conclusion. It would be like concluding that no one goes bald by losing one hair, but someone might go bald by losing two hairs. For the same reasons for which we think that it is impossible for two very different jobs to be *precisely* equal in value (so that *any* trivial improvement in A would make it clearly better than B, and *any* trivial worsening in A would make it clearly worse than B[33]), it is impossible for two very different jobs to be *trivially* different in value—just as it is impossible for 'tall' to have a tolerance principle formulated in nanometres but not in millimetres.

Here is a test that might focus hunches about whether incommensurabilities can be significant. Suppose A and B are the jobs in teaching and in law, and suppose we have concluded that they are incomparable: we know everything we could want to know about the jobs, and we just do not know whether to say that A is better, or that B is better (we know they cannot be precisely equal). Is it possible that there should be some *significant* improvement in A that would not make it clearly better than B? If so, then the incommensurability between the jobs is significant. If B is incomparable with both A++ and A, and A++ is significantly better than A, then incomparability is significant.

Of course, a significant improvement in A might make it easy to compare A with B: a big pay rise for teachers might be all it takes to make teaching clearly preferable to the law. Some significant changes put paid to some incomparabilities. But it certainly seems to be possible that a significant improvement in an option might not make it clearly better than the alternatives with which it had been incomparable. Suppose someone said,

I've been thinking about whether to go into teaching or into law, and I don't think that either career would be clearly better or worse than the other. The teachers have just received a huge pay increase, which makes teaching a lot more attractive. But I still see good reasons for each, and no reason to think one choice is better than the other.

I do not think that we can say that such a person is necessarily confused, or that the uncertainty is necessarily mere ignorance.

So it seems that Raz is right to deny that incomparable options are necessarily roughly equal. In that case, value incommensurabilities and indeterminacies in the application of value terms can be significant.[34] Yet it may seem that consequentialism is rescued from the incommensurability argument. It seems that consequentialism does not offer a *nonsensical* guide to action, but only a *vague* guide. The general consequentialist moral instruction 'do what will produce the best consequences' is only more *abstract* than a vague

---

[33] Griffin could agree that this is impossible, if A and B are within an 'area of indistinctness'.

[34] Could it be argued that incommensurabilities in the application of *non*-evaluative expressions are different in a way that guarantees that all incomparabilities are cases of rough equality? That may be the case for some expressions: perhaps if A and B are incomparable for baldness, and A becomes significantly less bald, A will necessarily become clearly less bald than B. But I think it would be very rash to make a more general claim than that. It seems, for example, that of two concerts that are incomparable for the application of the rave provision (say, one very loud, not very long concert and one very long, not very loud concert), it is possible that one could be made significantly worse without necessarily becoming clearly worse than the other.

instruction like 'choose the most competent applicant for the job'. Because 'best' is more abstract, its application can involve more far-reaching incommensurabilities than, for example, 'most competent'. And a consequentialist *would* be wrong to claim that there are no significant incommensurabilities in the application of either instruction. Perhaps the adverse implications of substantial value incommensurability for consequentialism are just that (i) consequentialism purports to give a *general, mandatory* guide to action, but in any rich field of options it yields no decisive guidance, and (ii) it wrongly recommends indifference between incomparable options.

It seems that a fundamental, general argument against consequentialism should not rely on incommensuracy of dimensions. It needs to address the 'constitutive' incommensurabilities between the moral value (I should probably say the 'rightness') of seeking to bring about good consequences, and the moral value of acting on the exclusionary considerations of justice that consequentialists have been accused of ignoring. There lies the fate of consequentialism; it is outside the scope of this book.

The Boundary Model: Conclusions

The boundary model describes vagueness as indeterminacy in the location of $x_?$ for F. It is a model of what makes it correct to apply an expression, and it can be shared by epistemic theorists and semanticists. The epistemic form of the boundary model needs to claim not only that there is an $x_?$ for F, but that *all* apparent incommensurabilities in the application of vague words are only epistemic. In the last chapter I argued that Williamson's version of the boundary model cannot support the claim that there are sharp boundaries.

A semanticist theorist, on the other hand, might admit incommensurabilities, and say that the boundary model gives a revealing picture of the indeterminacies in the application of vague language. When we try to describe the vagueness of real words in this way, vagueness becomes a complex of several varieties of indeterminacy. Combining the claims of this chapter and Chapter 6, there are indeterminacies:

1. in aggregation of idiolects, illustrated by the application of Arrow's impossibility theorem
2. (i) as to what slice of language use is being aggregated, or
   (ii) as to which dispositions count
3. in membership in a language community
4. arising from ethnolinguistic variation
5. arising from the model's inability to discern whether a particular disposition is mistaken
6. as to what the context is, and what effect context has on the location of boundaries.

It seems to me that the semanticist form of the boundary model is unattractive because it suggests that the expressions of a natural language have a function (drawing boundaries) for which they are necessarily inadequate. This problem is worse if the indeterminacies are significant, rather than a trivial fringe, and particularly if I was right to suggest that we should reject Griffin's notion that there are *roughly complete* orderings of objects for the application of evaluative expressions.

By abandoning the boundary model, we can avoid characterizing languages as necessarily inept. We can allow as much indeterminacy as there is in the application of vague language, while economizing in the description of its sources. That is, we can reject the complexities of the boundary model in favour of saying that the indeterminacies in the application of a vague word are indeterminacies in the similarities an object must bear to paradigms. That is a simpler account of the application of vague words.

Both the boundary model and the similarity model view meaning as determined (to the extent that it is determined) by use, at least for some expressions. The difference between the two models lies in the ambiguity of 'use': in the boundary model, 'use' can mean either 'way of using' (corresponding to dispositions), or 'incidence of use' (corresponding to actual applications). In the similarity model, 'use' means 'point, usefulness' (this is the sense in which something 'has a use' or 'is of use'; see Chapter 6.3). The use that determines the meaning of a word is the use that it has, not the use to which it has been put (although the three senses of 'use' are related). Vague words apply to objects to which it is generally useful to apply them; the indeterminacy of vagueness lies in indeterminacy of purposes and needs.

4. The Similarity Model

Frege compares a concept to an area and says that an area with vague boundaries cannot be called an area at all . . . But is it senseless to say: 'Stand roughly there'? Suppose that I were standing with someone in a city square and said that. As I say it I do not draw any kind of boundary, but perhaps point with my hand—as if I were indicating a particular *spot*. And this is just how one might explain to someone what a game is. One gives examples and intends them to be taken in a particular way. (Wittgenstein, *PI* 71)

In the similarity model, similarities to paradigms provide the normative regularity in which the meaning of an expression consists. Understanding an expression is taking examples in a particular way. A language is not an aggregate of idiolects that set *or* fail to set boundaries to the application of a vague word, and vagueness is neither a failure of idiolects to set boundaries, nor the impossibility of a determinate aggregation. To understand a vague word is to be able to use paradigms, and vagueness is flexibility in their use.

This account has the advantages of simplicity mentioned above, and gives a better account of two important features of vagueness that have been neglected in philosophical discussions: the fact that there may be no clear borderline cases (Chapter 5.5), and the parallel between semantic and pragmatic vagueness (Chapter 3.10). The problem with the similarity model is that it neither rescues classical logic from paradox, nor proposes to replace classical logic. We should consider three objections that Sainsbury has made to his own suggestion of using similarities to paradigms as a way of describing vagueness:

> But the suggestion has many vices. For one, it presupposes, without any justification, that every boundaryless concept must be instantiated. For another, the condition will not state anything which users of the concept have to know, since there may be more than one paradigm, and so one could master the concept just as well without knowing anything of [a particular paradigm]. Thirdly, anything which might have worried one about boundarylessness, for example any problems about the sorites paradox, naturally remain just as they were, though now attaching to the similarity relation.[35]

With regard to Sainsbury's first point, it seems that we need only draw on the flexibility of the notion of paradigms to avoid presupposing the instantiation of concepts. Paradigms can be described, or depicted—we can teach the use of 'dragon' with paradigms even if there are no dragons.

As for his second point, variation in paradigms is a crucial feature that a discussion of vagueness will have to account for. A paradigm is a clear case used as an object of comparison. It is tempting to think that a paradigm gives an agreed standard starting-point for a variable judgment of similarity. So we *agree* that a person who is literally as bald as an egg is bald, and we *disagree* in the judgments of similarity to that paradigm that are required for use of the word in borderline cases. But Sainsbury is obviously right to point out that paradigms vary. There is no reason to think that someone has to be perfectly hairless before we could use him as a paradigm bald man, and many expressions do not allow for absolute paradigms like the hairless man ('heap' is a good example). In the similarity model, being able to identify paradigm dragons as dragons is a criterion for understanding the word. But we could construct a sorites series for paradigms: 'If this picture is useful for teaching the meaning of the word "dragon", it will still be useful if we remove one tiny speck of ink . . .'. So not only do paradigms vary, as Sainsbury points out; the notion of a paradigm is itself vague.

Sainsbury's third claim seems to be true: the similarity model leaves the sorites paradox as it was. Moreover, we have just seen that the paradox attaches not only to the similarity relation, but to the very notion of a paradigm. Perhaps that is a virtue, if $x_?$ *necessarily* lacks a determinate location in

---

[35] Sainsbury, 'Concepts without Boundaries', n. 3 above, 20.

conceptual space. In any case, however, I think that, for the reasons tentatively proposed in Chapter 6.6, it is good policy neither to assert nor to deny bivalence.

The similarity model is worth pursuing if it offers a way of setting aside the paradoxical question of the location of $x_?$, and even if it only gives a clearer picture of what is unclear about the application of vague expressions. The best thing that can be said for it is that its vices and virtues correspond to the nature of the subject-matter.

5. Conclusion

We can draw a general conclusion from the discussion in Chapter 5.4 ('How Vague is a Vague Word?'), and the discussion of incommensurability in Section 3 above. Borderline cases are necessarily *intermediate* between clear cases of the application and non-application of vague expressions, but they are not necessarily (they typically are not) a trivial fringe. Cases in which a particular person is in doubt about the application of a vague expression in a known situation are not necessarily cases in which the application of the expression is indeterminate, but there are cases in which application is indeterminate. Perhaps a clear borderline case is one in which a speaker can know that the application of an expression is indeterminate; there may be no such cases for the application of some vague expressions.

It seems that the indeterminacies that arise from vagueness are not trivial. Although it is impossible to make any positive statement about *how* substantial they are, it is clear that they can be significant. So if they pose a threat to the ideal of the rule of law, it is a significant threat. Chapter 9 will argue that they pose no threat to the ideal.

8

Vagueness and Interpretation

AN interpretation is an answer to the question 'What do you make of this?' Interpretation is the process of coming up with an answer. Creativity and constraint complement each other in that process. If I ask, 'What do you make of this?', I ask you to *make* something, but it must be something made *of this*. As a result, there are critical differences and important similarities between interpretation and understanding, and between interpretation and invention.

Perhaps a general analysis of the concept of interpretation can say no more. The concept is abstract and malleable, and the extent of the creativity of interpretation depends on what the situation allows. That is a matter of the nature of the object, the questions that an interpretation must answer, the interpreter's purposes, the expectations of people to whom an interpretation is offered, and so on. If this is all we can say about the concept of interpretation, then some very general questions about how (for example) judges ought to interpret statutes and legal precedents are to be answered not by *in vitro* analysis of the concept, but by means that will have to do partly with the nature of a legal system, and partly with the individual characteristics of an indefinite variety of legal problems. In particular, we cannot say that interpretation eliminates indeterminacy in the application of legal rules, or even that it tends to reduce indeterminacy.

I will call this account of the concept of interpretation the simple account, and propose it as an alternative to more ambitious accounts of interpretation: first Ronald Dworkin's account, and then an account that Andrei Marmor developed in opposition to Dworkin's theory.

These issues of the nature of interpretation need to be addressed, in order to avert an important misunderstanding of the reach of the indeterminacy claim. That claim may seem to rely on a certain sort of picture of the law: a picture in which authorities issue linguistic formulations which judges then apply according to the rules of language. This picture concludes that the law is indeterminate in virtue of any indeterminacy in the rules of the language.

I will argue that the indeterminacy claim does not rely on any such picture of the law. I will do so by asking whether a different, 'interpretivist' picture of law could show that people's legal rights and duties are not indeterminate even if legislatures and judges use vague language in formulating the law. An interpretivist theory of law claims that to make any statement of law is to state the conclusion of an interpretation of the community's legal practice. Ronald Dworkin has developed the most sophisticated interpretivist theory, and this chapter will address the challenges that his interpretivism poses to the indeterminacy claim. Sections 1–3 will address the interpretivist claim that the law has sufficient resources to resolve any indeterminacies in the application of legal language. Theories that reject the indeterminacy claim treat juridical bivalence (see Chapter 4.4) as a model of the structure of the law, rather than as a legal technique. Section 3 discusses and rejects a suggestion of Dworkin's that juridical bivalence itself gives reason to deny the indeterminacy claim.

The point of discussing Marmor's work is to examine the relation between vagueness and interpretation in a non-interpretivist theory of law—a theory claiming that, in at least some cases, following the law is a matter of following rules that do not call for interpretation. The two questions I set out to ask of such a theory are 'How can we be following a rule when its requirements are indeterminate?' and 'Is legal interpretation best thought of as the task of dealing with legal indeterminacy?' I will claim that linguistic indeterminacy is not a prerequisite for interpretation, and that interpretation will not resolve all indeterminacies. It is not even generally a technique for resolving indeterminacies.

1. Hercules and the Quietest Rave

To an interpretivist, it seems that the vagueness of language is irrelevant to the determinacy of legal rights and duties. Recall the argument of Chapter 4. Dworkin has claimed that any indeterminacy in the application of vague language can be eliminated by a rule of interpretation providing that the language shall only be applied in clear cases. I argued that higher-order vagueness is an objection to that strategy, and that the objection survives Dworkin's elaborated defence of the strategy. But now we need to consider a deeper interpretivist claim: not that there may be rules of interpretation that resolve indeterminacies in the application of the law, but that the law itself is a holistic, constructive interpretation of the legal history of the community. The argument is that vagueness in the authorities' linguistic formulations of purported laws gives no reason to think that any legal rights or duties are indeterminate, because those formulations do not determine the law. They become part of the preinterpretive material that an interpretation of the law must fit.

Here I will argue that even an interpretive theory of law must accept indeterminacy in the law as a result of vagueness in the considerations that are relevant to a legal judgment. The argument has two parts: first, I illustrate the problem that even an interpretivist theory would face in the case of the million raves. That illustration is only the beginning of an argument, because an interpretivist will claim that the law offers resources that make vagueness irrelevant. So the second part of the argument (in Section 2) asks what can be said in general about the interpretive resources of the law. I claim that we have general reasons to say that they themselves are typically vague. Vagueness in the law is *not* just a problem of indeterminacy in the application of the words that lawmakers use.

I propose that the case of the million raves would cause a crisis, in which Hercules would have to make decisions that he cannot justify in principle. In fact, I will argue that the case *illustrates* a crisis that Hercules would suffer in *most or all* cases: he will not be able to portray the law as having integrity. If it succeeds, the argument is a fatal objection to Dworkin's theory of law as integrity. But the purpose here is to argue that an interpretivist theory of law should not deny indeterminacy in the law.

In prosecutions under the Criminal Justice and Public Order Act, Hercules would develop a conception of serious distress in the context of raves. That task would require him to develop a constructive interpretation of the law—an account of what the law requires that both fits the legal history of the United Kingdom and puts it in the best light. He would seek to portray the Act as a good piece of legislation, and to portray its requirements in the case before him as consistent in principle with the rest of British law. In any particular case, Hercules would find that a concert is a rave if that decision would portray the state's coercive interference with the organizer as justified by the political virtues that law ought to exhibit: justice, fairness, procedural due process and integrity.[1]

But suppose that Hercules were confronted with the whole series of concerts out of which we might construct a sorites paradox, all at once. One million rave organizers are in his court on charges of disobeying a direction to turn off their music, and they have all put on identical concerts—*except* that each successive defendant in the series of cases played the music at an imperceptibly lower volume than the one before. The first defendant tormented all of Shropshire; the last defendant played music that was scarcely audible.

As the volume goes down with each case, Hercules will have to choose a quietest rave, and a noisiest concert that is not a rave. He has no room to say that police interference was *somewhat* legally justified—he has to convict or acquit. Yet Hercules' fully developed conception of serious distress—the outcome of the interpretive method—cannot yield a quietest rave. It must *itself* be susceptible to sorites reasoning. His conception aims to be principled. But what scheme of principle, what constructive interpretation, could account for a statement of the requirements of the law according to which one organizer in our series is convicted and the next is acquitted? How can Hercules treat x_i in the same way as x_0, and treat x_{i+1} in the

---

[1] See *LE* 164–7.

same way as $x_{1,000,000}$, when x_i and x_{i+1} have done materially the same thing? Why should an imperceptible difference in volume make a polar difference to the legal outcome? An interpretation on which there is a sharp boundary will suffer in the dimension of justification, because it will lack integrity: there will be no consistency in principle between a conviction and an acquittal for materially equivalent conduct. Yet, faced with the series of defendants, Hercules himself can come up with no other result.

In this predicament it seems that Hercules would suffer a nervous crisis. He would convict one rave organizer for conduct materially the same as conduct for which the next is acquitted. He would not be able to portray those two decisions as consistent in principle. Law as integrity would fail by its own standards. And this is not the sort of breakdown that might result when the interpretive attitude cannot be sustained (when, for example, no scheme of principles that fits the history of the community makes it look at all attractive). It is a breakdown that results in any legal system in which legal rules can be stated in vague language. We can leave behind the 'application' view of law in favour of the interpretive view—and the problem remains. The problem arises not only if the requirements of the law are determined by authoritative formulations of law, but if the requirements of the law can be *expressed* (as the outcome of the interpretive process) in language that is susceptible to the sorites paradox. Unless the paradox can be resolved, those requirements will be indeterminate in some cases.

In fact, we should see that Hercules' problem is even worse than the case of the million raves suggests. Real judges do not ordinarily face a case like the case of the million raves. But that case only *brings to light* the problem that Hercules would face in *every* case in which the requirements of the law can be stated in vague language. In reaching every decision, Hercules seeks to achieve consistency in principle among all the requirements of the law;[2] it seems that, in any single rave case, he would seek to achieve consistency between the decision he renders and the decisions he would render in all other potential rave prosecutions. If that is what Hercules tries to do, then in *every* case in which the law can be stated in vague language, he will face a problem like the case of the million raves.

These claims seem to face a fundamental potential objection. Even if the claims hold when people's legal rights and duties *can be stated* in vague language, that does not mean that they hold whenever *a lawmaker has used* vague language. Perhaps, in the case of the million raves, a *complete* statement of the law would not use vague language at all: it would yield an answer to any rave case. Real judges do not have the time *or* the need to develop such a statement of the law; Hercules would be able to do so. The objection is that

---

[2] See *LE* 245, and the 'horizontal' dimension of integrity mentioned at *LE* 227 and *Freedom's Law* (Oxford: Oxford University Press, 1996), 83.

the law has other resources than the mere words in which the definition of a rave was framed, and those resources may enable Hercules to find the quietest rave.

2. The Resources of the Law

We want to say that there must be more to the requirements of the law than the mere application of words. If that is so, then perhaps vagueness is a defect in the latter that need not lead to indeterminacies in the former. Dworkin takes that view, and he is not alone. One of Hart's concessions about *The Concept of Law* might seem to support it:

the question whether a *rule* applies or does not apply to some particular situation of fact is not the same as the question whether according to the settled conventions of language this is determined or left open by the words of that rule. For a legal system often has other resources besides the words used in the formulations of its rules which serve to determine their content or meaning in particular cases.[3]

The suggestion is that *The Concept of Law* took a naive view of the relation between the conventions of language and the requirements of legal rules. But Hart does not withdraw the basic claim that the open texture of language leads to indeterminacies in the law. And we could read his concession simply as admitting that his book had not explained why, for example, a rule prohibiting vehicles from the park does not necessarily prohibit an ambulance, even though the word 'vehicle' applies to the ambulance by the settled conventions of language.[4]

But once Hart admits the distinction between the application of the *words* of a rule and the application of the *rule*, he seems to have conceded what Dworkin claims. Given the distinction, it seems that *no* claim about indeterminacy in the law follows from the vagueness of, for example, 'serious distress'. Linguistic indeterminacy does not entail legal indeterminacy.

Of course, it is true that a judge applying the Criminal Justice and Public Order Act has a great variety of resources as a guide. There may be a rule of interpretation requiring strict construction of penal legislation, so that only concerts that are *clearly* likely to cause serious distress count as raves. There will be other relevant considerations—such as the purposes for which the Act was passed, the principles of the legal protection of liberty on the one hand and of public order on the other, the implications of the role of the provision in a scheme of prior restraint, analogies with the principles of the law of nuisance (and the considerations that justify a statute treating *some* nuisances as criminal), and so on. It will be an important part of the judge's task to take

---

[3] Hart, *EJP* 'Introduction' 7–8.   [4] See Ch. 3.10 above, 'Pragmatic Vagueness'.

such considerations into account. And there is nothing peculiar about the Act in this regard: the use of similar resources is a pervasive feature of legal practice, as are legal duties to use such resources. Perhaps legal systems *always* have such resources.

As Dworkin might put it, the question whether those resources yield a quietest rave is a *substantive* question. It would take an internal, interpretive argument to support the notion that there is no quietest rave — an interpretive argument which has no *general* grounds for a claim that there cannot be a quietest rave, but has to compete, concert by concert, with the view that any particular defendant has a legal right to be acquitted, and with the view that the defendant ought (legally) to be convicted.

But there are two reasons to conclude that the interpretive considerations relevant to the decisions do not determine a quietest rave. The fact that the law has 'other resources besides the words' does not distinguish law from other uses of language, and there is reason to claim that the resources of the law are generally not precise.

The Resources of Language Use

It is very misleading to say that the law has other resources besides the meaning of words, because it suggests that this feature distinguishes law from other uses of language. We cannot contrast law with uses of language that have no resources other than the meaning of words, because there are no such uses. The idea that there are any such uses must rely on an incoherent notion of the 'semantic autonomy' of language (Chapter 2.4, above).

Perhaps Hart's concession suggests such a notion: a notion of what is determined by 'the settled conventions of language' — as if a *word* might apply to an object by those conventions, but a rule *using* such a word might not apply because of the resources of the law. But what does it mean to say, for example, that the word 'vehicle' applies to ambulances by the settled conventions of language? It cannot mean that a police officer is talking nonsense if he says, 'We must keep all vehicles away from the accident scene so that the ambulances can get through'. If that is not nonsense, then ordinary conversational uses of language do not lack 'resources besides the words'.

If any sorites paradoxes arise, they are not eliminated by the resources of communication that accompany *all* uses of language. If that is right, the fact that law has 'other resources besides the words' does not guarantee the elimination of indeterminacies that arise outside the law.

The Resources of the Law are Commonly Vague

Even if there is no coherent distinction between using language with and without 'resources besides the words' (and even if those resources do not generally eliminate indeterminacies), the resources of the law are certainly *different*. So there still seems to be an argument that the existence of indeterminacies in other uses of language does not show that indeterminacies in the law must arise from the use of vague language. We have to ask what, if anything, can be said in general terms about the varied resources *of the law*. And it may seem that all we can say is that those resources may or may not eradicate indeterminacies.

It is certainly *conceivable* that the interpretive resources of the law might yield precise requirements when a lawmaker uses vague language. If a town council passes a by-law requiring cyclists to use lights 'after dark', it might be right for a magistrate to interpret the by-law as requiring cyclists to use lights just at the precise times when other laws require cars to use lights.

But I think that there are general reasons to conclude that the resources of the law do not eradicate indeterminacy. We can say three things: (i) those resources are generally considerations of principle; (ii) they will only eliminate indeterminacies if they have a *special structural feature*—precision; and (iii) considerations of *principle* generally lack that feature.

Think of the considerations mentioned above, which might bear on the application of the rave provisions: strict construction, protection of liberty, analogies with other departments of the law, and so on. None of them is precise.[5] What is more, the reasons why they are imprecise give reason to generalize about the resources of the law. Strict construction is vague, unless there is no higher-order vagueness (see Chapter 5.2). General principles of consistency with other areas of the law are vague, because they are forms of analogical reasoning, and the operative notions of sufficiency and relevance of similarities are vague.[6] Principles of protecting liberty are vague, because they need to account for the interests with which freedom of action is in tension (so, for example, Mill's principle of liberty is vague (partly) because 'harm' is vague . . .). That is not to say that there could be no precise technique for protecting liberty. But such a technique would not be a *principle* — a starting-point for reasoning that could have *general* application to the treatment of a variety of behaviour. Among the arguments of principle that Dworkin has discussed throughout his work I expect that there is none for which we could not formulate sorites paradoxes. And there is no reason to think that a consideration of *all* of Hercules' sorites-susceptible arguments of principle would yield a view of the requirements of the law that is not susceptible to sorites reasoning.

---

[5] General principles of promoting the common good, or other values or interests, are also vague (if arguments above concerning the vagueness of evaluation (Ch. 6.4) and the incommensurability of values (Ch. 7.3) succeed). Note that, for present purposes, we do not need to identify the limits of the law. The problem of vagueness is not just that judges must take into account non-legal considerations; it is that legal and non-legal considerations will not ordinarily identify a quietest rave.

[6] See Ch. 6.3.

But can we rule out the possibility that, in any particular context, arguments of principle might identify some precise phenomenon as decisive? How can we come to a *general* conclusion that Hercules would not find that some such phenomenon marks the last point at which it is justifiable to convict concert promoters—and thereby marks the quietest rave? Let us presume that, in our series of 1 million raves, there are precise phenomena—there is a first concert which would lead to adrenalin being secreted in some precise quantity in the glands of some precise proportion of some precisely specified group of local inhabitants, and a first concert which everybody (or which somebody) in such a specified group would call 'distressing', and so on.[7]

The problem with the notion that Hercules could identify some such phenomenon as decisive is that no such phenomenon could *justify* the polar difference in treatment between conviction and acquittal. Picture a conclusion that x_i is the quietest rave because it is the last concert in the series that some precise proportion of inhabitants would view as seriously distressing. If x_{i+1} is so closely similar that the fact that it did not happen to provoke the same response is fortuitous, then the difference in treatment of x_i and x_{i+1} cannot be viewed as justified by principles that support a conviction in x_i, and that support an acquittal in x_{i+1}. A precise distinction, whose application is fortuitous, does not provide the distinction in principle that is required to achieve consistency in principle between the two judgments.

There would be something wrong, by Hercules' reckoning, if he picked a quietest rave by reference to some precise phenomenon: what would be wrong is that the technique would lack integrity. It is important not to overgeneralize, and perhaps we should say that such a technique *might* be justified in principle. We could still say that Hercules would *typically* be unable to achieve integrity on his own terms when legislation is vague. But I think that even this concession would be overly cautious. The wealth of resources available to Hercules means that people's legal rights and duties are *different* from what a naive view about the conventions of language might lead someone to think. But there is just no reason to think that those resources even make it likely that the law's requirements are *more precise* than the naive view would lead someone to believe. Which is vaguer: 'serious distress', or 'what ought to be treated as serious distress, given all the resources of the law'? There is no clear answer to that question. There is no reason to think that the latter is precise.

---

[7] I ignore here the vagueness of 'likely to' in the definition of a rave, which may in itself be an overwhelming objection to the notion that there is a quietest rave. It is outside the scope of this book to give an account of the vagueness of statements of the likelihood of future contingencies.

3. Dworkin and Juridical Bivalence

There *is* one consideration, which we might call a legal principle, which might seem to restore integrity in the million raves case. That principle is juridical bivalence (Chapter 4.4)—the requirement of legal practice that a court *must* give judgment for one side or the other on every issue (and must convict or acquit in a criminal case). That very duty, we might say, gives a principled reason for dividing the defendants at some point. Dworkin has recently suggested that this is an argument that supports his right answer thesis: that the duty to decide is a feature of adjudication that provides a resource which is distinct from the resources of other forms of communication, and which is a reason not to conclude that the requirements of the law are indeterminate.

We make sense of them [indeterminacy claims], if there is any sense to make, by treating them as internal, substantive positions based, as firmly as any other, on positive theories or assumptions about the fundamental character of the domain to which they belong. In law, for example, the functional need for a decision is itself a factor, because any argument that the law is indeterminate about some issue must recognize the consequences of that being true, and take these into account.[8]

But the need for a decision cannot support an argument that the requirements of the law are determinate. A duty to decide is a reason *to give a decision*, but is not a reason to conclude that the law requires one decision. That is so because the need for a decision is incapable of counting in favour of the plaintiff or in favour of the defendant—whatever the facts, and whatever the law. It is a need that will be met (and met equally well) by a decision either way. For every one of the million rave cases, the need for a decision will be met by a decision in favour of the prosecution *or* by a decision in favour of the defence.

In fact, the need for a decision is a fundamentally important feature of adjudication, and does justify *choosing* a quietest rave (see Chapter 9.5). But it does nothing to support the notion that the law (or morality) requires a particular choice.

4. Interpretation, Intention, and Understanding

I have argued that an interpretivist theory of law cannot successfully reject the indeterminacy claim. But I do not propose that anyone should accept an interpretivist theory of law. The simple account of interpretation suggests that identifying the law is not generally an interpretive task—that it is often

---

[8] 'Objectivity and Truth: You'd Better Believe It' (1996) 25 *Philosophy and Public Affairs* 87, 137 (see also 138, where the 'demand for action' made by legislation is treated as a reason against concluding that the demands of the legislation are indeterminate).

possible to understand what the law requires without any of the creative activity that deserves to be called interpretive. It is not the purpose of this book to elaborate that view of the role of interpretation in law. But for present purposes we should ask what implications the simple account would have for the relation between vagueness and interpretation. Is interpretation simply the process of resolving indeterminacies in the law? In what follows, I will address that question by considering Andrei Marmor's deflationary account of the role of interpretation in law.[9]

Dworkin's theory of interpretation is Andrei Marmor's prime target: Marmor proposes that there are good reasons for 'revising the theory altogether' (84). Marmor aims to deflate overblown notions of interpretation in legal theory and in the philosophy of language. His own view of interpretation emerges in the form of two distinctive theses opposed to interpretive theories of law: that every interpretation is an attribution of actual or counterfactual communication intentions to a real or fictitious author (I will call this the 'intention thesis'), and that interpretation is an exception to the standard way of understanding language (I will call this the 'exception thesis'). The exception thesis is a crucial conclusion that Marmor draws from Wittgenstein's discussion of following a rule. It is a reminder that interpretation does not mediate between a rule and the actions that accord with the rule—that, in Wittgenstein's words, 'There is a way of grasping a rule that is *not* an interpretation.'[10] Marmor presents his two theses as the basis of an analysis of interpretation that refutes interpretivist theories of law. I will argue that all that is needed for that purpose is something like the exception thesis, and that the simple account of interpretation meets the need.

The Intention Thesis

Marmor defines interpretation roughly as 'the imposition of meaning on a[n] object' (13), and sets out to analyse the concept of interpretation by identifying the appropriate notion of meaning (14). The available notions are (i) the 'meaning of' the object; (ii) what the author means by the object ('meaning that'); and (iii) what the object means to the interpreter ('meaning for') (30). Marmor discards 'meaning for' as amounting to emotional response and irrelevant to interpretation. He associates 'meaning of' with 'the semantic notion of meaning', and rejects it on the ground that semantics is rule-governed, and interpretation is not rule-governed. 'Meaning that' is not semantic but pragmatic, and is a matter of communication intentions (so that it is not determined by rules). 'Meaning that' is the notion that Marmor

---

[9] *Interpretation and Legal Theory* (Oxford: Clarendon Press, 1992). In this chapter I will refer to Marmor's book by page numbers in parentheses.

[10] *PI* 201.

deems essential to interpretation: he proposes that interpretation is the attribution of communication intentions to an author.

But if we give an account of the meaning of a poem that disregards the author's intentions, we may yet have interpreted the poem. To this objection Marmor gives an original answer: in such a case, 'meaning is assigned through a counter-factual statement . . . an interpretative statement is either a statement on the communication intentions of the actual speaker, or else it must be a counter-factual statement, characterizing the communication intentions of a fictitious speaker' (31). The claim is that an interpretation is necessarily a statement as to what a particular sort of author would have been trying to communicate by uttering *this* text in particular circumstances.

Three objections may be made to Marmor's ingenious forging of a conceptual link between interpretation and communication intentions. First, as Marmor admits, the link is inconsequential. Secondly, the thesis is deliberately restricted to interpretations of objects of communication intentions, and so is not an analysis of the concept of interpretation. A third objection relates to the unstable distinction between semantics and pragmatics on which the thesis is built.

Why should counterfactual propositions about intention matter? Marmor's peculiar answer is that they do not have to matter:

I suppose that there are philosophers who would want to argue that the attribution of counter-factual intentions does not concern intentions at all. . . . There is, of course, more than a grain of truth in these contentions (or complaints, as one may wish), but they are beside the point. My thesis is confined to the explication of the grammar of interpretation, and was not meant to imply anything further. (32)

This appeal to grammar adopts Wittgenstein's aspiration to dissolve philosophical problems by investigating grammar—that is, by reminding people 'of the kind of statement that we make' (*PI* 90). But Marmor's intention thesis does not actually point out the kind of statement we make; it points out a kind of statement we *could* make—i.e. that such-and-such an interpretation is what such-and-such an author would have intended to communicate by means of this object. If the fact that we could make a statement like that implies nothing further, it adds nothing to an understanding of interpretation.

In particular, the intention thesis does not contribute to Marmor's project of undermining Dworkin's constructive model of interpretation. In that model, the interpreter does not attribute an intention, but imposes purpose on the object 'in order to make of it the best possible example of the form or genre to which it is taken to belong'.[11] Marmor aims to counter this view of interpretation by pointing out that any interpretation can be stated as an

---

[11] *LE* 52.

attribution of intentions. But his claim can coincide with the constructive model, if we are willing to add that the real or fictitious author to whom an interpreter attributes intentions ought to be the best possible example of an author. Indeed, Dworkin ascribes a role to intention that is very similar to Marmor's intention thesis: 'even if we reject the thesis that creative interpretation aims to discover some actual historical intention, the concept of intention nevertheless provides the formal structure for all interpretive claims. I mean that an interpretation is by nature the report of a purpose.'[12] The slide in this passage from 'intention' to 'purpose' makes room for Dworkin's constructive model of interpretation, and Marmor's intention thesis does not forestall that move.[13]

A second objection to the thesis is that it pertains only to interpretation of objects of an intention to communicate. Marmor gerrymanders the concept of interpretation. He treats interpretations of 'acts or products of communication' (14) as paradigms of interpretation, which they certainly are. No grounds are offered, however, for his presumption that 'these standard uses of "interpretation" are considered to be the most appropriate ones' (13), or for his suggestion that scientific 'interpretation', for example, is a 'deviant' or 'dispensable' use of the word (13).

This gerrymandering might be supported by a suggestion of Dworkin's that the phrase 'scientific interpretation' is a metaphor that portrays data as speaking to the scientist.[14] Such an account of the concept of interpretation cannot work, because the use of the word 'interpretation' in science is integrated into its much wider use in an indefinite variety of everyday instances of non-demonstrative inference (think of interpretations of footprints, or enemy troop movements, or patterns of share price changes . . .), which cannot plausibly be called metaphorical.

The grammar of interpretation cannot be explicated by treating some paradigm cases as deviant or metaphorical. An account of the concept of interpretation should admit interpretations of dreams, novels, census data, seismograph records, constitutions, and the entrails of a chicken, without dismissing any as non-standard uses of the word.

This objection only amounts to a complaint that Marmor is not actually analysing the concept of interpretation. It leaves his theory untouched as a theory of the interpretation of objects of communication intentions. And those, after all, are the objects of greatest interest to legal theory. The simple account recommends itself only if it is a simpler or more accurate account of

---

[12] *LE* 58.

[13] But Marmor later raises direct objections to the constructive model, arguing that in some cases interpreters choose not to make the best of the object, and mentioning John Finnis's argument that there is often no best interpretation because interpretations are incommensurable (53–5).

[14] *LE* 51. But Dworkin concludes that even scientific interpretation may be 'constructive' in his sense (ibid. 53).

legal interpretation, too. Its approach to intentions is, at least, simpler. By asserting that attributions of intention may be counterfactual, Marmor's intention thesis obliquely emphasizes how *little* interpretation may be constrained by the actual intentions of an author. The simple account makes the same point by saying no more about intentions than that, if there are any, they are relevant to interpretation because they characterize the object.

A final objection to Marmor's intention thesis concerns the distinction between semantics and pragmatics on which it is built. We have seen that Marmor associates 'semantic meaning' with the 'meaning of' an expression, and with 'those aspects of communication which are determined by rules' (21). He associates pragmatics with 'meaning that' (speaker's meaning), and with 'that aspect of communication which is not explicable in terms of following rules or conventions' (28). So on the semantics side we have sentence meaning and rules and determinacy, and on the pragmatics side we have speaker's meaning, non-rule-governed activity, and indeterminacy. Marmor places interpretation on the pragmatics side of the divide.

The associations Marmor draws are suggestive, but very rough. The indeterminacies in semantic rules (lexical and syntactical ambiguities, vagueness) cannot be herded into whatever corral we fence off for pragmatics. Much of pragmatics is perfectly determinate (e.g. the references of the pronoun 'I' in a typical conversation, or the implications of most uses of 'but' instead of 'and'). Pragmatics is not entirely a matter of speaker's meaning, and is partly rule-governed.[15]

So, while creativity typically characterizes interpretation, we should question the generality of Marmor's claim that 'interpretation . . . is not a rule- or convention-governed activity' (28). That claim would make 'rules of interpretation' a contradiction in terms. If there are any rules of interpretation, then the motivation for Marmor's intention thesis is undermined, because interpretation cannot be restricted to a field of 'pragmatics' that is conceptually associated with intention. Marmor insists on insulating interpretation from rules: he admits that interpretations can be guided by paradigms, but he distinguishes paradigms from rules: paradigms 'can be respected and emulated, but not followed as are, for instance, rules of the correct use of language. Deviating from an established paradigm—unlike failing to follow the rules of language—does not necessarily manifest a misunderstanding' (21). This distinction is misleading: many rules can be stated in the form 'do the same as *this*', with a reference to a paradigm. If, as Marmor suggests, the meaning of a word is a rule for its use, there is reason to think that it is typically a rule that can be communicated by reference to paradigms.[16] As Wittgenstein repeatedly pointed out, there may be no better way of teaching

---

[15] See the discussion of pragmatics in Ch. 3.10 above.
[16] On the notion of the meaning of a word as a rule for its application, see Ch. 6.3.

a rule (including a rule of language) than by pointing out paradigms.[17] A teacher who explains a rule by pointing out paradigms need not be hiding anything from the pupil. Part of the point of Wittgenstein's remarks on following rules is that failing to follow a rule *is* deviating from a paradigm.

Having questioned the generality of the claim that interpretation is not rule-governed, we can do the same with the association between interpretation and indeterminacy. When a rule formulation determines the result in a case, Marmor considers it vacuous or wrong to say that the rule is being interpreted (151). Suppose that a complex and difficult statutory regime, once it is unknotted, turns out to resolve a dispute unequivocally. A judge might say that there was only one available interpretation; Marmor would say that the judge is not interpreting at all, but only applying the rule (127).

Finally, we can question the generality of the association of interpretation with speaker's meaning, on which Marmor's intention thesis stands. The associations of interpretation with pragmatics, and of pragmatics with speaker's meaning, are too rough. The speaker's intentions become surplus to an understanding of interpretation when the intentions become counterfactual, and the speaker fictitious.

The Exception Thesis

Marmor's second distinctive thesis is that interpretation is an exception to understanding. It is supported by the claim discussed above that understanding is rule-governed while interpretation is not, and by a claim that interpretation requires understanding of the language of an expression being interpreted (22).

While Marmor uses the argument explicitly only against Lon Fuller, it should be understood as underlying his attack on interpretive views of law in general.

In a variety of formulations Marmor characterizes interpretation as something to be distinguished carefully from understanding: 'interpretation is an exception to the standard understanding of language and communication, as it pertains only to those aspects of understanding which are underdetermined by rules or conventions' (12).[18]

It may be objected that interpretation is not an exception to the standard understanding of language, because interpretation and understanding belong to different categories. This fact is implied in a footnote of Marmor's: 'the concept of interpretation typically designates an activity; interpretation

---

[17] *PI* 71, 208–11; see also *Remarks on the Foundations of Mathematics*, 3rd edn., ed. G. H. von Wright, R. Rhees, and G. E. M. Anscombe, trans. G. E. M. Anscombe (Oxford: Blackwell, 1978), 228, 343–4.

[18] Cf. also pp. 22, 34, 122.

is something which must be carried out' (23 n.). So there is a more straight-forward grammatical difference between understanding and interpretation than Marmor states, and it is not a difference between norm and exception. Understanding is an ability, and interpretation is an activity.[19]

Marmor evidently calls interpretation an exception to the standard under-standing of language because, for example, 'How do you interpret this?' seems to mean the same as 'How do you understand this?' The fact that the two concepts coincide in this way could mislead us into thinking that under-standing *is* interpretation, or that understanding is a state which can only result from an act of interpretation. Those misconceptions are the target of Marmor's thesis.

So the point of the thesis is that interpretation is not a prerequisite for understanding, and that understanding *is* a prerequisite for interpretation. To be able to interpret, we must be able to follow rules. But don't we have to interpret a rule in order to follow it? What connects a rule with its applica-tions, if not interpretation? These are the philosophical problems that Wittgenstein set out to dissolve.

Marmor closely follows the interpretation that Gordon Baker and Peter Hacker developed in their commentary on Wittgenstein's *Philosophical Investigations*[20] (see Chapter 2.5). They insist that understanding a rule is being able to follow the rule.[21] Wittgenstein does not deny that a rule deter-mines its applications, but tries to dispel the notion that this is a queer process. He does not come up with something that bridges a gap between rule and application, but points out that there is no gap. Thus Baker and Hacker write,

Nothing can be inserted between a rule and its application as mortar is inserted between two bricks. It is a grammatical platitude that a rule determines what acts are in accord with it, just as a desire determines what satisfies it and a description deter-mines what must be the case for it to be true. . . . The rule and its 'extension' are not two things that can be grasped independently of one another, but are internally related. The rule 'Add 2' would not be the rule it is if writing '1002' after '1000' were not in accord with it. It is in language that a rule and the act in accord with it (or a rule and its 'extension') make contact.[22]

On this view, Wittgenstein is trying to point out that there is no room for interpretation to mediate between rule and application. Indeed,

---

[19] So, for example, the verb 'to interpret' has an ordinary imperfect tense; the verb 'to under-stand' does not.

[20] See G. P. Baker and P. M. S. Hacker, *Wittgenstein: Rules, Grammar and Necessity* (Oxford: Blackwell, 1985); see also *Scepticism, Rules and Language* (Oxford: Blackwell, 1984).

[21] Ken Kress gives a similar account, succinctly: 'For Wittgenstein, understanding a rule sim-ply consists of the ability to apply it.' Ken Kress, 'Legal Indeterminacy' (1989) 77 *California Law Review* 283, 333.

[22] Baker and Hacker, *Wittgenstein: Rules, Grammar and Necessity*, n. 20 above, 91.

interpretation is one of the possibilities that the interlocutor clutches at as a bridge between rule and application. Baker and Hacker's view is supported by Wittgenstein's response:

any interpretation still hangs in the air along with what it interprets, and cannot give it any support. Interpretations by themselves do not determine meaning. (*PI* 198)

there is a way of grasping a rule which is not an interpretation, but which is exhibited in what we call 'obeying the rule' and 'going against it' in actual cases.

Hence there is an inclination to say: every action according to the rule is an interpretation. But we ought to restrict the term 'interpretation' to the substitution of one expression of the rule for another. (*PI* 201)[23]

From these remarks, Marmor and Baker and Hacker draw the point that there is an absurd regress in the notion that an interpretation makes a transition from rule to action in accord with the rule: if every rule needs an interpretation to be followed, the interpretation also needs an interpretation, and we will never get as far as following the rule (152).[24] Thus Marmor says, 'A rule, in other words, is a sign and its meaning cannot be determined by another sign; the meanings of rules, like those of all symbols, must be determined by the actions themselves, that is, by the way the rules are used' (149). Rules can be expressed in signs, but it is idiosyncratic to call a rule a sign (let alone a symbol).[25] The important point is clear, though: following a rule is acting, not interpreting. Someone who understands a rule can follow it. That ability is not interpretation, but understanding. The exercise of that ability is not interpretation, but following the rule. The result of its exercise is not an interpretation, but an action in accord with the rule. In the terms of the simple account of interpretation, this is simply a reminder that, if we drove up to a red light, it would be some sort of joke (in ordinary circumstances!) if I asked you, 'What do you make of that?'

What is the place of this argument in jurisprudence? The simple reminder that there is no gap to be bridged between 'add 2' and writing '1002' after '1000' is crucial. Marmor rightly applies the argument to defend Hart against

---

[23] It is uncharacteristic of Wittgenstein to propose to 'restrict' the word 'interpretation' to a technical sense ('the substitution of one expression of the rule for another'). We do not necessarily substitute expressions when we interpret: if you ask me for a jack, and I decide that you want the telephone connecting device and not the ship's flag, I may not reformulate anything, though I certainly could articulate my interpretation by reformulating your request. Wittgenstein adopts his technical sense to prevent the misconception that leads to absurdity, by highlighting the possibility of articulating an interpretation of a rule as a reformulation of the rule. Elsewhere he uses 'interpretation' in its ordinary sense, e.g. *PI* 34.

[24] And see *Wittgenstein: Rules, Grammar and Necessity*, n. 20 above, p. 149. Wittgenstein expressed this regress in *Zettel* : 'So when we wanted to say "Any sentence still stands in need of an interpretation", that meant: no sentence can be understood without a rider.' *Zettel*, ed. G. E. M. Anscombe and G. H. von Wright, trans. G. E. M. Anscombe (Oxford: Blackwell, 1978), s. 229.

[25] With the same idiosyncrasy Marmor considers law a 'form of communication' (122), rather than a form of social ordering that needs communication.

Lon Fuller's claim that no application of a rule can be decided except in view of the purposes of the rule. But Marmor does not use the argument in his campaigns against other interpretive views. Ronald Dworkin never appears in Marmor's discussion of following a rule, and yet that discussion is a powerful argument against the claim that 'law is an interpretive concept'.[26] To Dworkin, an 'easy case' is a special instance of a hard case.[27] The court must still interpret the law, using the same method as in a hard case (though there hardly seems to be a method at work, because the result is so straightforward). To Marmor, an 'easy case' is one in which understanding a rule is knowing how the rule applies, so that it would be a mistake to say that the court interprets the rule.

If we accept this approach to Wittgenstein's remarks, it seems that constructive interpretation has no foothold in some cases: for a court to apply the rule will not put legal practice in anything that can sensibly be called the best light; there is no other light. Coupled with Marmor's argument that an interpreter does not necessarily make the best of the object,[28] this argument attacks the foundations of Dworkin's interpretive theory of law.

5. Interpretation and Indeterminacy

To accept Wittgenstein's argument, as Marmor presents it, is to abandon both Dworkin's view of interpretation, and also the scepticism that denies that there are rules. But it may seem that a less virulent but more persistent form of scepticism survives. Wittgenstein used a rule that is not vague. Most legal rules are vague. Many are ambiguous. When circumstances make it seem that a rule should not be applied as it is ordinarily understood, it may be unclear whether the problem is one of interpretation or of deciding whether to follow the rule. In all those cases, perhaps there is a more tenuous relation between rule and application, if there is any at all.

The new sceptical problem emerges if we accept Marmor's claim that 'it does not make sense to say that one has understood a rule yet does not know which actions would be in accord with it' (153). If that claim were made *generally*, it would make nonsense of saying that we understand a vague legal rule, because there are cases in which we do not know what action would accord with the rule. But that conclusion would be misguided (and also un-Wittgensteinian): it would set an impossibly high standard of understanding. If we understand *any* rules, we understand vague rules.

If there is a connection between the rule 'add 2' and ordinary vague legal rules, it must lie in the idea of paradigms. If there are such standard examples of the application of a vague rule, then they are the actual cases in which

---

[26] *LE* 87.   [27] Ibid. 266; cf. also 353–4.   [28] See above, n. 13.

'what we call "obeying the rule" and "going against it"' (*PI* 201) exhibits a grasp of the rule. The same internal relation holds between understanding the vague rule and knowing its application to paradigms, as between understanding 'add 2' and knowing that 1002 comes after 1000.

The claim that there are paradigms of the application of general terms provides the 'core' in Hart's distinction between a core and a penumbra in the application of legal rules.[29] Marmor argues persuasively that Hart's claim had a Wittgensteinian grounding (125 ff.). But Marmor attributes to Hart a stronger version of the thesis than Hart (or Wittgenstein) expressed: 'Since the meaning of a concept-word consists in (inter alia) its use, there must always be standard instances in which the application of the concept word is unproblematic' (126; cf. 134–5). The bare fact of use does not imply that there are paradigms. Hart and Wittgenstein make a less general claim, attributing the existence of paradigms not to the fact that words are used, but to our communication needs: there must be paradigms, Hart claims, 'if we are to communicate with each other at all',[30] and if 'we are to express our intentions that a certain type of behavior be regulated by rules'.[31] And he puts the claim in terms of 'agreement in judgments', which Wittgenstein also emphasized:

The plain case, where the general terms seem to need no interpretation and where the recognition of instances seems unproblematic or 'automatic', are [*sic*] only the familiar ones, constantly recurring in similar contexts, where there is general agreement in judgments as to the applicability of the classifying terms. (*CL* 126)

If language is to be a means of communication there must be agreement not only in definitions but also (queer as this may sound) in judgments. (*PI* 242)[32]

Wittgenstein and Hart claim that in order to use language in ordinary communication, we need agreement in particular judgments that provide standards for criticism and explanation. Then perhaps Marmor's formulation of their claim is sound if his appeal to 'use' is modified to refer to general facts about the use of language, and not to the fact that a particular word is used.

Let us call cases on which there is agreement in judgments (in Hart and Wittgenstein's sense) 'paradigms'. Michael Moore has ascribed the view that there are such paradigms to Joseph Raz, and presented two objections to the notion: (i) 'the nonvagueness of some statute as applied to some case is no

---

[29] See Ch. 2.1 above.

[30] 'Positivism and the Separation of Law and Morals' (1958) 71 *Harvard Law Review* 593, 607. Cf. 'General terms would be useless to us as a medium of communication unless there were such familiar, generally unchallenged cases.' *CL* 126.

[31] 'Positivism and the Separation of Law and Morals', n. 30 above, 607.

[32] Cf. 'We say that, in order to communicate, people must agree with one another about the meanings of words. But the criterion for this agreement is not just agreement with reference to definitions, e.g. ostensive definitions—but also an agreement in judgments. It is essential for communication that we agree in a large number of judgments.' *Remarks on the Foundations of Mathematics*, n. 17 above, 343.

guarantee at all of there being a similar absence of vagueness in all other legal standards that could bear on that case'; and (ii) the claim that there are paradigms 'does not specify what gives any predicate in a natural language a "core" of easy applications'.[33] The first point is true, but immaterial. The possibility of uncertainty in some standard relevant to a case is a good reason for lawyers to give cautious opinions; but there is no guarantee at all that vagueness in some other relevant legal standard *will* affect the case. There are countless breaches of contract (and performances of contracts), criminal offences, transfers of property, administrative decisions, and so on to which no legal standard has an indeterminate application. We could not talk about running a red light if potential uncertainty in legal standards made it doubtful whether anything counted as running a red light.

Moore's second point is also true. But it complains of a failure to fill a gap that does not exist. In fact, Moore's complaint is just how Wittgenstein's interlocutor could have put the philosophical problem that Wittgenstein was trying to dissolve: the interlocutor thinks there has to be something that *makes* 1002 follow 1000 when we are adding 2. Wittgenstein points out that that is what 'add 2' means. It is as if Moore claimed that no one has shown what *makes* someone with no hair 'bald'.

If this is the right way to view Moore's objection, then it is attractive to think that Hart's notion of paradigms ties ordinary vague legal rules into Wittgenstein's discussion of following a rule. That eliminates any scepticism of the form 'a rule is not really a rule if it is vague'. But we are still faced with Marmor's suggestion that we do not understand a rule if we do not know what accords with it.

The trouble is that it seems as if we *do* need interpretation to make the transition from a vague rule to action in accord with the rule in a borderline case. But then Wittgenstein's dilemma resurfaces: 'Whatever I do is, on some interpretation, in accord with the rule' (*PI* 198). In that case, 'there would be neither accord nor conflict' (*PI* 201). That is Kripke's paradox; it seems to be a genuine paradox in a borderline case.

Vagueness and Normal Circumstances

Marmor expresses the grammatical nature of the relationship between rule and application as follows: 'Understanding a rule consists in the ability to specify which actions are in accord with the rule' (153). This notion of understanding is crucially indefinite: does understanding consist in the ability to specify for every conceivable action whether it is in accord with the rule? No: Marmor follows Baker and Hacker in warning against that conception of

---

[33] 'Authority, Law and Razian Reasons' (1989) 62 *Southern California Law Review* 827, 892.

completeness.[34] It would be pointless to say that we can never understand a rule completely because an action could always be conceived for which we are unprepared. This idea of complete understanding is not an unattained ideal, but makes no sense.

Then how do we qualify the generality of Marmor's account of understanding a rule? He proposes that there is a quite sensible notion of completeness: 'one has a complete grasp of a rule, if under normal circumstances, one is able to specify which acts are in accord with the rule' (153). Wittgenstein drew on this notion of 'normal circumstances',[35] and it was valuable for his purpose of clearing away the incoherent notion of complete understanding that he attributed to his own earlier philosophy and to Frege. It was valuable because, if you think that you need to know every possible application of a word in order to understand it, you need to be reminded that you can use the word 'chair' even though you would not know whether to call something 'a chair' if it kept disappearing and reappearing (*PI* 80).

Can we use the same notion of 'normal circumstances' to explain what amounts to complete understanding of vague words? We cannot. If someone asks you whether so-and-so is tall (or tactful, or honest, or sensitive), and you think that so-and-so is a borderline case, there may be nothing abnormal about the circumstances. Under perfectly normal circumstances, you may be at a loss to say what is in accord with a rule. It would be disastrous to say that we only understand a vague word if we know how to apply it in normal circumstances.

Perhaps we cannot frame a criterion for complete understanding of words like 'tall' or 'tactful' that is more demanding than the ability to identify paradigms, and to make sensible judgments of similarity. For some legal rules it is no doubt true that if we understand them, we know how they apply in normal circumstances—but those are precise rules. With vague rules there are still paradigms, but uncertainty and disagreement may be widespread.[36] In the latter case, a complete understanding of a rule is consistent with uncertainty about a multitude of perfectly normal cases.

This may sound like a sceptical position that survives the anti-sceptical interpretation of Wittgenstein's remarks. But it is only a claim that some real indeterminacies are extravagant. When we clear away the theoretical indeterminacies of a sceptical interpretation of Wittgenstein, we have not yet said anything about the extent of determinacy of any rule.

---

[34] G. P. Baker and P. M. S. Hacker, *Wittgenstein: Meaning and Understanding* (Oxford: Blackwell, 1983), i. 224–5.

[35] *PI* 87, 141–2.

[36] This distinction corresponds roughly to the rather tentative distinction that Hart drew in *The Concept of Law* between rules 'with only a fringe of open texture' (*CL* 133) or 'determinate rules' (*CL* 135) on the one hand, and 'vague' or 'very general' or 'variable' standards (*CL* 131–5). See also *CL* 263.

6. Interpretation and Invention

If we have a notion of understanding a rule that is consistent with not knowing how to apply a rule in some very normal (borderline) cases, how do we describe what people do with rules in those cases? How is interpretation to be distinguished from invention? Perhaps by describing interpretation as the application of a rule in an unclear case, and invention as the substitution of a new rule. But if a case is unclear, how can we say that the rule is being applied? Or that it is not being applied?

Marmor suggests that interpretation tends to become invention as the counterfactual characterization of an author becomes 'more abstract' (33). But by 'more abstract', perhaps we should read something like 'less plausible': there could be very concrete characterizations of a hypothetical author that would correspond to proposals that are not interpretations.

Marmor discusses the distinction between interpretation and invention only to the extent of claiming that Dworkin cannot draw the distinction, because his theory cannot show that fit constrains interpretation (70, 82–4). This is a serious charge: in Dworkin's theory judges must not invent, since one party has a legal right to a decision.

But Marmor draws no clear distinction either. In explaining Wittgenstein's remarks on rules, he equivocates: 'Interpretation is just another formulation of the rule, substituting one rule for another, as it were' (149). This ambivalence about the distinction between different rule formulations and different rules amounts to ambivalence about the distinction between interpreting (reformulating a rule) and inventing (substituting a new rule). The ambivalence is restated when Marmor says that it is arguable that Joseph Raz's preemption thesis 'puts too strong a constraint on interpretation of the law'. Marmor says, 'When judges interpret the law, they often have to rely on considerations about that which the law is there to settle, yet—within certain limits—they can still be said to be following the law, not inventing it' (122). Here, of course, 'certain limits' means uncertain limits.

Ambivalence is justified, because judicial interpretations can be more or less inventive. On the one hand, there is sometimes one obviously right interpretation. 'Invention' can be a term of reproach, and there are irreproachable interpretations. On the other hand, if we define 'invention' as the substitution of a new rule, and 'interpretation' as reformulation of a rule, it will be unclear in many cases whether someone is interpreting or inventing.

Two points might clarify the issue, or at least articulate its unclarity. First, we might say that every legal interpretation is an invention, in the weak sense that it is a new answer to some legal question. But here we are interested in inventions that are not applications of an existing rule (and I take it that we cannot say that no interpretation is an application of a rule). 'Invention' in this strong sense will presumably mean creating a new answer to a legal question either (i) where there is no rule to apply, or (ii) in place of an existing rule.

The second point is that the question of how to distinguish interpretation from invention has two aspects:

(1) When does an interpretation become so outrageous that it can be condemned as an invention?

(2) If a rule does not determine an action in a case, can a court be said to apply the rule at all? If not, then interpretation must simply be a subcategory of invention.

The first aspect of the question is important in interpreting art. In Marmor's theory the distinction at this level is between attributing intentions to a (real or fictitious) author, and saying something that no plausible author could have intended to communicate. On the simple account of interpretation, the distinction is between making something *of this*, and making something up. As a general issue the distinction is extraordinarily vague, though it can be perfectly clear in some situations.

In the quite different context of attempts to apply rules, it seems that Marmor's theory supplies a simple solution to this aspect of the question: we should call it an invention when a decision-maker gives the wrong answer in an easy case.

The second aspect of the problem of distinguishing interpretation from invention arises only in the context of attempts to apply rules. Marmor suggests that 'interpretation' is a term for the resolution of indeterminacies in the application of the language of rules.

It should be emphasized that all this is not meant to imply that, in all cases of disagreement on the applicability of a given rule (due to vagueness, for example), Wittgenstein would maintain that 'anything goes', as it were. . . . If the formulation of a particular rule is inadequate for purposes of determining a particular result in certain circumstances, then there is nothing more to explain or understand about its meaning; what is required is a new formulation of the rule — one which would remove the doubt — and this is what the term 'interpretation' properly designates. (153)

These views need close examination. What is at stake for a 'conventionalist' like Marmor in distinguishing interpretation from invention is the ability to give a differentiated description of judicial law-making. Judges may apply a vague or ambiguous rule in a way that makes its application more determinate, or may create a new rule by analogy with an existing rule, or may resolve a conflict between rules, or may create a new rule even without an analogy, or may decide not to apply an existing rule even without a conflict. It is unclear which of these activities are interpretive, and in what circumstances.

Consider the court's reasoning in giving effect to a dummy standard: recall the requirement of 'sufficient interest' for standing to seek judicial review of administrative action (Chapter 3.9). In a case where it is not clear to a judge whether an applicant has a sufficient interest, is the judge's task to interpret the provision? Possibly: the judge may need to decide what to make of such a provision, and to work out what the legislature was trying to do, and those are interpretive tasks. But if the judge does that, and comes to the conclusion that the legislature was leaving it to the courts, it seems necessary to reach a determination based on considerations that are not interpretive, but inventive. It seems that deciding whether the applicant's interest is sufficient in an unclear case is not necessarily a matter of interpreting the provision, any more than deciding how to exercise an express discretion is necessarily a matter of interpreting the provision that grants discretion. In giving effect to the 'sufficient interest' provision, there may be nothing to interpret. What is more, I claimed in Chapter 3.9 that *vague* standards bear a similarity to dummy standards. The similarity means, for present purposes, that in borderline cases for the application of a vague standard, there may be no *interpretive* technique that will help to decide the case. Interpretive considerations may even make the requirements of the law more vague than they would appear to someone who reads a provision without knowing of the interpretive requirements that the law imposes (see Section 2 above). An understanding of pragmatic vagueness suggests that interpretation may not even *tend* to make the requirements of the law precise. An invitation to come at five o'clock sounds precise, but it may need to be interpreted in light of a vague convention of coming fashionably late. It only takes a purposive interpretation to give a vague legal effect to a precise form of words. The statute prohibiting alms to a valiant beggar is *more vague* if it is interpreted not to apply in foul weather (see Chapter 3.10).

It might seem that interpretation of a vague statute must at least *narrow down* the indeterminacies in its application. But we cannot even say that, unless we have a clear notion of what indeterminacies there are before and after the interpretive task is performed. In the case of the million raves, a good interpretation would take into account all the considerations mentioned in Section 1, above. Perhaps cases in which the application of the statute *appropriately interpreted* is indeterminate will be fewer than the cases in which the application of the phrase 'serious distress' would be indeterminate if the interpretive resources of the law were not brought to bear. But that is not obviously the case. Interpretive techniques make a difference to the requirements of the law, but it seems that we have no grounds for a general conclusion that they make the requirements of the law more precise. And if a court declared a sharp cut-off to the application of the provision, the court would *not* be reporting the result of an interpretation, but would be *adopting a measure* by which to resolve the cases.

If this is correct, then the court does not necessarily interpret when it applies vague standards in unclear cases. That is inconsistent with Marmor's suggestion that 'interpretation' properly designates the process of providing a new formulation of the rule which would remove the doubt. But we should be careful not to overstate the generality of Marmor's commitment to the view that interpretation resolves indeterminacies, for two reasons: (i) although he insists that the interpretations that resolve indeterminacies can be based on reasons (153), he never claims that there are always reasons for an interpretation that yields a determinate outcome, and (ii) Marmor's nimble intention thesis can provide an account of indeterminacies left unresolved by interpretation: a court would not be interpreting in a case in which no plausible author could have uttered the formulation in question with the intention of communicating any solution to such a case.

7. Conclusion: The Charm of Legalism

What does a consideration of these issues say about the general question of the place of interpretation in legal reasoning? It seems that interpretation shares features with the application of rules on the one hand, and with the invention of new rules on the other hand. In central cases of applying a rule, there is no need to interpret. In central cases of inventing a new rule, either there is nothing to interpret, or a rule that might have been applied or interpreted is overturned, or derogated from, or ignored.

If the simple account is right, detailed conclusions about the place of interpretation would require specific description of what judges and other people can appropriately make of the law in various specific legal situations. I suggested in Section 6 that vague rules share features with dummy standards, and with express grants of discretion, and that decisions as to their applicability in unclear cases may better be described as inventive than as interpretive.

Marmor's answer, by contrast, suggests that interpretation has the general role of answering questions left unanswered by the language of the law: interpretation is needed 'if the formulation of a particular rule is inadequate for purposes of determining a particular result in certain circumstances' (153). This view refutes the claim that law is an interpretive practice, but it still gives interpretation too broad a role in legal reasoning. It suggests that interpretation provides a decision whenever a pertinent rule does not determine an outcome.

Perhaps, even after making his concerted arguments against Dworkin, Marmor feels a vestige of the charm of legalism. The charm of legalism is the inclination to take juridical bivalence not for the 'technical device' that Finnis calls it, but as a picture of the structure of judicial duty. The charm of legalism is seductive, for it seems much more attractive for a judge to say, '*these* are the legal rights and duties of the parties' (Dworkin), or even '*this* is an interpretation of the requirements of the law' (Marmor), than for a judge to say, 'anything goes; here is what I've come up with'. Marmor is anxious to preserve his view of law from saying 'anything goes'.

If the argument of Sections 1 and 2 was right, there are cases (and they are not a trivial margin of cases) in which all the resources of judicial interpretation of the requirements of vaguely formulated laws yield no right answer. That conclusion seems to raise the horrible spectre of saying 'anything goes'. It seems mischievous to propose that there are cases in which there is no help for the conscientious judge who wants to do justice according to law—to propose that reason itself may have nothing to say that will decide the outcome of important litigation. Yet that is the implication of the case of the million raves.

I try to face up to the 'anything goes' spectre in Chapter 9. But it should be made clear from the start that I do not propose that there are cases in which a judge can rightly put aside the pursuit of justice according to law. If there are no clear boundaries to the application of vague rules, it will not be clear to a court (i) that the case is not easy, or (ii) that the interpretive resources of the legal system do not offer a resolution to the dispute. The possibility that a rule does not answer a dispute, and that a good interpretation of the law would not make something of the rule that would decide the case, is never a reason for a court to abandon its attempt to give effect to the law, or its responsibility for the wise development of the law. This claim underlies the account that I propose, in Chapter 9, of the role of judges in pursuing the ideal of the rule of law.

9

The Impossibility of the Rule of Law

THE rule of law is unattainable. Communities never completely achieve it. It requires, among other things, that government officials conform to the law. But they may not do so, and presumably there is no large community in which they always do so. To the extent that officials do not conform to the law, the community fails to attain the ideal of the rule of law. Perhaps no community has even got very close to the ideal. People do not always follow rules.

I will argue that that is the only respect in which the rule of law is unattainable. Vagueness in the law may seem to contradict that claim, because vagueness seems to make arbitrary government, to some extent, unavoidable. If arbitrary government is unavoidable because of vagueness, it seems that the ideal of the rule of law is, to some extent, unattainable—and for a reason other than infidelity to law.

Avoiding that conclusion will require a revised account of the ideal of the rule of law. Perhaps because communities do not come very close to the ideal, there has been little discussion of what would count as achieving it completely. Yet the question is basic to understanding the ideal, and trying to answer it raises some puzzles that have not been addressed.

Legal philosophers have argued over what virtue there is in the rule of law, but there is a consensus about the *requirements* of the ideal: laws must be open, clear, coherent, prospective, and stable, legislation and executive action must be governed by laws with those characteristics, and there should be courts that impose the rule of law.[1] The organizing principle of these requirements is, as Joseph Raz puts it, that 'the law must be capable of guiding the behaviour of its subjects'.[2] Law that fails altogether to meet the requirements would not be law at all, and a legal system that lacks them to some degree is defective in a legal sense. In John Finnis's phrase, a legal system must meet the requirements if it is to be 'legally in good shape'.[3]

The requirements of the rule of law seem to offer an answer to our question of what would count as achieving the ideal: if the ideal is to be completely met, the requirements must be completely met, and to pursue the rule of law is to maximize conformity to the requirements. On that view, we might say that the requirement of *clarity* requires that vagueness must be eliminated, and that a community does not achieve the rule of law to the extent that its law is vague. I will argue that such a view would make the ideal not simply

---

[1] See Lon Fuller, *The Morality of Law*, 2nd edn. (New Haven: Yale University Press, 1969), ch. 2, and lists derived from Fuller's in Raz *AL* 214–18 and Finnis *NLNR* 270–1.
[2] Raz, *AL* 214.   [3] *NLNR* 270.

unattainable, but incoherent (Section 2). I will propose a revised account of the ideal, in which vagueness is not necessarily contrary to the rule of law (Section 3).

The revised account will be supported by discussion of three puzzles about the ideal, concerning legal change, finality in adjudication, and the opposition of the rule of law to anarchy (Section 4). The puzzles arise if we think that the rule of law requires maximum stability, and judicial review of every decision, and that the life of a community be completely ruled by law. Those puzzles might make it seem as if the rule of law is necessarily unattainable, and unravelling them will help to unravel the puzzle about vagueness. A conclusion addresses the implications for understanding the role of courts in the rule of law, and argues that it is a basic duty of courts to decide cases that the law does not resolve: i.e. to impose resolution (Section 5). Resolution is a basic requirement of the rule of law.

1. The Content of the Ideal

A community attains the ideal of the rule of law when the life of the community is governed by law. So the rule of law can be opposed to anarchy, in which the life of the community is not governed.[4] The rule of law can also be opposed to *arbitrary* government. So Aristotle wrote that it was better for the law to rule than for any one of the citizens to rule.[5]

Arbitrary government is a particular form of unreasonable government. It abandons constraints of reason, ordinarily to do the will of the rulers. One technique of arbitrary government is to dispense with law altogether. It is much more common to maintain a legal system, and to suspend laws, or to ignore them, or otherwise to violate the requirements of the rule of law, when convenient.

People tend to think of government as 'arbitrary' if it has any or all of three characteristics:

(1) Government is arbitrary if it gives effect to the unconstrained will of the rulers—as in an absolute dictatorship.
(2) Government is arbitrary if it does not treat like cases alike—if it does not treat people consistently.[6]
(3) Government is arbitrary if it is unpredictable—if it does not tell its citizens where they stand, what their rights and duties are.

---

[4] But see n. 11 below.   [5] *Politics* 3. 16, 1287ª19.

[6] Cf. John Rawls: 'The rule of law . . . implies the precept that similar cases be treated similarly. Men could not regulate their actions by rules if this precept were not followed.' *A Theory of Justice* (Cambridge, Mass.: Harvard University Press, 1971), 237.

It seems that government will be arbitrary if it lacks constraint, consistency, or certainty. The rule of law seems to be opposed to government that is arbitrary in these senses, because it offers constraint, consistency, and certainty. Yet, as I will argue in Section 2, government by law unavoidably lacks all three characteristics to some extent. Does that mean that the ideal of the rule of law is incoherent, because it both requires and prohibits arbitrary government?

I do not think that the ideal is incoherent, and I think that we should conclude, instead, that lack of constraint, inconsistency, and unpredictability *are not necessarily arbitrary* in the ordinary, pejorative sense of the term (although for convenience I will continue to call them 'arbitrary government in the first three senses'). I will argue that there is not necessarily anything at all wrong with a legal system that does not achieve complete constraint of officials, complete consistency, and complete predictability. Note, however, that this approach has some work to do: it needs to give an account of what *is* arbitrary in the ordinary, pejorative sense. We need a fourth sense of 'arbitrary'—a sense necessarily opposed to the rule of law, which I will state here and try to explain below:

(4) Government is arbitrary if its actions depart from the reason of the law.

The need to reconcile lack of constraint and inconsistency with the rule of law should be readily apparent: rulers can and do use the law *to achieve* their will. The formal constraint of the rule of law may impose little substantive constraint on the will of the rulers. So government may conform to the rule of law, and yet leave the rulers free from constraints that justice and the common good require. And a legal system that conforms to the rule of law may treat like cases alike only in the thin sense of treating alike those cases to which the law applies in the same way. The law may offer citizens the *certainty* that they will be dealt with arbitrarily.

So we have a puzzle about the content of the ideal: it seems to demand constraint, and yet lack of constraint is inevitable. This puzzle is insoluble if we think that lack of constraint on the rulers is necessarily contrary to the ideal. But we can solve the puzzle by saying that the rule of law is *technically* opposed to arbitrary government. That does not mean that the opposition is trivial, but that the rule of law is a technique that stands in the way of arbitrariness in our first three senses. Making laws is *also* a technique for achieving the will of the rulers (and it *may* be a technique for acting inconsistently). But this should not be more puzzling than the proposition that, for example, promise-making is a way of achieving your will and also a way of constraining your will. The puzzle should evaporate if we consider that it may suit the interests of the rulers to ignore a law which it has suited their interest to enact and to keep in force.

2. Vagueness and Arbitrary Government

Vagueness may seem to pose a much worse puzzle. Vagueness in the law makes arbitrary government in the first three senses unavoidable. This book has argued that, if the law is vague, judges are sometimes called on to resolve disputes for which the law provides no resolution. With respect to such disputes, the law does not constrain the will of the judge. It is impossible for a court always to treat like cases alike when the law is vague. And a vague law lacks certainty in some cases.

These claims may sound extreme. They certainly go against the ideology of lawyers in various communities. We think that applying the law and treating like cases alike are the heart and soul of the judge's task. But if these things cannot always be done, then it seems that the rule of law is unattainable because of the vagueness of language. An impossible ideal seems romantic at best, and at worst absurd.

Consider the claim that, because of the vagueness of 'within a reasonable time', there is no last day on which charges of murder against a particular defendant may lawfully be heard in a community in which defendants have a legal right to trial within a reasonable time. Notice what sort of claim it is: it is a statement of law, to the effect that the law does not provide an answer to a question that a court may have to answer. Imagine a series of many defendants, like the series of defendants in the million rave cases. In this series, all the cases are identical except that each successive defendant is prosecuted a day later. Imagine that the first is clearly prosecuted with a reasonable time, and that there is clearly unreasonable delay in prosecuting the last in the series (so that the court ought to dismiss the charges). In each case, the court has just two options: to allow the prosecution to proceed, or to dismiss the charges. If every pair of adjacent defendants in the series is in the same legal position, then there is no first defendant against whom the law requires that the charges be dismissed. If the first defendant may lawfully be prosecuted and the last defendant may not, then for some pair of adjacent defendants, the court must allow the prosecution to proceed against one, but dismiss the charges against the other. The court cannot even solve this problem by appealing to considerations of justice, or of the interests of the public or of individuals.

The result is that the court will have to *choose* the last defendant to be tried. The court will not be able to decide all of the cases according to law: the decision in some cases will be an unconstrained act of will. In choosing which defendant is to be the last in the series to be prosecuted, the court will not be able to reach a better decision than it would reach by flipping a coin. Flipping a coin (even secretly) is not ordinarily a justifiable judicial technique, but in this situation that is *not* because the court could have reached a preferable outcome by using any other technique. Moreover, the court will have to mete out opposing treatment to people whose cases are alike. Finally, the decision will be unpredictable, because some of the defendants have no way of knowing whether the court will find them guilty or not guilty. In our first three senses of 'arbitrary government', the decision in some of the cases will be an act of arbitrary government.

So, when the law is expressed in vague language, the result is some degree of arbitrary government in the first three senses. If this is a problem, it is a wide-ranging problem, because vague language is a pervasive legislative tool. Lawmakers very often use very vague terms. Consider, for example, the term 'riot', which defines a qualification to the right to life in Article 2 of the European Convention on Human Rights, or the term 'torture' in Article 3. With these terms and many others in the European Convention (and in every bill of rights) we could illustrate the same problem illustrated here using 'within a reasonable time'.

We can make this claim stronger: vague language cannot be eliminated from the law, and therefore arbitrary government in the first three senses cannot be eliminated. The ineliminability of vagueness may seem obvious, but it is worth pointing out some reasons for that conclusion.

Many legal standards could be made more precise. Article 6 of the European Convention provides a right to trial on criminal charges 'within a reasonable time', and a right to be informed 'promptly' of charges, and a right to 'adequate' time to prepare a defence. Those vague standards could all be replaced with time limits. There might be reasons not to use precise standards: if we chose a precise time limit suitable to prosecutions for shoplifting, it would not give the prosecution the time it needs in cases of stock market fraud. A precise time limit suitable to the prosecution of stock market frauds would give the prosecution too much time in a shoplifting case. It would be cumbersome to develop a tariff of time limits for different offences—and it would be fruitless: there might be wide variations in the time the prosecution needs for different instances of the same type of charges.

Here it is tempting to say, 'Vagueness *can* be eliminated, but there may be good reasons not to do so. The rule of law is never quite achieved, so long as vague legislation provides the possibility of arbitrary government. But there are other values besides the rule of law, which need to be balanced against it.' This approach seems attractive because it is certainly true that conflicts can arise between the rule of law and other values. The most familiar is the conflict with national security. If allowing due process in civil disputes runs the risk of disclosing the plans of our submarines to enemies, then the rule of law conflicts with national security.[7] It may seem that the rule of law requires precision, and that reasons to have vague rules are reasons not to pursue the rule of law.

---

[7] Cf. *Duncan* v. *Cammell Laird and Co. Ltd.* [1942] AC 624. On the question of when it is right to suspend the rule of law, see Finnis, *NLNR* 275.

But in fact we cannot give a coherent account of the rule of law as requiring precision, because vagueness cannot be eliminated. Consider the qualification on the right to life in case of riot, and the prohibition on torture. It is inconceivable that we could replace *those* vague terms in the way we pictured replacing the time requirements, with regulations that are similar, but precise. We could not come up with a useful list of prohibitions or permissions that would give a *precise* answer to the question of what the police may do in response to public disorder. A list would be useless because it would be rigid and incapable of coping appropriately with the complexity of public disorder. It would also be useless because any itemization detailed enough to be even somewhat precise would be unwieldy. It would be of no use to the police as a guide for their conduct—so it would be no advance towards the rule of law. It is similarly inconceivable that we could replace the vague definitions of offences of violence in criminal law (or definitions of torts that involve personal injury) with precise standards. And even if those legislative feats were possible, a legal system purged of vagueness would have to refuse to enforce vague agreements (which would ruin, for example, legal regulation of the sale of goods).

Vagueness is ineliminable from a legal system, if a legal system must do such things as to regulate the use of violence among citizens, and commercial agreements between citizens. Every legal system does such things. There would be no reason to call anything a legal system if it regulated no such aspects of the life of a community. No community would be ruled by law if such things were not done. Not every law need be vague, but legal systems necessarily have vague laws. So we can go so far as to say that vagueness is an essential feature of law. If we could conceive of a form of regulation of the life of a community that used only precise rules, it would be so fundamentally different from any legal system that it would not be part of what an explanation of law has to explain. We can put the claim even more strongly: we cannot conceive of a community regulated with precise laws. *Law is necessarily vague.*

But now we have come round in a circle, and we face a paradox. The rule of law is the absence of arbitrary government. Vagueness in the law leads to arbitrary government in the first three senses. Law is necessarily vague. So arbitrary government—the antithesis of the rule of law—is a necessary feature of the rule of law. The rule of law entails both the presence and absence of arbitrary government. It is not just an unattainable ideal, it is a *necessarily* unattainable ideal. It is incoherent.

3. Reconstructing the Ideal

How do we reject this apparently inescapable notion that the rule of law is necessarily unattainable? It might seem that a dose of common sense is all that is needed — and that is probably true. After all, while we could probably imagine a community that *would have* attained the ideal, except that its laws were too vague, there has probably never been such a community. But there remains a puzzle, because rejecting the notion that the rule of law is necessarily unattainable will require reconciling arbitrary government, in the first three senses, with the ideal of the rule of law.

Perhaps the simplest way to do *that* is to admit that a community lacks the rule of law to the extent that its law is vague, just as it lacks the rule of law to the extent that its officials ignore the law. On this view, it might be a fair generalization to say that the community is ruled by law if there is not *too much* vagueness, just as it is a fair generalization to say that the treatment of suspects is ruled by law if official illegality is rare. A commitment to the rule of law would include a commitment to *minimize* vagueness. In this regard, the ideal of the rule of law would be like the ideal of a goalkeeper: every goal goes against the ideal, but even great goalkeepers allow *some* goals.

I propose that we can do more than that to make sense out of the ideal of the rule of law. We can start with the notion of a 'deficit' in the rule of law. A community suffers from a deficit when it lacks the rule of law in some respect. The most obvious sort of deficit is official illegality. If the law requires police not to torture suspects, then there is a deficit in the rule of law every time an officer tortures a suspect. If the officer gets away with it, that is another deficit. If such deficits occur, the community does not fully achieve the ideal of the rule of law. If they are widespread and systematic, the treatment of suspects is not ruled by law. If there are significant deficits in other areas too, we might say that the community is not ruled by law at all. Every deficit in the rule of law (e.g. every incident of torture by the police) takes the community further from the ideal. Every success in eliminating such a deficit brings the community closer to the ideal. If success is general, and torture is an extraordinary exception, then it is a fair generalization to say that police conduct is ruled by law.

Vagueness is different. I propose that a vague law does not necessarily represent a deficit in the rule of law. Replacing a vague law with a precise law does not necessarily bring a community closer to the ideal of the rule of law. For example, there is no reason to think that European countries would approach the ideal more closely if they replaced Article 6 of the European Convention with a regime of precise time limits for steps in the criminal process. That step might not even increase certainty: the history of the English Statute of Frauds shows that precise laws stimulate the interpretive ingenuity of lawyers and judges — and interpretive ingenuity can give extravagant pragmatic vagueness to precisely formulated laws. Whether a judge will evade the effects of a precise rule may be as uncertain as how a judge will apply a vague rule. More importantly, a regime of precise time limits would introduce arbitrariness in our *fourth* sense: the sense in which a *law* is arbitrary if its requirements do not reflect the reasons on which such a law ought to be based.[8]

A time limit of, for example, precisely seven months for prosecutions on serious criminal charges would be arbitrary in our fourth sense. It would be met by prosecutions that (whatever the rationale for limiting delay) should not be allowed, or it would not be met by prosecutions that should (according to that rationale) be allowed, or both.

Increasing precision can *increase* arbitrariness. So an increase in precision is not a guaranteed step closer to eliminating arbitrary government. So even if the rule of law is simply the absence of arbitrary government, an increase in precision would not necessarily be a step towards the ideal. A more precise law could conceivably be farther from *or* closer to the ideal, or neither. In regulating criminal procedure, lawmakers face a complex question of legislative craft; they do not necessarily face a choice between pursuing the rule of law with precise time limits, and relinquishing it with a vague law. In regulating more complicated affairs, such as violence, the question of whether to use precise terms does not even arise: regulation cannot be precise.

4. Three Puzzles

We should be able to take a similar approach to three other puzzles, in which it seems to be impossible to meet the requirements of the rule of law. Each will be introduced with a mistaken claim about the impossibility of the rule of law.

Legal Change

> Law-making is necessarily free, to some extent, from legal control. Legislation is not ruled by law. *Stability* is one of the requirements of the rule of law. A minor change in the law does not rob a legal system of all its stability, but it is a deficit in stability. So every act of law-making (by court or legislature or executive) is a deficit in the rule of law.

Again, it might be tempting to say that a legal system with rules of change is *close enough* to the rule of law, as long as there is not *too much* change. But we can say more than that: we can reject the notion that a change in the law is necessarily a deficit in the rule of law. It is too obvious that, in order to be *legally* in good shape, a legal system needs not only rules of change, but also active lawmakers.

---

[8] An exercise of a discretionary power is arbitrary in the same sense, even if it is not illegal, if it does not reflect the reason of the law. Cf. the similar sense of arbitrariness in the exercise of a power that Raz describes; *AL* 219.

A legal system with no rule of change is conceivable. But there is just no reason to think that it would approach the ideal of the rule of law more closely than ordinary legal systems do. It is inconceivable that a healthy legal system in any large industrialized society could lack a rule of change, and the reasons why are reasons to think that rules of change do not necessarily license deficits in the rule of law. In such a society, if the law did not provide for its own change, it would commit itself to increasing irrationality—to increasing arbitrariness in our fourth sense—by refusing to respond when existing regulations or forms of regulation are seen to be (or to become) pointless, and when new regulations and forms of regulation are needed: when the reason of the law demands a change in the law.

When *is* a change in the law a deficit in the rule of law? We can appeal again to the organizing principle of the rule of law—that the law must be capable of guiding behaviour. That principle does not require that the law's guidance never change. It requires that the prospect of change should not make it impossible to use the existing law as a guide. So the government does not necessarily incur a deficit in the rule of law if it imposes a new curriculum on schools. But it does incur a deficit if its behaviour gives teachers reason to think that they cannot guide themselves by an existing curriculum, because it is liable to be replaced before the lessons are taught or the exams are written.

Finality in Adjudication

> The rule of law is conceptually impossible, because it requires judicial control of official decisions. Judges are themselves officials, and adjudication is itself the standard technique for legal control of any form of decision-making. Adjudication is not ruled by law. No legal system has an infinite hierarchy of courts, and that is what it would take for adjudication itself to be ruled by law. In any hierarchy of courts, the highest court is not ruled by law.

It is impossible for a community to have an infinite number of courts. But an infinite *hierarchy* of courts is not impossible: that would only take two courts, each of which has power to reverse the decisions or to control the process of the other.

It might be argued that there was such a hierarchy in England in 1616— that the Court of Chancery had power to issue injunctions against enforcement of judgments of the Court of King's Bench, and that the King's Bench had power to issue judgments against litigants who questioned its judgments in another court. But the better view is doubtless that the courts did not *both* have the power they claimed (and it may be indeterminate which court, if either, had the power it claimed). The Lord Chancellor claimed the power to interfere with King's Bench judgments, and the Chief Justice claimed the power to indict litigants for seeking that interference, but neither they nor anyone else thought that *both* claims were valid. An infinite hierarchy of appeals is repugnant to the rule of law. The idea is not repugnant because of any logical inconsistency. It is easy to conceive of such a system. But there would be something very wrong with a legal system without finality in adjudication. It would not carry out a basic function of legal systems. It would not be legally in good shape.

We may seem to have reached a paradox, in which finality in adjudication is both required for the rule of law, and fatal to the rule of law. But that is only a muddle arising from an inadequate account of the ideal. The paradox arises only if we claim that a decision is not ruled by law unless it is subject to judicial review. Judges often talk as if judicial review of administrative action were a necessity of the rule of law, or of logic itself:

Subjection in this respect to the High Court is a necessary and inseparable incident to all tribunals of limited jurisdiction; for the existence of the limit necessitates an authority to determine and enforce it: it is a contradiction in terms to create a tribunal with limited jurisdiction and unlimited power to determine such limits at its own will and pleasure — such a tribunal would be autocratic, not limited.[9]

That attitude is a symptom of Albert Dicey's confusion of the rule of law with the rule of the High Court. Not even Diceyan judges take the view that the House of Lords is necessarily autocratic, and yet no one can legally review its determinations of the limits of its powers.

People can follow rules without anyone else enforcing them. If you make a rule for yourself of making breakfast for your cat before you make breakfast for yourself, you may not keep to it. And you may be more likely to keep to the rule if someone checks up on you. But there is nothing impossible about following rules without a review process. And having someone check up on you may improve your compliance just as well, whether or not that someone has the power to reverse your decisions.

The same goes for the House of Lords: because there is no legal recourse from its decisions, it has opportunities that lower courts do not have, to ignore the law and to get away with it. To the extent that it ignores the law, Britain is not ruled by law, but by judges.[10] But freedom from review does not make it impossible for the highest court to follow rules.

When *is* lack of judicial review of administrative, legislative, or judicial decision-making a deficit in the rule of law? Simply when judicial review is *needed* to achieve official conformity to the law. So we can avoid the paradox

---

[9] *R.* v. *Shoreditch Assessment Committee, ex parte Morgan* [1910] 2 KB 859 *per* Farwell L.J. at 880.

[10] It would be a confusion to think that Britain is not ruled by law to the extent that the House of Lords *changes* the law — see above on legal change. To the extent that it lawfully changes the law, Britain is ruled by law *and* by the judges.

by reworking the ideal in a way that makes more sense. Judicial review of official decision-making is not logically required for a community to achieve the ideal of the rule of law, in the way that, for example, it is logically required that the officials generally adhere to the law. Judicial review is an instrumental requirement—a *check* against departures from the rule of law. It may be a very effective instrument, if judges are more impartial than other officials, or more faithful to the law. If that is not the case, then judicial review has no value in achieving the ideal—judicial review may hinder the rule of law. In any case, questions as to how much judicial review should be available, of which decisions or actions, in what form, and on what standard, are questions of legislative craft, and not necessarily questions of whether to adhere to the rule of law or to relinquish it. Lack of judicial review is not necessarily a deficit.

But finality in adjudication is a *condition* of the rule of law. People may conduct themselves according to law even without being held to do so. But people cannot conduct themselves according to law to the extent that there is no end to disputes.

It still makes sense to say that some form of judicial review of administrative action is a requirement of the rule of law: because of the contingency of infidelity, it is hard to imagine a community ruled by law, with no form of legal remedy against official illegality. But it does not even make sense to talk of a community ruled by law, with an infinite hierarchy of courts. The ideal of the rule of law does not require even the potential for judicial control of every official decision. The ideal *forbids* it.

The Rule of Law Opposed to Anarchy

> The rule of law is opposed not just to arbitrary government, but also to anarchy. If the rule of law is to be attained, the life of a community must be ruled by law. But then the rule of law would only be attained completely if the life of the community were completely ruled by law. That would be impossible (and undesirable). So the rule of law is unattainable and undesirable; we can achieve the rule of law only incompletely.

The impossible scenario, in which every event in a community is governed by law, would make no sense as an ideal. It would be nonsensical, and not just detrimental, for a lawmaker to pursue it. Complete attainment of the rule of law must be something quite different, if the rule of law is to make sense as an ideal. To make sense of the rule of law, we must conceive of it as a complex mean between anarchy and over-regulation.[11]

---

[11] Some people have treated the rule of law as by definition a purely procedural ideal—a formal characteristic of laws, and not a state of affairs in a community. It is only a verbal question whether to say that 'the rule of law' is achieved when the requirements are met, regardless of the

What would count as attaining such a mean? We cannot say, unless we have an account of what the law ought to regulate. The rule of law is like the ideal of self-control: we cannot say whether someone has achieved self-control unless we know what needs controlling. A community achieves the rule of law only if the law regulates just what it is its function to regulate—if it does what it is good at. But good from what point of view? The question is evaluative, but it leaves unaddressed the question of whether the rule of law is positively valuable in itself. If we admit that it must be possible for the rule of law to be completely achieved by a vicious system, then we have to say, 'good from the legal point of view'. From that point of view, it may be unclear what ought to be regulated. The law may have no clear or consistent point of view towards its function.

We seem to need an account of the legal point of view, and of the general principles of the law of a community (which I have been loosely calling 'the reason of the law'). The general task cannot be carried out here, but an example might show what it is that we need to understand.

Does Britain under Elizabeth II come closer to the ideal of the rule of law than England did under Henry II? Probably it does, but we should say that it does not do so merely in virtue of the fact that, for example, there was no workplace safety legislation under Henry II. Was the lack of workplace safety legislation under Henry II a deficit in the rule of law? That depends on whether the reason of the law demanded workplace safety legislation in that community. A community is legally in good shape if the law regulates what, from the legal point of view, it ought to.

There is a genuine puzzle here. In any decent legal system there is a fairly clear answer to the question 'What is regulated?' But there is not necessarily any clear answer, from the legal point of view, to the question 'What ought to be regulated?' Finnis has pointed out the important fact that concern for the rule of law 'works to suggest new subject-matters for authoritative regulation'.[12] That concern may itself identify respects in which the life of the community ought to be regulated, and is not. But if Henry II's jealous concern for the rule of law did not suggest workplace safety legislation, then its lack was not a deficit. The reason of the law did not call for such regulation. From a point of view unrestricted by the principles of the law of twelfth-century England, it might have been better if there had been workplace safety regulation. That would not have brought England closer to the rule of law; it would have changed the principles of the law.

We might say that a lack of regulation (or an undeveloped form of regulation) in some area is a deficit just when it is inconsistent with the reason of the

content of the law, or (as I have done) that the rule of law is achieved only if the life of the community is ruled by law. If the former approach were taken, then this section on anarchy and the rule of law would be a discussion of a different ideal—something like the ideal of government.

[12] *NLNR* 271.

law—with the principles of the law. Those principles may be muddled, or fragmentary, or incommensurable, or inconsistent, or simply unclear. So the ideal of the rule of law is vague. It may be unclear, in some cases, whether a lack of regulation of workplace safety runs contrary to the principles of the law—whether it is a deficit in the rule of law. That does not mean that the ideal of the rule of law is incoherent, any more than a vague request is incoherent. But if the law of a community were entirely unprincipled, the rule of law *would* be impossible.

I do not claim that there are no deep puzzles about the content of the ideal. One puzzle relates to the question of the virtue of the rule of law: it is the puzzle of how to articulate the ideal as a technical ideal, without building into it all the requirements of good law. We might say that it is a puzzle of how to account for the functions of law entirely by reference to the reason of the law.[13]

I only claim that no such puzzles arise from vagueness, just as none arise from rules of change or from finality in adjudication. The rule of law is unattainable, but it is not inconceivable.

5. Resolution

> Where it seems that the law cannot draw a boundary, it would seem impossible for a human being to identify one. Yet the law trains officials for that very purpose, and appoints them to judge and to regulate that which it leaves undetermined, as rightly as they can.
>
> (Aristotle, *Politics* 3. 16)

Aristotle was aware that the rule of law might seem to be impossible because of legal indeterminacy. He mentions the point as a potential objection to his claim that it is preferable for the law to rule than for one citizen to rule. His response is, in the first instance, that if the law is indeterminate, the right outcome is unknowable for any person—so that indeterminacy in the law does not mean that the rule of people is preferable. But his complete response is to identify the law's capacity to provide for the resolution of its own indeterminacies. The law provides for the resolution of its own indeterminacies, just as it provides for its own identification, and its own change, and its

---

[13] For another puzzle about the content of the ideal, see Raz, *Ethics in the Public Domain* (Oxford: Clarendon Press, 1994), 362, on the denial of access to justice and alienation from the law that arise from the very procedures and institutions that promote the ideal: 'To some extent there is no escape from these blemishes.' John Gardner has identified another similar puzzle about the rule of law: there are different and potentially incompatible ways in which the law might achieve the requirement of clarity: 'Rationality and the Rule of Law in Offences against the Person' (1994) 53 *Cambridge Law Journal* 502, 511–20.

own enforcement. These are all senses in which, as Kelsen said, the law regulates its own creation.[14]

To make sense of the ideal of the rule of law, we need to make a basic claim about the role of courts: their role in securing the rule of law for a community is not just the forensic role of fact-finding and the watchdog role of ensuring compliance; it is also the creative role of resolving unresolved disputes about the requirements of the law. Such disputes need to be subjected to the rule of law. The rules that give courts jurisdiction do not just identify the sphere within which a court is to apply the law. By authorizing (and requiring) the court to impose resolution, those rules regulate what the law does not regulate in any other way. The unsurprising consequence is that there is no escaping the rule of people. To make sense of the ideal of the rule of law, we have to make sense of the necessarily creative role of judges. This means that 'the rule of laws, not of men' is a rhetorical figure for the rule of laws, *free from abuse* by men. The ideal of the rule of laws still makes perfect sense.

The conclusion is that judges have a duty to give (in fact, to *impose*) resolution. Resolution is a basic requirement of the rule of law. The plaintiff in a libel case may have a legal right to substantial damages—and nothing more determinate. Then we might say that the court would do justice if it ordered the defendant to pay 'substantial damages'. But such an order would be a dereliction of duty, because part of the court's duty is to impose resolution.[15] A judge faced with the whole series of murder prosecutions discussed earlier would speak the truth if she said, 'there is no legal answer to the question "Who is the last defendant who can be tried?"' But she would fail in her duty if she did not either dismiss the charges or allow the prosecution to proceed in each case.

Resolution is a critically important duty of judges.[16] It is important when it is indeterminate what justice or the law requires, and when the various incommensurable requirements of good judicial decision-making conflict with each other, and even when there is no just outcome. It is a reason for appeal courts to have an odd number of judges and simple majority voting, and a reason for finality and for the doctrine of *res judicata*. The ability and responsibility of judges to impose resolution is a major source of their legitimacy. But it is not an especially noble duty, like their duty to do justice. They cannot help but carry it out, unless they quit or throw up their hands. They

---

[14] Hans Kelsen, *General Theory of Norms*, ed. Michael Hartney (Oxford: Clarendon Press, 1991), 124, 126, 132, etc.

[15] Perhaps it is better to say that the plaintiff has a legal right to substantial damages, *and also* a legal right to have that right determined in a precise sum. Then the duty of the court to impose resolution is itself a duty of justice. I do not think that that conclusion would affect what I say here about the independent and basic nature of the duty to impose resolution.

[16] Cf. Raz's account of the functions of law, in which settling unregulated and partly regulated disputes is a 'primary function' that shows 'the key position of the court system in all legal systems.' *AL* 174–5.

can fulfil it even when they decide without giving reasons, even when they decide wrongly, and even when they decide corruptly. Their ability to impose resolution is enhanced to the extent that their justice and good sense enhances acceptance of the courts' decisions. So they fail to fulfil it if they decide cases in a way that brings the administration of justice into such disrepute as to endanger the rule of law, by prompting executive contempt, or rebellion, or mob violence. Yet even that failure is to some degree independent of the justice of their decisions, since just decisions too may prompt such breakdowns in the rule of law. Imposing resolution is a basic and independent duty, but it is not paramount. There is no reason to think that judges have an absolute duty to promote acceptance of the resolutions they claim to impose.

The many duties of judges cannot be listed neatly, but they include maintaining the integrity and decency of the process of the court (including supervising the law of evidence and the law of contempt), managing and directing the jury fairly and according to law in a jury trial, and finding the facts in a trial without a jury. In their decisions and in the remedies they give their duties are to do justice according to law, to take responsibility for the development of the law so as to promote the public interest and the doing of justice, to impose resolution on disputes, and to give clear and forthright reasons. They ought to uphold respect for and understanding of the law in all of their actions (especially in making procedural decisions and in writing their reasons). And they must do all of this impartially, without bias or prejudice.

There are many potential tensions among these duties — conflicts between justice and legality are only the most poignant. The important point for our purposes is that the duty to impose resolution on disputes is, ordinarily, not in conflict with any of the other duties in decision-making.[17] It is independent and basic. It implies the duty to resolve incommensurabilities among the other requirements of a good decision.

If a coordination problem is a problem in which the need for a solution is important in itself (independently of the importance, if any, of which solution is adopted), then every judicial decision is a solution to a coordination problem. A community's need for resolution is related to its need for coordination, because resolution coordinates, and every coordination problem needs some degree of resolution for its solution. The legislature and the executive need to give resolution. Resolution is needed in politics (especially in democratic politics), just as it is in law. That explains rules of closure on legislative debates, and the universal use of precise numerical tests (simple or weighted majorities) for the outcome of voting in elections and in legislatures. The

---

[17] Exceptions may arise in some crises in which a court can only promote acceptance of its decisions by making a decision that would be wrong in the absence of the need to promote acceptance.

support reflected by a 50.6 per cent vote in a referendum is virtually the same as the support reflected by a 49.4 per cent vote, but the tiny difference in support may make all the difference to the result, because of a rule of voting that reflects the need for resolution.

Not all coordination problems, however, need the form of resolution that courts give. Problems faced by the legislature and the executive (what to do about unemployment, where to build a road . . .) do not generally present the bivalent form of judicial disputes. When they do, as in the question whether a bill is to be passed, or who is to be elected, rules of legislation and of voting provide bivalent outcomes, just as judges do. Ordinary politics — the making of executive decisions, and of decisions as to what legislation to propose — is different. The legislature and the executive can respond to their problems by deferring decisions, by compromising, by finding a third way, by consultation, and so on.

In adjudication the general political need for resolution in decision-making crystallizes into a formal, structural demand. Every judicial dispute is a coordination problem with a special feature (a feature shared by some political decisions, such as elections): it demands that one of two outcomes be given, and the force of that demand is independent of the importance, if any, of the considerations for and against either outcome.

One immediate puzzle that arises from this need for resolution is why it should be a special responsibility *of judges*. To take the example of the use of powers in administrative law, it seems that we could achieve resolution much more effectively and simply by prohibiting judicial review than by allowing judicial review.[18] So it might seem that there is no particular virtue in entrusting resolution of disputes to judges.

That view would be mistaken, because the need for resolution never overrides the need for justice and the need for legality. If judicial review is a better technique for meeting *those* requirements, then the resolution of disputes is generally better entrusted to judges. If the judges are independent, their independence by itself is often enough to make judicial review preferable. Prohibiting judicial review runs the risk of prejudice — which is a form of arbitrariness in our fourth sense. Unreviewable official decision-making may abandon the reason of the law for purposes that are biased or corrupt or simply foreign to the law.

It sounds grand to say that, at least sometimes, there is no one better than a judge to impose resolution on disputes about the requirements of the law. But the conclusion that it may not matter what the resolution *is* suggests a rather *bitter* prospect for a judge who wants to do justice according to law.

---

[18] We could illustrate the same point by asking why legal disputes in private law should be resolved by courts rather than by self-help, or by governmental commissioners, or by some other means.

The outcome of an action may matter terribly to the parties, and yet there may be no legal or moral reason to choose one resolution rather than another.[19] Yet a resolution must be given. However dedicated the judge, it seems as if legality and justice do not matter in such a case: there is nothing the judge can do to give a decision that is more consistent with the law or more just than the alternative decision would be, and there is no way to avoid arbitrariness in our first three senses.

One consolation for the conscientious judge might be to consider that the resolution in such a case need not be arbitrary in any sense repugnant to the rule of law. Our first three senses of arbitrariness are *not* necessarily opposed to the rule of law. If 'arbitrary' is a pejorative, it is misleading to call them 'arbitrary'. Lack of constraint, inconsistency, and unpredictability are, to some extent, entailed by the rule of law. No doubt we can say that there is a deficit if the law is characterized by *too much* of any of those features. But we can say something more: lack of constraint, inconsistency, and unpredictability are not deficits in themselves. The resolution in an unclear case need not be arbitrary in any pejorative sense. It will not be arbitrary in our fourth sense of abandoning the reason of the law, because the need for resolution is itself a general legal reason to resolve disputes, and there is no conclusive reason against the resolution in question.

But that is a hollow consolation for a judge intent on legality and justice, because it seems to say that those virtues are unimportant and unhelpful in the case in question. If all that is needed is resolution, and it does not matter what the resolution is, *why not* adopt the paradigm technique of arbitrary decision-making — and flip a coin? After all, flipping a coin can be a legitimate way of making very important decisions, as long as it is appropriate that the decision should not turn on reasons that support the outcome. And it must be *appropriate* that a judicial decision not turn on such reasons, if it is *impossible* for it to turn on such reasons.

There is a reason not to flip coins, and there should be nothing bitter about it, although it is humbling for judges. It is the need for judicial discipline. A constant determination to carry out the rest of the judge's duties provides a discipline against corruption and prejudice and wilfulness. This judicious attitude always tries to give effect to the rights of the parties, and to develop the law wisely, and so on. It does not at any stage give up and say that there is no answer. The need for judicial discipline is a conclusive reason not to flip coins, even in secret, even when (if ever) it is clear to the judge that the law does not resolve the matter.

---

[19] Cf. Finnis, 'Reason and Authority in *Law's Empire*' (1987) 6 *Law and Philosophy* 357, 376: 'in some cases there is only one answer which is not wrong, while in other (not infrequent) cases there is more than one such answer, and reason itself (whether legal or even moral) lacks the resources to identify one as best'.

If judicial discipline requires a judge always to attend to other duties than the duty to impose resolution, we might ask whether that duty has any consequences at all for the way a judge ought to act. One consequence traditionally associated with the view that the requirements of the law are indeterminate in some cases is that, when the law does not answer a question, judges need to act on the considerations that would motivate a good legislature. That is true, but it does not make indeterminacy into a source of a special duty, and recourse to legislative considerations cannot always fulfil the independent need for resolution. First, indeterminacy in the law is not a precondition of justifiable judicial lawmaking. The judge may also need to act (and may, like the House of Lords, be empowered by law to act) as a lawmaker when the *clear* requirements of the law need changing. Secondly, legislative considerations are not necessarily enough to give resolution. When it is unclear what the law requires, it may also be unclear what legislative considerations require. Those considerations may not identify a last defendant who may rightly be prosecuted—and yet the judge needs to resolve the matter.

Nevertheless, the need for resolution does have consequences for how judges ought to act. It is a reason for judges to avoid giving long-winded or confusing reasons for judgment, and a reason for courts with more than one judge to pursue consensus, to avoid acrimony, and to eliminate inconsistencies in outcome in complex proceedings. It is ordinarily a reason for courts to give precise remedies—while laws are characteristically vague, judicial remedies are typically precise. And it is a reason either to avoid giving remedies that need judicial supervision, or else to provide effective judicial facilities for supervising remedies. There may be other ways in which courts can promote the rule of law by enhancing their capacity to impose resolution on disputes. But the duty to impose resolution cannot tell us more about how judges ought to act than that they ought to guard their capacity to carry it out. It tells us nothing new about the duty to do justice according to law, but it is a reminder that that is not the only duty of judges.

When is Vagueness a Deficit in the Rule of Law?

Vagueness in the law is not necessarily a deficit in the rule of law. And by a similar argument we can generalize and say that *discretion*, whatever its source, is not in itself a deficit. There is no coherent way to characterize the rule of law as an ideal that is intrinsically opposed to discretion; and while it is no doubt the case that *too much* discretion is a deficit, we can say more about what counts as too much discretion, and we can say more about when vagueness is a deficit.

If we return to Raz's organizing principle—that people must be able to use the law as a guide—then it is tempting to keep on insisting that vagueness is always a deficit, because there are ways in which people really cannot guide themselves by a vague rule (where they *could* guide themselves by a similar, precise rule). Prosecutors really cannot use the European Convention to answer the question 'How long can we put off the trial?' This approach would make the ideal incoherent, after all.

Questions such as 'How long can we put off the trial?' are common, and we should not underestimate the challenge that they pose to our attempt to make sense of the ideal of the rule of law. We might say that the ideal of the rule of law is incoherent if it requires that a lawyer must be able to give *precise* answers to such questions. But it is not incoherent if it simply requires that the law must be useful to the lawyer in advising a client.

To make sense of the organizing principle of the ideal, we need to distinguish between using the law as a guide, and using the law to dictate an outcome in every possible case. We need to find a sense of 'guide' in which a requirement of trial within a reasonable time *can* guide behaviour. And, of course, it can—not by giving the prosecution a deadline, but by giving them a reason to act as soon as they are able to (not *simply* in order to avoid the hazard that a delay will be held unreasonable, but in order to be able to account for themselves as having reasons for the time they take). The notion of a 'guide', in turn, would be an incoherent notion if we counted nothing as a guide unless it answered all questions. No map, for instance, would be a guide, and no vague promise could guide our behaviour. The notion of a guide can only be coherent if we have a notion of what can be asked of a guide, and count something as a guide when it meets that need.

Again, it is tempting to say that vagueness is a deficit when the law is *too* vague. But vagueness is unquantifiable, and in any case there is no reason to think that every *very* vague rule (e.g. standards of fairness, reasonableness, satisfactory quality...) represents a deficit. So what can we say that would be more illuminating than that the law must not be *too* vague?

If we consider even one case in which vagueness has *clearly* amounted to a deficit in the rule of law, that will help to answer this question. Consider Stalin's murderous abuses of law. His 1932 decree collectivizing Ukrainian agriculture ordered 'dekulakization'. The vagueness of the ideologically loaded jargon turned agricultural confiscations into a reign of terror by local officials. That vagueness was a technique for achieving a legally sanctioned abandonment of the rule of law.

Vagueness is a deficit when it lends itself to arbitrariness in our fourth sense—to abandoning the reason of the law. Authorities can use vagueness to exempt their actions from the reason of the law, or even to make it impossible to conceive of the law as having any reason distinguishable from the will of the officials. Then vagueness is a deficit in the rule of law.

Bibliography

ARROW, K. J., 'Arrow's Theorem', in *The New Palgrave: A Dictionary of Economics*, ed. John Eatwell *et al.* (London: Macmillan, 1987).
—— *Social Choice and Individual Values*, 2nd edn. (New York: Wiley, 1963).
AUSTIN, JOHN, *The Province of Jurisprudence Determined*, Hart edn. (London: Weidenfeld & Nicolson, 1954).
BAKER, G. P., and P. M. S. HACKER, *An Analytical Commentary on Wittgenstein's Philosophical Investigations* (Chicago: University of Chicago Press, 1980).
—— *Scepticism, Rules and Language* (Oxford: Blackwell, 1984).
—— *Wittgenstein: Rules, Grammar and Necessity* (Oxford: Blackwell, 1985).
BIX, BRIAN, *Law, Language and Legal Determinacy* (Oxford: Clarendon Press, 1993).
BROOME, JOHN, 'Is Incommensurability Vagueness?', in Ruth Chang (ed.), *Incommensurability, Incomparability, and Practical Reason* (Cambridge, Mass.: Harvard University Press, 1997), 67.
CARDOZO, BENJAMIN N., *The Nature of the Judicial Process* (New Haven: Yale University Press, 1921).
CARLSON, DAVID GRAY, 'Liberal Philosophy's Troubled Relation to the Rule of Law' (1993) 43 *University of Toronto Law Journal* 257.
COLEMAN, JULES, 'Truth and Objectivity in Law' (1995) 1 *Legal Theory* 33.
—— and BRIAN LEITER, 'Determinacy, Objectivity, and Authority', in Andrei Marmor (ed.), *Law and Interpretation* (Oxford: Clarendon Press, 1995), 203.
COLLINI, STEFAN, 'Introduction: Interpretation Terminable and Interminable', in Umberto Eco, *Interpretation and Overinterpretation*, ed. Stefan Collini (Cambridge: Cambridge University Press, 1992), 1.
CULLER, JONATHAN, 'In Defence of Overinterpretation', in Umberto Eco, *Interpretation and Overinterpretation*, ed. Stefan Collini (Cambridge: Cambridge University Press, 1992), 109.
—— *On Deconstruction* (London: Routledge & Kegan Paul, 1982).
DERRIDA, JACQUES, 'Force of Law: The "Mystical Foundation of Authority"', in Michel Rosenfeld and D. G. Carlson (eds.), *Deconstruction and the Possibility of Justice* (London: Routledge, 1992), 3.
—— 'Letter to a Japanese Friend', in David Wood and Robert Bernasconi (eds.), *Derrida and Différance* (Coventry: Parousia Press, 1985), 7.
DWORKIN, RONALD, *Freedom's Law* (Oxford: Oxford University Press, 1996).
—— *Law's Empire* (Cambridge, Mass.: Harvard University Press, 1986).
—— *A Matter of Principle* (Oxford: Clarendon Press, 1986).
—— 'No Right Answer?', in P. M. S. Hacker and Joseph Raz (eds.), *Law, Morality and Society* (Oxford: Clarendon Press, 1977), 58.
—— 'Objectivity and Truth: You'd Better Believe It' (1996) 25 *Philosophy and Public Affairs* 87.
—— 'On Gaps in the Law', in Neil MacCormick and Paul Amselek (eds.), *Controversies about Law's Ontology* (Edinburgh: Edinburgh University Press, 1991), 84.
—— *Taking Rights Seriously* (London: Duckworth, 1977).

EDGINGTON, DOROTHY, 'Vagueness by Degrees', in Rosanna Keefe and Peter Smith (eds.), *Vagueness: A Reader* (Cambridge: MIT Press, 1997), 294.

——'Wright and Sainsbury on Higher-Order Vagueness' (1993) 53 *Analysis* 193.

ENDICOTT, TIMOTHY A. O., 'Questions of Law' (1998) 114 *Law Quarterly Review* 292.

FINE, KIT, 'Vagueness, Truth and Logic' (1970) 30 *Synthese* 265.

FINNIS, J. M., *Fundamentals of Ethics* (Oxford: Clarendon Press, 1983).

——*Natural Law and Natural Rights* (Oxford: Clarendon Press, 1980).

——'On Reason and Authority in *Law's Empire*' (1987) 6 *Law and Philosophy* 357.

FISH, STANLEY, *Doing What Comes Naturally* (Durham, NC: Duke University Press, 1989).

——'How Come you Do me Like you Do? A Reply to Dennis Patterson' (1993) 72 *Texas Law Review* 57.

FISS, OWEN, 'Objectivity and Interpretation' (1982) 34 *Stanford LR* 739.

FREGE, GOTTLOB, *Grundgesetze der Arithmetik*, ii (Jena: Hermann Pohle, 1903).

FULLER, L. L., *The Morality of Law*, 2nd edn. (New Haven: Yale University Press, 1969).

——'Positivism and Fidelity to Law: A Reply to Professor Hart' (1958) 71 *Harvard Law Review* 630.

GARDNER, JOHN, 'Rationality and the Rule of Law in Offences against the Person' (1994) 53 *Cambridge Law Journal* 502.

GRICE, H. P., *Studies in the Way of Words* (Cambridge, Mass.: Harvard University Press, 1989).

GRIFFIN, JAMES, 'Mixing Values' (1991) 65 *Proceedings of the Aristotelian Society (Supplement)* 101.

——*Well-Being* (Oxford: Clarendon Press, 1986).

HALE, BOB, and CRISPIN WRIGHT (eds.), *A Companion to the Philosophy of Language* (Oxford: Blackwell, 1997), Glossary, s.v. 'Higher-Order Vagueness'.

H. L. A. HART, *The Concept of Law*, 2nd edn. (Oxford: Clarendon Press, 1994).

——*Essays in Jurisprudence and Philosophy* (Oxford: Clarendon Press, 1993).

——'Introduction' to Chaim Perelman, *The Idea of Justice and the Problem of Argument* (London: Routledge & Kegan Paul, 1963), p. vii.

——'Positivism and the Separation of Law and Morals' (1958) 71 *Harvard Law Review* 593.

——'Theory and Definition in Jurisprudence' (1955) 29 *Proceedings of the Aristotelian Society (Supplement)* 239.

KELSEN, HANS, *General Theory of Norms*, trans. Michael Hartney (Oxford: Clarendon Press, 1991).

——*Introduction to the Problems of Legal Theory*, trans. Bonnie Litschewski Paulson and Stanley L. Paulson (Oxford: Clarendon Press, 1992).

——*The Pure Theory of Law*, trans. Max Knight (Berkeley: University of California, 1967).

KIM, JAEGWON, *Supervenience and Mind* (Cambridge: Cambridge University Press, 1993).

KRESS, KEN, 'Legal Indeterminacy' (1989) 77 *California Law Review* 283.

KRIPKE, SAUL, *Wittgenstein on Rules and Private Language: An Elementary Exposition* (Oxford: Blackwell, 1982).

KUTZ, CHRISTOPHER L., 'Just Disagreement: Indeterminacy and Rationality in the Rule of Law' (1994) 103 *Yale Law Journal* 997.

LANDERS, SCOTT, 'Wittgenstein, Realism and CLS: Undermining Rule Scepticism' (1990) 9 *Law and Philosophy* 177.

LANGILLE, BRIAN, 'Legal Realism', in Dennis Patterson (ed.), *A Companion to Philosophy of Law and Legal Theory* (Oxford: Blackwell, 1996), 261.

LEITER, BRIAN, 'Revolution without Foundation: The Grammar of Scepticism and Law' (1988) 33 *McGill Law Journal* 451.

LEVINSON, SANFORD, 'What do Lawyers Know (And What do they Do with their Knowledge)? Comments on Schauer and Moore' (1985) 58 *Southern California Law Review* 441.

LIPKIN, ROBERT JUSTIN, 'Indeterminacy, Justification and Truth in Constitutional Theory' (1992) 60 *Fordham Law Review* 595.

LUZZATI, CLAUDIO, 'Discretion and "Indeterminacy" in Kelsen's Theory of Legal Interpretation', in Letizia Gianformaggio (ed.), *Hans Kelsen's Legal Theory: A Diachronic Perspective* (Turin: Giapicchelli, 1990), 123.

LYONS, DAVID, Book review (1995) 111 *Law Quarterly Review* 519, 520, reviewing Hart, *The Concept of Law*, 2nd edn. (Oxford: Clarendon Press, 1994).

—— 'Constitutional Interpretation and Original Meaning' (1986) 4 *Social Philosophy and Policy* 75.

McDOWELL, JOHN, 'A Natural Law Theory of Interpretation' (1985) 58 *Southern California Law Review* 277.

—— 'The Semantics of Judging' (1981) 54 *Southern California Law Review* 151.

—— 'Wittgenstein on Following a Rule' (1984) 58 *Synthese* 325.

MACHINA, KENTON F., 'Truth, Belief, and Vagueness' (1976) 5 *Journal of Philosophical Logic* 47.

MARMOR, ANDREI, *Interpretation and Legal Theory* (Oxford: Clarendon Press, 1992).

PATTERSON, DENNIS, 'The Poverty of Interpretive Universalism: Towards the Reconstruction of Legal Theory' (1993) 72 *Texas Law Review* 1.

PEIRCE, CHARLES S., *Collected Papers of Charles S. Peirce*, ed. Charles Hartshorne and Paul Weiss (Cambridge, Mass.: Harvard University Press, 1934).

PLATTS, MARK, *Ways of Meaning* (London: Routledge & Kegan Paul, 1979).

PUTNAM, HILARY, 'Are Moral and Legal Values Made or Discovered?' (1995) 1 *Legal Theory* 5.

QUINE, WILLARD, 'What Price Bivalence?' (1981) 78 *Journal of Philosophy* 90.

—— *Word and Object* (Cambridge, Mass.: MIT Press, 1960).

RADIN, MARGARET JANE, 'Reconsidering the Rule of Law' (1989) 69 *Boston University Law Review* 781.

RAWLS, JOHN, *A Theory of Justice* (Cambridge, Mass.: Harvard University Press, 1971).

RAZ, JOSEPH, *The Authority of Law* (Oxford: Clarendon Press, 1979).

—— 'Legal Principles and the Limits of Law', in Marshall Cohen (ed.), *Ronald Dworkin and Contemporary Jurisprudence* (London: Duckworth, 1983), 73.

—— *The Morality of Freedom* (Oxford: Clarendon Press, 1986).

—— *Practical Reason and Norms* (London: Hutchinson, 1975).

RORTY, RICHARD, *Consequences of Pragmatism* (Brighton: Harvester, 1982).

—— 'The Pragmatist's Progress', in Umberto Eco, *Interpretation and Overinterpretation*, ed. Stefan Collini (Cambridge: Cambridge University Press, 1992), 89.

ROSENFELD, MICHEL, 'Deconstruction and Legal Interpretation: Conflict, Indetermin-
acy and the Temptations of the New Legal Formalism', in Michel Rosenfeld and
D. G. Carlson (eds.), *Deconstruction and the Possibility of Justice* (London:
Routledge, 1992), 152.

ROSS, KENNETH A., *Elementary Analysis: The Theory of Calculus* (New York:
Springer-Verlag, 1980).

RUNDLE, BEDE, *Wittgenstein and Contemporary Philosophy of Language* (Oxford:
Blackwell, 1990).

RUSSELL, BERTRAND, 'Vagueness' (1923) 1 *Australasian Journal of Psychology and
Philosophy* 84.

SAINSBURY, R. M., 'Concepts without Boundaries', inaugural lecture, King's College,
London, 1990.

——'Is there Higher-Order Vagueness?' (1991) 41 *Philosophical Quarterly* 167.

——*Logical Forms* (Oxford: Blackwell, 1991).

——*Paradoxes*, 2nd edn. (Cambridge: Cambridge University Press, 1995).

SAINSBURY, R. M., and TIMOTHY WILLIAMSON, 'Sorites', in Bob Hale and Crispin
Wright (eds.), *A Companion to the Philosophy of Language* (Oxford: Blackwell,
1997), 458.

ST GERMAN, CHRISTOPHER, *St. German's Doctor and Student*, ed. T. F. T. Plucknett
and J. L. Barton (London: Selden Society, 1974).

SCHAUER, FREDERICK, 'Formalism' (1988) 97 *Yale Law Journal* 509, 514 (*LL* 434).

——(ed.), *Law and Language* (Aldershot: Dartmouth, 1993).

——*Playing by the Rules* (Oxford: Clarendon Press, 1991).

SCHIFFER, STEPHEN, 'The Epistemic Theory of Vagueness' (1999) 13 *Philosophical
Perspectives* 480.

——'Two Issues of Vagueness' (1998) 81 *The Monist* 193.

SEN, AMARTYA, *Collective Choice and Social Welfare* (San Francisco: Holden-Day,
1970).

——'Social Choice', in *The New Palgrave: A Dictionary of Economics*, ed. John
Eatwell *et al.* (London: Macmillan, 1987).

SORENSEN, ROY, 'Vagueness, Measurement and Blurriness' (1988) 75 *Synthese* 45.

VON WRIGHT, GEORG HENRIK, 'Truth and Logic', in *Truth, Knowledge and Modalities*
(Oxford: Blackwell, 1984), 26.

WAISMANN, FRIEDRICH, 'Verifiability', in A. Flew (ed.), *Logic and Language*, 1st ser.
(Oxford: Blackwell, 1952).

WILLIAMSON, TIMOTHY, *Identity and Discrimination* (Oxford: Blackwell, 1990).

——'Schiffer on the Epistemic Theory of Vagueness' (1999) 13 *Philosophical Perspectives* 505.

——'Vagueness and Ignorance' (1992) 66 *Proceedings of the Aristotelian Society
(Supplement)* 145.

——*Vagueness* (London: Routledge, 1994).

——'What Makes it a Heap?' (1996) 44 *Erkenntnis* 327.

——'Wright on the Epistemic Conception of Vagueness' (1996) 56 *Analysis* 39.

WITTGENSTEIN, LUDWIG, *Philosophical Grammar*, ed. and trans. Rush Rhees and
Anthony Kenny (Oxford: Blackwell, 1974).

——*Philosophical Investigations*, trans. G. E. M. Anscombe (Oxford: Blackwell, 1958).

——*Remarks on the Foundations of Mathematics*, 3rd edn., ed. G. H. von Wright, R. Rhees, and G. E. M. Anscombe, trans. G. E. M. Anscombe (Oxford: Blackwell, 1978).

WRIGHT, CRISPIN, 'The Epistemic Conception of Vagueness' (1994) 33 *Southern Journal of Philosophy (Supplement)* 133.

——'Further Reflections on the Sorites Paradox' (1987) 15 *Philosophical Topics* 227.

——'Is Higher Order Vagueness Coherent?' (1992) 52 *Analysis* 129.

——'Language-Mastery and the Sorites Paradox', in G. Evans and J. McDowell (eds.), *Truth and Meaning* (Oxford: Clarendon Press, 1976), 223.

YABLON, CHARLES M., 'Law and Metaphysics' (1987) 96 *Yale Law Journal* 613.

ZIFF, PAUL, *Semantic Analysis* (Ithaca, NY: Cornell University Press, 1960).

Index

The use of technical terms is explained at places marked in italics.

Lightning Source UK Ltd.
Milton Keynes UK
UKHW022350230220
359073UK00003BB/46